101 Good Ideas

How to Improve Just about Any Process

Also available from ASQ Quality Press

Creativity, Innovation, and Quality
Paul E. Plsek

Quality Problem Solving
Gerald F. Smith

Root Cause Analysis: A Tool for Total Quality Management
Paul F. Wilson, Larry D. Dell, and Gaylord F. Anderson

Mapping Work Processes
Dianne Galloway

Quality Quotes
Hélio Gomes

Let's Work Smarter, Not Harder: How to Engage Your Entire
Organization in the Execution of Change
Michael Caravatta

The Change Agents' Handbook: A Survival Guide for Quality Improvement
Champions
David W. Hutton

Understanding and Applying Value-Added Assessment: Eliminating
Business Process Waste
William E. Trischler

To request a complimentary catalog of ASQ Quality Press publications,
call 800-248-1946.

101 Good Ideas

How to Improve Just about Any Process

Edited by

Karen Bemowski
and
Brad Stratton

ASQ Quality Press
Milwaukee, WI

101 Good Ideas: How to Improve Just about Any Process
Karen Bemowski and Brad Stratton

Library of Congress Cataloging-in-Publication Data

101 good ideas : how to improve just about any process / edited by
    Karen Bemowski and Brad Stratton.
        p.   cm.
    Collection of articles originally published in ASQC's magazine,
Quality progress.
    Includes bibliographical references (p.   ).
    ISBN 0-87389-391-3
    1. Quality control. 2. Quality assurance. I. Bemowski, Karen,
1961—   . II. Stratton, Brad, 1957—   . III. Quality progress.
TS156.A23   1998
658.5'62—dc21   98—8553
                                                             CIP

10 9 8 7 6 5 4 3 2 1

ASQ Mission: To facilitate continuous improvement and increase customer satisfaction by
identifying, communicating, and promoting the use of quality principles, concepts, and
technologies; and thereby be recognized throughout the world as the leading authority on, and
champion for, quality.

Attention: Schools and Corporations
ASQ Quality Press books, audiotapes, videotapes, and software are available at quantity
discounts with bulk purchases for business, education, or instructional use. For information,
please contact ASQ Quality Press at 800-248-1946, or write to ASQ Quality Press, P.O. Box 3005,
Milwaukee, WI 53201-3005.

For a free copy of the ASQ Quality Press Publications Catalog, including ASQ membership
information, call 800-248-1946.

Printed on acid-free paper

American Society for Quality

Quality Press
611 East Wisconsin Avenue
Milwaukee, Wisconsin 53202

Contents

Acknowledgments

From both of us: Four *Quality Progress* administrative staff members—Debbie Magerowski, Mary Rose Wallus, Anne Calek, and Lyn Reimer—supported the One Good Idea manuscript review process during our tenure at the magazine. We couldn't have done this without them. And we'll always appreciate the fact that Nancy Karabatsos heard the idea for One Good Idea and said, "Yes."

From Karen: Thanks to Mike, Del, Carlene, Debbie, and Brad for encouraging me to pursue my one good idea: to become a writer and editor.

From Brad: Jane, Joshua, and Jack have endured me talking about quality for more than 10 years now. I appreciate their endless support.

Introduction

The Origins of 101 Good Ideas

Ever have a boss who listened? We had one back in 1988, and the roots of this book can be traced to that relationship. You see, Brad Stratton first proposed developing a continuing series of articles titled "One Good Idea" back in 1985. At that time, he worked for a restaurant trade magazine with a less-than-ideal boss whose response to the proposal was a shrug of the shoulders and an "I don't know about that." Actually, he didn't know much about a lot of things. He eventually was promoted to vice president (the Peter Principle at work) before being fired.

A few weeks after Brad arrived at *Quality Progress* magazine, he told that story to his editor, Nancy Karabatsos.

"So what happened to your idea?" she asked.

"Nothing," Brad said.

"Well, I think we should do it," she said.

And we did.

After getting the green light from Nancy, Brad oversaw what was dubbed One Good Idea for the next few years. Shortly after Nancy left the magazine in May 1990, Brad became editor and Karen Bemowski was promoted to associate editor—Brad's old position. Within a few months, Karen took over the monthly editing of the column.

A group effort

101 Good Ideas, therefore, is a collection of the One Good Idea articles that appeared in *Quality Progress*, the monthly magazine of the American Society for Quality, between April 1988 and January 1998. While Brad and Karen edited the majority of the articles and now this book, the book's strength comes from the experiences of the authors who submitted the articles and the members of the magazine's review board who reviewed them and offered suggestions to make the articles better. Without their contributions, this book would not be in your hands.

We know the articles have value because readers have consistently ranked them at or near the top of all continuing series in the publication, according to a monthly opinion ranking conducted by an independent survey organization. It also has a relatively high monthly readership when compared to all other items in a typical issue. That's quite a compliment, considering One Good Idea is always located on the last editorial page of the magazine.

What this book isn't—and is

There are dozens of books that explain the basics of items such as the tools of quality (including controls charts, Pareto and fishbone diagrams, and flowcharts) or prevalent quality improvement approaches. This book isn't one of them.

People searching for such resources should examine texts such as *Juran's Quality Control Handbook* by J.M. Juran (in its fourth edition with a fifth expected in 1998), *Out of the Crisis* by W. Edwards Deming, *The Quality Toolbox* by Nancy Tague, and the delightfully concise (and pocket-sized) *Memory Jogger* by GOAL/QPC. We provide references to these books and others throughout the text.

What this book is, therefore, is a collection of real-world applications of common tools and approaches. You could read several books about quality improvement and not find as many implementation examples as can be found on the following pages.

Where the book differs from what has appeared on the pages of *Quality Progress* is that the articles have been arranged in groups with similar articles. Where several months (or years) might have passed between articles about how to promote quality or analyze data, this book places them on consecutive pages. We also link the various articles in each chapter with an introduction.

Our hope is that regardless of whether you are a long-time reader of *Quality Progress* or a first-time visitor to the world of improving processes, you will find value in the information. We can both honestly report that we have learned a great deal from these articles and enjoyed revisiting them while preparing this book.

Karen Bemowski
Fort Collins, CO

Brad Stratton
Milwaukee, WI

"The column's longevity and popularity among readers proves that the column itself is one good idea."

—Nancy Karabatsos, *former editor, Quality Progress*
January 28, 1998

How to Improve a Process

Improving processes is at the core of improving quality. There might be no better way to improve processes than to study one of Walter A. Shewhart's greatest contributions to quality: what has become known as the plan-do-check-act (PDCA) cycle.[1] It is also known as the plan-do-study-act cycle, the Shewhart cycle, and because he popularized it with the Japanese, the (W. Edwards) Deming cycle. Brian L. Joiner provides what might be the best perspective on it: "The basic notion of PDCA is so simple that when I first heard it, I felt I understood it in five minutes. Now, more than a decade later, I think I might understand it some day."[2]

Directly or indirectly, all the authors in this chapter have a bit of Shewhart's basic idea imbedded in their articles. The most obvious example is Gerry Fay's "Here's a PIP of an Improvement Plan." Fay expands on what Shewhart had to offer by presenting a 10-step plan showing how his company interpreted the four different cycle phases.

William Kearney and Cathy Heflin explain how Bechtel Corporation takes "Eleven Steps to Improved Processes." Those steps are collectively known as the Work Process Improvement (WPI) and are arranged in a very simple flowchart that has four sections: planning, analysis, recommendation, and implementation. The WPI has a nice track record, as the authors credit it with "saving a few million dollars in operating costs."

Joel A. Skellie offers a six-step method to reduce cycle time in "Optimizing the First-Article Inspection Process." The issue of cycle time was especially critical for Skellie's work at Compaq Computer Corporation because of its potential effect on new product introductions.

Steven E. Rigdon's contribution to this chapter, "How Do You Improve a Process?," actually has as its backdrop another great Shewhart contribution: the control chart. Rigdon suggests that you must know the state of a process before it can be improved. Therefore, he presents a simple figure to be used in cooperation with control charts.

Dennis Sowards and Pat Temple propose a straight-line improvement process in "COPIS Focus." Their approach to continuous improvement can be appreciated because it puts the customer first when teams work to satisfy customer requirements.

The chapter concludes with a story that is rooted more in common sense than anything else. Samuel M. Chacon reveals that one quality manager was able to improve a difficult situation with a simple action: "All He Had to Do Was Ask."

References

1. Shewhart, *Statistical Method from the Viewpoint of Quality Control.*
2. Joiner, *Fourth Generation Management*, p. 44.

Here's a PIP of an Improvement Plan

by Gerry Fay

One of the biggest challenges facing a facilitator or team leader of a process improvement project is to keep the team focused on the current problem. To do so, he or she must also communicate progress to the team and sponsors. Many teams use meeting minutes to deliver progress information and next actions, but meeting minutes provide only a snapshot of what the team accomplished at the last meeting.

The use of a process improvement plan (PIP) provides more information than normal meeting minutes and helps standardize all process improvement efforts. The PIP displays the current process flow, highlighting the process steps affected by the team's efforts. It also displays an up-to-date schedule that shows overall progress, including schedule slips and completions (see top section of Figure 1.1). The PIP can be reviewed at a summary level, for management briefings, or in detail. The PIP format is an excellent tool for illustrating the plan-do-check-act cycle.

The following explanation of the 10-step PIP process used at Raab Karcher Electronics Inc., San Diego, CA, demonstrates its effectiveness.

In the plan phase

1. *Name the process owner; define the objective and current process.* In the first meeting, the team defines the problem or objective and identifies the process owners and customers. All are documented on the PIP. The PIP is reviewed by all members prior to the second meeting to ensure concurrence.

2. *Document and measure the current process.* The team creates a flowchart of the current process down to the task level. Team members then identify, on the flowchart, where measurements are currently taken. The completed flowchart is added to the PIP.

3. *Develop an action plan to improve the process.* Through the use of the flowchart and other quality improvement techniques, such as Pareto charts, cause-and-effect diagrams, and nominal group technique, the team identifies the areas where improvements can yield the greatest return. These tools are the basis for root-cause analysis. The detailed actions for performing the analysis are documented on the progress plan to ensure clear communication of responsibilities and expectations. The process steps affected are identified on the PIP flowchart by highlighting them.

In the do phase

4. *Develop process improvements and schedule the implementation.* The team develops a plan to implement changes to the process that will improve efficiency or robustness. The overall project schedule is documented on the PIP. Detailed actions are documented on the TQM (total quality management) Progress Plan (see bottom section of Figure 1.1). Listed are the initiative, benefit of the initiative, estimated completion date, and person responsible for the initiative. This is used at each meeting to track progress. Any improvements that significantly alter the process flow are also documented on the PIP flowchart.

Figure 1.1.

Process Improvement Plan and Progress Report

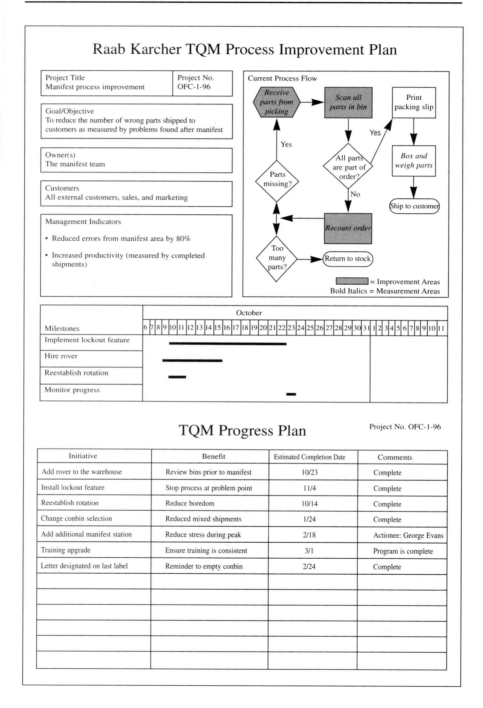

Raab Karcher TQM Process Improvement Plan

Project Title	Project No.
Manifest process improvement	OFC-1-96

Goal/Objective
To reduce the number of wrong parts shipped to customers as measured by problems found after manifest

Owner(s)
The manifest team

Customers
All external customers, sales, and marketing

Management Indicators

• Reduced errors from manifest area by 80%

• Increased productivity (measured by completed shipments)

Current Process Flow

█ = Improvement Areas
Bold Italics = Measurement Areas

Milestones	October
Implement lockout feature	6 7 8 9 10 11 12 13 14 15 16 17 18 19 20 21 22 23 24 25 26 27 28 29 30 31 1 2 3 4 5 6 7 8 9 10 11
Hire rover	
Reestablish rotation	
Monitor progress	

TQM Progress Plan
Project No. OFC-1-96

Initiative	Benefit	Estimated Completion Date	Comments
Add rover to the warehouse	Review bins prior to manifest	10/23	Complete
Install lockout feature	Stop process at problem point	11/4	Complete
Reestablish rotation	Reduce boredom	10/14	Complete
Change conbin selection	Reduced mixed shipments	1/24	Complete
Add additional manifest station	Reduce stress during peak	2/18	Actionee: George Evans
Training upgrade	Ensure training is consistent	3/1	Program is complete
Letter designated on last label	Reminder to empty conbin	2/24	Complete

5. *Develop management indicators of process improvement.* Once the team has implemented the process improvements, team members establish quantifiable indicators of expected improvement with the customers. Once approved, the indicators are documented on the PIP in the management indicators section. This is the basis for deter-

mining if the proposed changes result in significant improvements and should be standardized, or if they were ineffective and further root-cause analysis is necessary. This occurs in the act phase.

In the check phase

6. *Verify improvements and ensure process remains capable.* The team continues to meet and use the PIP and TQM Progress Plan to stay on track. The responsibilities for data collection and analysis are documented and tracked on the TQM Progress Plan. The schedule is reviewed to ensure progress is being made.

7. *Determine whether further action is required.* If further action is required based on the results of data collection or other process indicators, the schedule and who is responsible for actions are documented on the PIP and TQM Progress Plan.

In the act phase

8. *Verify improvement effectiveness.* The team collects process data to verify that changes were effective and achieved the desired results. The schedule for data review and who is responsible are communicated on the PIP and TQM Progress Plan. The process data are reviewed against the management indicators that were documented on the PIP in the do phase. Based on the results, the changes are either determined to be effective or ineffective. If effective, the changes are standardized. If ineffective, a new root-cause analysis is conducted. The PIP history is vital for quickly moving into the plan phase if the process changes were ineffective.

9. *Standardize and document the new process.* If the process changes are effective, the new process is standardized into a policy or procedure for consistency. The PIP serves as a useful tool for guiding the documentation effort. It is a historical document that accurately records the entire process change effort from what it was to what it is.

10. *Continue to monitor and audit the process.* The PIP serves as the baseline for future process improvement efforts. It already contains the current process flowchart and can be modified to address any new efforts undertaken.

Raab Karcher Electronics keeps PIPs and TQM Progress Plans on the company computer network so they can be viewed by anyone interested in a given team's progress. The template for the PIP is done in Microsoft Power Point. Visio for Windows is used for the flowcharting. Microsoft Project is used to create the schedule data.

The use of the PIP has proven to be instrumental in the success of the company's process improvement efforts and has greatly reduced the time needed in meetings to report progress. Information that used to be kept on several pages in a team binder can now be displayed on two pages. Having the information on the company network also ensures that all interested parties, from top management to team members, have access to the same data with no filtering.

And the success of PIP got a great boost from the first Raab Karcher Electronics team to use it. That team reduced returned material inventory from $500,000 to under $1,000.

When this column was published in October 1997, Gerry Fay was the quality assurance manager for Raab Karcher Electronics Inc., San Diego, CA. He received a bachelor's degree in business administration from the University of Redlands in California. Fay was an American Society for Quality member and certified quality auditor.

Eleven Steps to Improved Processes

by William Kearney and Cathy Heflin

Process flowcharting consistently hooks people on quality management. Bechtel Corporation, which provides engineering and construction management services, has used a tool for flowcharting processes called Work Process Improvement (WPI) for three years. It is one of the most beneficial quality management tools being implemented at Bechtel.

WPI is usually introduced during Bechtel's Commitment to Continuous Improvement training. This training, which takes less than two days, includes three classes: "Introduction to Quality Management," "Work Process Improvement," and "Introduction to Statistical Process Control." The classes include many hands-on activities, from conducting the classic red bead experiment to flowcharting a trip to the post office. Virtually all of the exercises are taken from actual office operations. The classes provide enough breadth for everyone to immediately start implementing WPI and other quality management techniques.

The most powerful aspects of WPI are its simplicity and effectiveness. The WPI approach involves 11 steps:

1. Identify a process for improvement.
2. Don't re-invent the wheel. Consider previous improvement suggestions that you or others have made.
3. Determine characteristics to be measured that are important to your customer and that will document improvement to the process.
4. Challenge existing assumptions and accepted procedures.
5. Flowchart the process. Support the flowchart with statistics.
6. Share the flowchart with others. Brainstorm and solicit ideas.
7. Gather statistics that further define the problem in the process and that would support the benefits if the process were improved.
8. Sell your suggestions for improvement.
9. Implement the improvements.
10. Reevaluate and refine the new process. Give it your commitment.
11. Assess your measures. Is the process better? How do you know?

Figure 1.2 shows the WPI flowcharting path.

WPI implemented companywide

WPI has been used to analyze and measure processes in many of Bechtel's service organizations, job sites, and international offices. Departments rapidly gained many benefits from their flowcharting efforts. They obtained initial measurements of their processes. They quickly learned of obvious inefficiencies and the number of people involved in what they might have previously perceived as "simple" processes. They learned what measurements needed to be taken relative to the quality of the processes.

Figure 1.2.

Flowcharting Path

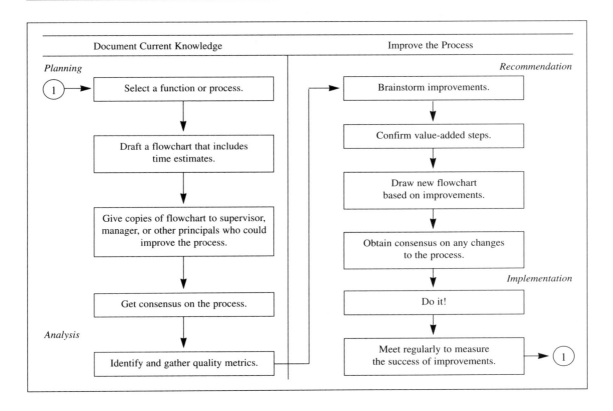

Statistics were often pursued enthusiastically to further identify rework or rerouting of work. Control charts and Pareto charts for measuring process performance emerged. The company's computer systems were used as tools when it was discovered that they could be tapped for valuable data extracts for process measurement.

It became commonplace to see employees trying to determine "how many" and "how come" for process tasks that, previously, they wouldn't have been able to identify as tasks. Process tracking and sharing data with other departments revealed many process improvement opportunities and nurtured friendships between internal suppliers and customers.

Potential process changes were frequently apparent and sometimes embarrassing. Wasteful activities—such as redundancies and excessive inspections and reviews—were commonly found in processes. It was also discovered that some processes needed significant revamping.

Improvements in processes led to other successes, mainly because process changes were inspired by the employees themselves. It was their efforts and innovations that made continual analysis of processes fruitful and fun. Management's support of adopting new methods and listening to new ideas and approaches has created an environment that makes WPI that much easier to apply.

The formula for success

The formula for the success of WPI is straightforward: training and education, then dissecting processes for measurement and improvement. With training and assistance from Bechtel, some of its major clients have even started similar initiatives using the WPI model, proving that WPI can work in any corporate culture. After three years of injecting new fire into old routines, WPI is gaining momentum and saving a few million dollars in operating costs along the way.

When this column was published in July 1991, William Kearney and Cathy Heflin were quality advisors in Bechtel Corporation's Quality Resources Group in San Francisco, CA. Kearney received a bachelor's degree in computer science from American University in Washington, DC. Heflin received bachelor degrees in accounting and business administration from Southeastern Oklahoma State University in Durant, OK.

Idea 3

Optimizing the First-Article Inspection Process

by Joel A. Skellie

Standard first-article inspections (FAIs) have been structured with little regard for cycle time. Yet in new products, with their associated marketing windows, cycle time is paramount. Because of the critical effect it can have on new product introductions, the FAI process must be optimized to ensure a minimal effect on cycle time.

A recent re-assessment of the FAI process was conducted by the Supplier Quality Engineering and Component Engineering groups involved with electrical components at Compaq Computer Corporation. They took a six-step total quality control approach to solve the problem of excessive cycle time.

1. Identify customers, expectations, and problems

The first step was to identify the customers of the FAI process and their expectations and perceived problems. Manufacturing groups expected high-quality raw materials to be available when they needed them. The problem was that manufacturers thought the new product build schedules were being delayed because raw materials were in the FAI process.

2. Set priorities

The related corporate priorities were defined as quality, cycle time, and asset utilization.

3. Characterize the process

A process flowchart was developed to identify actual FAI procedures. It was found that FAIs were performed on:

- The first lot received from a supplier for a given part number.
- All parts with revised specifications.
- Any part from a supplier that has not supplied parts in more than one year.

The scope of the FAI was all specifications within the primary and secondary documents. If problems were found during this FAI, containment and permanent corrective actions caused significant delays in product release. Engineering evaluations performed before receiving the first production lot were later duplicated as an FAI.

4. Select performance measures

The selected performance measures included:

- FAI cycle-time data
- FAI reject rate
- Manufacturing (customer) feedback
- Number of engineering evaluations later duplicated with an FAI

5. Collect and analyze data

Six months of data on the performance measures indicated:

- An FAI cycle time of four to five days
- A 27 percent FAI reject rate
- Customer dissatisfaction with the cycle time associated with FAI
- More than 500 engineering evaluations later duplicated as FAIs

In addition, data on FAIs (number pass, number fail, and parameters failing) indicated that, of all FAIs performed, only 6.75 percent were rejected for critical parameters that would not have been caught in the standard incoming inspection.

6. Improve the process

Brainstorming generated ideas for improving the FAI process. The following ideas were implemented in the refinement of the process:

- Use FAI as a prevention tool (i.e., initiate, conduct, and complete FAI before receipt of first lot).
- Perform FAI only on the parts and suppliers that have caused problems in the past.
- Perform FAI only on critical parameters in generic secondary specifications (packaging and mechanical) and other primary specification parameters.
- Consider FAI only for new sources or for tightening specifications related to critical parameters.

Implementation notes and results

The most difficult part of refining the FAI process is phasing in the new procedure. To properly manage the risks, guidelines relating to previous and ongoing FAIs have to be followed. New parts that arrive during the first six weeks have to be handled on a case-by-case basis because no FAI and preventive action will have taken place.

The results of optimizing the FAI process were astounding. Manufacturing no longer had to wait for material delayed by FAIs; the FAI process was completed before the first production lot arrived. The inspection cycle time dropped from 3.2 days to 2.1 days—a 34 percent reduction! And there was no longer duplicated effort relating to engineering evaluations or low-risk parts and suppliers.

When this column was published in October 1990, Joel A. Skellie worked on the supplier quality engineering staff for Compaq Computer Corporation in Houston, TX. He was a member of the American Society for Quality.

How Do You Improve a Process?

by Steven E. Rigdon

It comes as a surprise to many that a process can be in control but still produce a significant proportion of nonconforming units. It is also possible to have a process that is not in control but still makes all units within specification. Such statements, which might appear paradoxical, are true because the ideas of an in-control process and a capable process are completely independent. You can have both, neither, or one and not the other. Thus, there are four possible states for a process, to which Donald L. Wheeler and David S. Chambers attach the following descriptive terms:[1]

- Ideal (a process that is in control and capable)
- Threshold (a process that is in control but not capable)
- Brink of chaos (a process that is capable but not in control)
- Chaos (a process that is incapable and not in control)

The most common reason for using control charts is to detect when special causes of variability creep into the process so that they can be identified and eliminated. Control charts also provide a tool for learning about the process. But there's another good reason to use SPC charts: You need to know which of the four states a process is in if you're going to improve it. You'll perform different tasks to move it to the ideal state accordingly. Without control charts, you can't determine which state the process is in. (Usually, everyone knows whether a process is capable, but control charts are needed to see whether the process is in control.)

Consider the three states other than the ideal and the steps necessary to bring the process to the ideal state. The threshold state describes a process that is in control but not capable of producing most units within specification. Moving from this state to the ideal state is often the most difficult transition because the process must be changed. Either the variability of the process must be reduced or the process mean must be shifted closer to the target. To achieve this, it is often necessary to design experiments to find factors that affect the important quality characteristics. The evolutionary operation procedure of George E. P. Box and Norman R. Draper is also useful for moving from the threshold state to the ideal state.[2] If it is not possible to change the process, then either the product specifications must be widened or there must be 100 percent inspection to separate the good units from the bad ones.

The brink-of-chaos state describes a process that is capable but not in control. In this situation, the process is improved and brought to the ideal state by using SPC to detect, identify, and eliminate special causes of variability. (Of these three tasks, control charts can help with only the first: detection. Once special causes have been identified, it is up to you to use your knowledge of the process to eliminate them.) Attempts to reduce the variability or center the mean of a process are not likely to be fruitful if the process is capable but not in control.

If the process is in the chaos state, the first thing to do is to use control charts to detect special causes of variability. After identifying and eliminating these special causes, the process might be perfectly capable of meeting specifications. In this situation, the process has moved from the chaos state to the ideal state. If the process is still producing nonconforming units after being brought into control, then it has moved from the chaos state to the threshold state. To reach the ideal state, the process would have to be changed.

It is helpful to think of the chaos state as being divided into two states: correctable chaos, in which bringing the process into control achieves the ideal state, and uncorrectable chaos, in which bringing the process into control achieves the threshold state. In practice, it is usually not possible to determine which of the two chaos states the process is in until the process is brought into control. Figure 1.3 summarizes the four states and the actions required to reach the ideal state.

Figure 1.3.
The Five States and Their Required Actions

References

1. Wheeler and Chambers, *Understanding Statistical Process Control.*
2. Box and Draper, *Evolutionary Operation.*

When this column was published in August 1990, Steven E. Rigdon was an assistant professor of statistics at Southern Illinois University at Edwardsville. He was an American Society for Quality associate member and certified quality engineer.

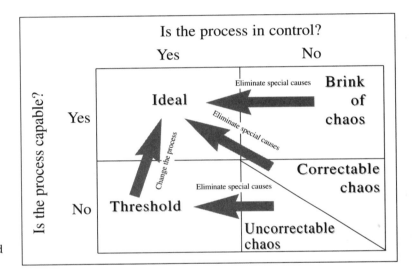

<table>
<tr><td>Idea
5</td><td><h1 style="text-align:center">COPIS Focus</h1> by Dennis Sowards and Pat Temple </td></tr>
</table>

If quality is meeting customers' requirements, the real key to continuous improvement is defining those requirements. COPIS can help you do just that. It can be applied to any level of detail to meet the needs of any situation. It helps those people involved focus on the key elements of the work process.

COPIS is the acronym for "customer, output, process, input, supplier." It reminds people to work backward (from right to left) when defining the elements of the system shown in Figure 1.4. Some people call this process SIPOC, but that interpretation puts the supplier rather than the customer first; COPIS is more customer-focused and efficient.

Figure 1.4.

The System

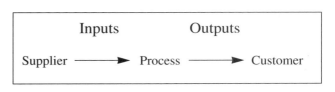

COPIS can be applied to a process, department, division, or organization. It defines all work as a process. All processes have outputs (which are used by internal or external customers) and inputs (which are provided by internal or external suppliers).

Defining all the elements of COPIS and those elements' requirements can improve work processes, create awareness of customer requirements, clarify requirements for suppliers, and facilitate communication across functional and organizational boundaries. COPIS is most effective when it is applied by a cross-functional team representing the major players in the process. Groups or departments can also apply it to their products and services. Many participants have said that the act of identifying their customers, processes, and outputs was educational and valuable in itself.

The steps

Here are the steps to apply COPIS:

1. *List your customers.* Who receives your work? Your customer is the person or area in the total system that receives your work. You might also have a final customer who needs to be identified, but the major focus is on your immediate customer. You might have several customers or different customers for different products and services.
2. *List your outputs.* What service or product do you produce? What work do you do?
3. *Match customers and outputs.* Do you have a customer without an output or an output without a customer?
4. *Define your customers' requirements.* What do your customers want your output to do? Are they satisfied with your output? You can explore this issue with team members by answering the question: "What would our customers say is wrong with our product or service?" Then ask your customers that question.

5. *Define your process.* What is your current process? Is it producing an output that meets the customers' requirements? How can you improve the output? The first time through, your team just needs to perform a simple process analysis; otherwise, it could become mired in the details of steps that might not need to be explored. Stay at the macro level to start the analysis. As opportunities for improvements are identified, more detailed process analyses can be performed in the particular areas in question.

6. *List your inputs.* What do you need to do your job? Most inputs can be divided into the categories of capital, manpower, materials, and information (e.g., methods, standards, and data). Are the requirements for each of these categories clearly defined?

7. *List your suppliers.* Who provides the needed inputs?

8. *Match inputs and suppliers.* Do you have a supplier without an input or an input without a supplier?

9. *Define your requirements for your suppliers.* What is required of the inputs? Are you satisfied? Talk to your suppliers to get their views.

Implementation suggestions

When applying COPIS, you should:

- Communicate with your customers and suppliers. Establish a customer feedback mechanism to monitor your progress in meeting customers' requirements. Provide feedback to your suppliers on how they are meeting your requirements. Make sure all persons involved in the process understand the entire COPIS picture and their roles in it.
- Establish performance targets and measures to track conformance to requirements. Measure the process not the people.
- Document your findings. Designate a person to own each COPIS. This person should maintain the records, answer questions, and document changes as they occur.

COPIS is a way to think always of the customer first. It is especially effective when teams use it, but it can also be used by an individual for his or her work function. COPIS can help any team or individual focus on the priority elements of the work process. It ensures that the process is focused on the customer.

When this column was published in December 1992, Dennis Sowards was the president of Quality Support Services in Mesa, AZ, and the executive director of the Arizona Quality Alliance in Phoenix. He received a master's degree in business administration from Arizona State University in Tempe. He was an American Society for Quality member and certified quality auditor. Pat Temple was the senior industrial engineer at the Salt River Project in Phoenix, AZ. She received a master's degree in industrial engineering from Arizona State University in Tempe.

<table>
<tr><td>

┌─────────┐
│ Idea   │
│   6   │
└─────────┘

</td><td>

All He Had to Do Was Ask
by Samuel M. Chacon

</td></tr>
</table>

In my 21 years as a quality assurance specialist with the Defense Contract Administration Services in the Los Angeles region, only one quality assurance manager of an electronics firm had the courage to ask me what I would do to improve the quality of his company's products. He was in serious trouble with a Navy contract and was desperate. I told him what to do; he did it. Within six months, the defective rate dropped from more than 10 percent to less than 0.5 percent. His company went from being unable to ship products to shipping products on time. My suggestions involved three steps.

Step 1.   Do as I do

To improve the inspection process so that his inspectors could find the defects I was finding, I suggested he have the inspectors look over my shoulder and take notes on how I performed inspections. The inspectors should then:

- Inspect the products as I did.
- Get a sheet of notebook paper to list the defects and tack a copy of the list on the wooden post next to each inspection station.
- Continue inspecting the normal way and keep adding newly found defects to the list, but reinspect the same products using the list of defects to see whether the defects continued.

Step 2.   Review continually

Have the production supervisors review the list of defects every hour. Bring defects to the attention of the employees who manufactured them, and help those employees eliminate the causes of the errors.

Step 3.   Define quality terminology

Employees had to clearly understand the parts they were to play in the quality improvement exercise. Therefore, I redefined important quality ideas to help everyone understand each term:

- *Quality* was redefined as that which makes the product what it is and its degree of excellence. A characteristic checklist detailing all requirements (such as geometric and linear dimensions, materials, workmanship, and finish specifications) is necessary to describe that which makes the product what it is. When each characteristic is measured, the degree of excellence is determined. If a dimension is within tolerance, it meets the acceptable deviation from perfection. Dividing the total defects by the total characteristics inspected and multiplying that number by 100 gives the quality level of the product in percentage of defects. Taking 100 and subtracting the quality level gives the degree of excellence. The quality level of each subassembly by part number was plotted to show improvements.

- *Quality control* was redefined as work instructions and training to understand those instructions. This helped employees understand that they were the true controllers of quality.
- *Quality assurance* was redefined as supervisors making certain that employees have adequate work instructions and training. This made supervisors aware that they were truly in charge of quality assurance. Supervisors were instructed to monitor all characteristics produced, to approve the product as ready for inspection, and to measure the control of quality.
- The *inspection system* was redefined as the quality control measurement system to clearly distinguish the auditors as part of a system that measures the degree of excellence of production supervisor—in other words, the degree of excellence of the supervisor's quality assurance effort.

Putting it all together

The quality assurance manager at the electronics firm listened with an open mind. He took the initiative to implement the ideas immediately. He developed a weekly training program. Internal research of the company's data revealed the need to stop production for about two months to redesign part of the product. The supervisors took advantage of the production stoppage to ensure that every employee was properly trained to do the job right the first time.

When production resumed, the whole company was working like a well-trained team. Morale was high and every member of the team knew what part to play and played it well.

I received a big handshake and a big thank you from the quality assurance manager.

When this column was published in May 1988, Samuel M. Chacon taught quality control management courses at Los Angeles Pierce College in Woodland Hills, CA. He received an associate degree in electronics technology from San Bernardino Valley College in California.

How to Communicate Quality

In December 1997, Robert Kallstrom retired from the Federal Bureau of Investigation. An FBI assistant director, Kallstrom served as head of the bureau's New York office. He became well-known after TWA Flight 800 blew up and his office was assigned to the criminal investigation of the air disaster. Just prior to his retirement, Kallstrom was interviewed on National Public Radio by Robert Siegel. The interview was broadcast on December 11. To conclude the interview, Siegel asked Kallstrom to recall one main lesson from his 25 years with the FBI.

One can only imagine the many thoughts that went through Kallstrom's head and the many different subjects he could have discussed. The one he quickly settled on, however, was communication. "I learned the lesson over and over again that we need to talk more together," he said. "The FBI needs to tell the public what it does, who we are, and why we do it. The public needs to appreciate that and support us. The notion that we're an island floating over here, the public is another one, and corporate America is another is nonsense."[1]

Communication is no less important when it comes to quality improvement, as the authors in this chapter demonstrate. John F. Graham, in "Just Talk to Me," stresses the importance of listening and provides a dynamic example from former Secretary of State Henry Kissinger. Graham's thinking is reminiscent of Stephen Covey's principles of empathetic communication in *The 7 Habits of Highly Effective People*.[2]

Gerald W. Wooley in "Speaking About Quality" and Madhav N. Sinha in "Communicating Quality Without Using That Word" both provide ideas about how to explain quality without having the audience's eyes glaze over. Donald Ponge's "The Socratic Method Produces Enlightened Employees" suggests using the Socratic method to educate people about quality. You could just as easily argue that this could be called the W. Edwards Deming method because he often answered questions with questions.

In "The Buchanan Scale Identifies the Best and the Worst," Dennis Grahn offers a tool to communicate to line managers that they have a role in the quality process. Don't worry if the name Buchanan isn't familiar. Who Buchanan is isn't as important as what Buchanan is trying to communicate: Change is important, so managers must be committed to it.

The chapter concludes with Noel Flynn's "The Communicate-Listen-Act System." Flynn believes that employee involvement requires an effective internal communication system. So he developed a system that lets employees communicate their ideas and that gives management a process with which to listen to and act on employees' ideas. The system resulted in hundreds of suggestions.

References

1. Robert Siegel, interview of Robert Kallstrom on "All Things Considered," National Public Radio, Dec. 11, 1997.
2. Covey, *The 7 Habits of Highly Effective People*, pp. 235–60.

Idea 7

Just Talk to Me
by John F. Graham

Many people believe that quality improvement is limited to charting something. While charting variables and occurrences can go far to improve quality and while quality improvement techniques such as flow diagrams, fishbone diagrams, and experimental design can be powerful tools, the real key to quality improvement is communication. Quality improvement charts and tools are forms of communication. Data or information fed into charts and tools tell the user something—perhaps something the user doesn't yet know—or confirms situations that are already suspected. Charts and tools let users make confident decisions and help explain those decisions to others.

If communication is an important part of quality improvement, quality should improve when communication improves. Typically, communication connotes talking. Everyone does a lot of talking at home and work, but what is often forgotten is that communication is incomplete without listening. All too often, excited co-workers talk but do not listen to each other. When walking by a room of these people, it sounds as though the room is full of radios.

Keep communication lines open

Even when odds against improvement are high, it is best to keep communication lines open. When U.S.-Soviet relations were poor, the United States maintained that keeping the communication lines open would keep relations from worsening. Former Secretary of State Henry Kissinger said, "The great tragedies of the world happen not when right meets wrong, but when right meets right." So, the United States kept talking to the Soviets, never adopting the position "We're right, and we don't want to discuss it."

As humans, we must communicate to survive. Communication requires only minimal effort yet can take us a long way past survival. Among other things, open communication contributes to a more pleasant working environment.

Don't assume

Supposition is no substitute for communication. Don't assume co-workers are aware their efforts are appreciated. They might not be aware. If their work really is appreciated, tell them. If they are producing unacceptable work, tell them that too, but remain positive. Tell them what you would like to see without focusing on their flaws. Many times, mistakes are made because employees don't want to appear stupid by asking the boss too many questions. If you are in charge, say exactly what you mean. After all, it is the boss's responsibility to make sure a message is communicated completely and correctly. Too often, a sharp rebuke is a substitute for patient clarification. Such impatience does not demonstrate leadership.

When thinking about quality improvement, remember that the foundation is built by communication. Clear and complete communication must flow throughout work areas, among departments, and among companies before quality can improve.

When this column was published in February 1991, John F. Graham was the coordinator for the Ethyl Quality Improvement Process at the Ethyl Corporation's Houston Plant in Pasadena, TX. He was a member of the American Society for Quality.

<table>
<tr><td>

**Idea
8**

</td><td>

Speaking about Quality
by Gerald W. Wooley

</td></tr>
</table>

As a quality engineer, I have often been asked to give impromptu and planned presentations about quality. I have spoken at seminars, technical society meetings, community college classes, crew meetings, graduations, civic organization meetings, and even award banquets. In spite of how varied these groups are in terms of technical and educational background, I found six principles to be helpful when speaking about quality.

The six principles

The six principles are:

- *Emphasize continuous improvement.* Explain that improvement is ongoing. Explain that an organization currently might not be where it wants to be, but it is continuously working toward that goal.
- *Use simple tools to illustrate points.* Use run charts, Pareto charts, or histograms to emphasize important points. They can be hand-drawn on a blackboard or sketched on a flip chart. Three-dimensional, four-color graphics aren't needed to get a point across.
- *Reassure the audience about the use of statistics.* Don't let statistics scare people away. A good definition to use is "Statistics is messing around with numbers after something has already happened." Keep the discussion on statistics at this level of simplicity. Remember, calculations are usually the shortest part of any project.
- *Use recent, real-life examples.* Stay away from examples about processes used to manufacture widgets. Use process examples that the audience can relate to. Draw on the audience's experiences and processes when possible. Make up examples if needed.
- *Emphasize the importance of customer-supplier relationships.* Suggest that the audience members talk to their customers and suppliers. Tell them to leave their desks, stations, and machines and make the first move in establishing this important communication link. Unlike chess, it does not matter who—the customer or the supplier—makes the first move.
- *Tell the audience members what's in it for them.* Illustrate how quality affects them daily. Tell them how important it is to their companies'—and ultimately their own—financial security. Quality activities at work lead to more quality activities at home.

Use all or use some

You might not be able to incorporate all six principles in every speech, but it is not uncommon to use most of them. If you consider what would be of interest to your audience in the context of these principles, you will give an effective presentation.

When this column was published in November 1991, Gerald W. Wooley was a statistical quality engineer at the Boeing Spokane plant, Boeing Commercial Airplane Group in Washington. He received a bachelor's degree in mechanical engineering from the University of Idaho in Moscow. Wooley was an American Society for Quality member.

Communicating Quality Without Using That Word
by Madhav N. Sinha

The 1990 American Society for Quality/Gallup survey revealed a serious problem: Many respondents said the quality programs in their companies had either no effect or a negative effect on internal communication.[1] Are quality professionals poor communicators?

Communicating the quality message in an organization has never been an easy task, but it is an important one. Poor communication can hurt organizations, especially when they are trying to launch a systematic attack on waste and customer dissatisfaction. An even greater challenge lies in communicating and educating the entire U.S. population about quality.

How can the concept of quality be simplified so that it is easier to understand? It has always struck me that quality professionals aren't speaking the same language as the rest of the country. And the abstract definitions and carefully crafted semantics found in quality textbooks and standards don't do much to improve communication either.

In my 15 years' experience as a teacher, researcher, and promoter of quality, I have found telling others about quality very rewarding. I have found that quality is best communicated by using words that are the opposite of what most people think of as conventional. Instead of using words conveying goodness, I use words conveying problems (see Figure 2.1). These are words most people are familiar with and know as blunt truths of the times.

Figure 2.1.
Conveying the Problems of Poor Quality

❏ **What is quality?**
It is about defects, defectives, nonconformance, errors, inconsistencies, delays, unreturned phone messages, broken or unfulfilled promises, frustration, headaches, problems at work, repair, redoing jobs, late or wrong deliveries, quick fixes, being under pressure, administrative hassles, poor attitudes, low morale, poor motivation, lack of trust in products and services, wasted time, unutilized human talent, unbalanced inventories, and friction between employees, managers, customers, and suppliers.

❏ **What is quality control?**
It is defect control, error control, frustration control, and the control of all the negative and disheartening problems just mentioned.

❏ **What is quality assurance?**
It is assuring that some or all of the problems just described are not allowed to occur in any community or organization so that human suffering, hassles, and loss of pride in workmanship can be avoided.

When unconventional words are used to describe quality, listeners seem to get a real, down-to-earth picture in their minds about its true meaning and why it is important. Major hurdles are thus overcome. People can relate quality imperatives to their everyday life. A spark ignites in them, and they start looking for tools and techniques they can use to improve quality.

These unconventional words have grabbed management's attention as well as the attention of all those who can make a real difference. including teachers, politicians, doctors, lawyers, husbands, wives, and children. Fellow passengers on airplanes and buses—people who have never heard anything about quality management—have found the conversation very interesting. After giving lectures and seminars, attendees have often said, "I've never been told about quality control [or quality assurance or total quality management] this way before."

I urge readers to communicate quality using these unconventional terms on every possible occasion to help arouse the masses to the nation's No. 1 priority.

Reference

1. Ryan, "A Job with Many Vacancies."

When this column was published in March 1991, Madhav N. Sinha was the technical development officer in the Labor Inspectorate Division in the provincial government of Manitoba, Canada. Sinha was a senior member of the American Society for Quality.

The Socratic Method Produces Enlightened Employees

by Donald Ponge

Did you ever try to convince someone that you can't inspect quality into products and that inspection is costly, but when you were through, you weren't sure whether you got your point across? Next time, don't try to sell your point; instead, let people convince themselves. Using the Socratic method—asking leading questions so that individuals discover and learn the answers for themselves—is effective in teaching quality and manufacturing concepts.

An example of how it works

At Lutron Electronics, three manufacturing facilities supply products to headquarters, which, in turn, ships the products to the customers. Although each facility has its own quality control process, headquarters had historically performed a series of quality audits before shipping the products. To reduce the lead time to customers and reduce quality costs, an off-trailer shipment (OTS) program was initiated. In this program, the headquarters' quality audit was eliminated when a production facility was certified based on its product quality level. When developing and implementing the OTS program, however, it became obvious that not all manufacturing employees clearly understood the benefits of certifying their facilities.

Here is how the Socratic method helped. Groups of 10 to 15 employees were asked to construct a flowchart of the manufacturing quality inspection process. To start the discussion, the beginning and end of the inspection process (i.e., getting components from suppliers and delivering the final product to the customer) were placed on a board in front of the group. With prompting, the employees created the flowchart shown in Figure 2.2.

Two questions were then written on the board. The questions and the employees' typical responses were:

1. We should perform a final audit at headquarters. Why?
   - "To be positive that the products are good."
   - "We make and sell a high-quality product, and an extra check can't hurt."
   - "Damage during shipping could occur."
2. We should not perform a final audit at headquarters. Why?
   - "Because the facility is confident that the products are good."
   - "It is costly to audit again at headquarters."
   - "It takes time to audit again at headquarters."

A vote was then taken to determine which practice was better. The vote usually yielded mixed results. After allowing some debate (if the group was one-sided, the

Figure 2.2.

The Flowchart Created by the Employees

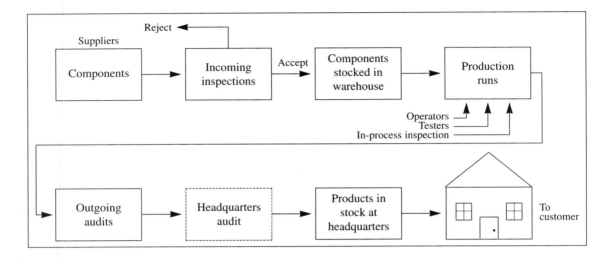

group leader spurred a debate by arguing the other side), the following scenario was presented to the employees:

You go home from work today at 5 p.m. and stop at the market. You smell freshly baked bread and ask the baker for a loaf. He responds, "You'll have to come back at 8 p.m. I need to inspect the bread first."

When asked whether they'd wait, the employees said they wouldn't even wait until 5:05 p.m. "Who has the time?" responded one employee. "Besides, if the baker has to inspect the bread, what's wrong with it?"

Suddenly, the headquarters audit didn't seem like such a good idea to the employees. The need for high quality at the source became more obvious to them.

Currently, all three Lutron Electronics manufacturing facilities are certified, and the headquarters audit has been eliminated. Headquarters audits the facilities to continuously monitor their activities. This audit, however, is much smaller in scope than the headquarters audit, is not very costly, and doesn't delay products from reaching the customer.

Another use

In addition to teaching quality and manufacturing concepts, the Socratic method is effective in combating resistance to change if it is used before the change is introduced. For example, once the headquarters audit was eliminated, the employees were asked again to look at the flowchart and determine what else could be done to save time and money. They suggested purchasing components just in time for production runs and eliminating the warehouse. Then they worked to implement those suggestions.

When this column was published in January 1992, Donald Ponge was the quality control supervisor for the Caribbean Manufacturing Operations of Lutron Electronics in Coopersburg, PA. He was an American Society for Quality member and certified quality engineer.

The Buchanan Scale Identifies the Best and the Worst
by Dennis Grahn

Menasha Corporation's total quality management process—the Menasha Excellence Process—has been implemented corporatewide for a number of years. Menasha has had some success, but it admits that it is just in the beginning stages.

The Menasha Excellence Process demands that management changes the way it manages products, services, processes, and, most important, people. The problem is that some managers do not want to change. Although managers at all levels have resisted, the change has been particularly hard for first-line supervisors, who see their primary job as directing, controlling, and disciplining the work force rather than being a mentor, coach, trainer, and team builder. Another factor that sometimes inhibits commitment to the Menasha Excellence Process is that many divisions have a stable financial history. This stability leads to the if-it's-not-broke-don't-fix-it syndrome.

To encourage commitment, the company uses the Buchanan Scale (Figure 2.3), a tool to communicate to line managers that they have a role in the Menasha Excellence

Figure 2.3.
The Buchanan Scale

Worst	Better, but not good enough	Best
1. Covert resistance The line manager torpedoes the process behind the scenes. **2.** Overt resistance The line manager openly says, "I will not change my style, which has worked well for 20 to 30 years!" **3.** Impassive The line manager believes that this too will pass, believing, "If I ignore it long enough, it will go away as all 'management programs' eventually do." **4.** Acceptance The line manager says, "You mean IBM, GM, Ford, Chrysler, 3M, Polaroid, Kimberly-Clark, James River, etc., require it? Okay, I accept!"	**5.** Support The line manager says, "Okay, I understand, I support you, and I'm committed. You go do it!" (Some line managers call this commitment.) **6.** Sponsorship The line manager says, "As a line manager, I spend visible amounts of my highly prioritized time making the process work."	**7.** Zealot The line manager says, "I passionately sponsor this process."

Process. The scale was developed by Bruce Buchanan, the company's vice president of corporate support services.

The Buchanan Scale communicates the need for change. It also helps the corporation address an important goal in the Menasha Excellence Process: that people know what's expected of them and how they're doing in meeting those expectations. When used properly, the scale is a strong communications tool.

The Buchanan Scale answers the question, "How do line managers respond to the Menasha Excellence Process?" More specifically, it answers the question, "How do managers respond when they realize top management is asking them to significantly change their role, exchanging (which is sometimes perceived as giving up) some of their traditional directing and controlling responsibilities for other kinds of responsibilities?"

Top management asks the line managers where they are in the Buchanan Scale. The only place to be is 6 (sponsorship) or 7 (zealot); 5 (support) is not good enough for the process to work. Line managers are given assistance and time to become at least a sponsor, but, ultimately, it is their responsibility to get there.

When this column was published in September 1989, Dennis Grahn was the director of corporate quality management for Menasha Corporation in Neenah, WI.

The Communicate-Listen-Act System

by Noel Flynn

One of the most important factors in a quality program is communication. Most quality programs, however, do not include a system for employees to communicate their ideas.

While attempting to develop an effective internal communication system, I saw the answer sitting on the receptionist's desk: a phone memo log. Whenever the receptionist answers the phone and cannot reach the desired individual, she writes a message in the log. She keeps one copy, and the other copy goes to whomever the message was intended for.

Borrowing this approach, I created a customized quality improvement memo book. It contains triplicate copies: one copy goes to the quality manager, another goes to the manufacturing manager, and the third stays with the employee. This memo book is the foundation of Mitek Systems' three-step communication system:

1. Enable employees to communicate their ideas.
2. Listen to what employees are saying.
3. Act on employees' ideas.

The memo book has been distributed to the 110 employees at Mitek Systems, a manufacturer of computers, printers, and fax machines based in San Diego, CA. Its purpose and use have been explained to employees.

How it works

Employees can fill out memos on any problem or suggestion concerning the company's quality, from the quality of products to the quality of facilities. Everyone who submits a problem or suggestion for improvement is guaranteed a response. Sometimes after investigation, the perceived problem is found not to be an issue or the suggestion is determined not to be viable. In either case, the outcome is always sent in writing to the originator. It is important that the originator be informed that, although no action was taken, the communication is appreciated and valued and that he or she should continue submitting memos.

It is also important that memos be responded to quickly. The average time to process a suggestion is one to two weeks. Some memos require more time to evaluate and resolve because of their complexity. Throughout the evaluation and resolution process, the originator is kept informed of the memo's status. Urgent memos (such as a memo about a problem that stops a production line) are responded to immediately.

All memos are reviewed by one of two quality improvement teams consisting of employees from all company areas. Team members are rotated every four months to ensure that everyone in the organization participates on a team.

Before participating, team members receive training. They learn about the memo system's goals (companywide continuous quality improvement and improved communication) and their roles in the system (to become efficient problem solvers and implementers of quality improvements). They attend a session on problem-solving techniques and five three-hour classes that cover problem statements, storyboards, flowcharts, Pareto diagrams, and cause-and-effect diagrams. After being taught how and where to apply these techniques, team exercises are conducted to ensure that each member thoroughly understands them.

A quality improvement steering committee oversees the system. This committee, consisting of managers, offers support and resources for investigating and implementing improvements.

A data base keeps track of the memos generated. It stores the names of the originators, problem and suggestion descriptions, dates, and teams assigned. When a memo is completed, information on the outcome is entered. A printout of the completed memo is then returned to the originator so he or she can see the results.

The rewards of this program are primarily nonfinancial. Team members are formally recognized for their participation in and contribution to the program: At the end of their four-month term, they are each given a wristwatch bearing the Mitek logo. Employees who submit memos are recognized informally through feedback from the quality improvement steering committee and are rewarded by seeing their suggestions implemented.

When the memo books were distributed throughout Mitek, employees were extremely enthusiastic about the prospect of sharing their ideas. In less than three months, more than 150 memos were submitted. Fifteen months into the program, about 280 memos were submitted.

Everyone benefits

As a result of this communication system, substantial and quantifiable improvements have been made in such areas as product quality, manufacturing processes, documentation, and inspection. Employees have gained a sense of involvement and accomplishment. The increased interaction with people from other departments has given employees a better understanding of each other's jobs and their interdependence.

Because the changes at Mitek Systems are clearly evident, they serve as a motivator. When employees know they can communicate their ideas and that someone will listen to and act on them, they participate more often.

When this column was published in June 1993, Noel Flynn was the quality assurance manager at Mitek Systems in San Diego, CA. He was an American Society for Quality member.

How to Train for Quality

One Good Idea contributors frequently write about the subject of training. In fact, this is the largest chapter in this book. Why is this so? Our first guess is that for most people (especially in the baby-boom and older generations), training in quality-related areas never happened in high school or college classrooms. Even today, according to the annual education listing in *Quality Progress* magazine, the schools offering quality training number in the hundreds while the total number of schools in the United States is in the thousands.

The 16 ideas in this chapter fall best into three groups: overall training approaches, getting started, and specific training subjects.

Overall training approaches

Applying the same rigor to its training curriculum as it does to its problem solving is a key to success for Colonial Penn Insurance Company, according to Jill Ellis Feninger in "Quality Quality Training."

Using the teaching material that you study is the best way to ensure your comprehension of it, says Forrest Kessler. This can be done by implementing "The Learn-Use-Train-Facilitate System."

Cooperative learning programs can quickly create well-trained workers. But that won't happen when such systems are improperly organized. Henry Kling describes how to prevent disorganization in "Co-Op Program Is an Important Process."

Quality improvement shouldn't be approached as an isolated activity, according to Tom Troczynski. Quality's role throughout the production process is illustrated as "The Quality Chain."

Dealing with a workforce for which English is not the primary language, and perhaps not even a second language, is challenging enough without introducing the new language related to improving quality. Robert Smith, in "Training for Non-English-Speaking Employees," contends that providing training in employees' native languages increases the chance that a quality effort will succeed.

Getting started

Even if all employees do understand the same language, consider the daunting task of learning the language of quality. Hedy G. Abromovitz believes trainers must be aware of buzzwords, but encourages them to have a little fun with the situation, in "Get Quality Meetings Buzzing."

With buzzwords under control and common terminology in hand, participants can understand any instructions they are given, right? Maybe not, according to John F. Thiele. His "Experiment Shows the Importance of Training" argues for operational definitions of the words people are expected to use.

A roomful of people awaiting the wisdom of the trainer might be in need of an icebreaker. "TQ Scramble: A Participatory Process That Works for Teams" is just the mixer needed, according to Dolly Berthelot.

Cheese isn't at the top of our list of training props (even if we have spent many years living in Wisconsin), but John J. Lawrence and John S. Morris have found yet another use for this dairy product. They describe this new use in "Cheese Isn't Just for Eating Anymore: Use It to Introduce Basic Quality Concepts."

Specific training subjects

Considering the article title "Companies Need to Help Employees Cross the Grand Canyon," you might believe that Richard Yingling was writing about wilderness survival. Instead, he is writing about how his organization helps employees visualize the challenges of solving problems.

Few subjects merit more attention than variation. Understanding this concept can lead to a better understanding of processes and people. Carolyn K. Amy and Ann Strong cover a lot of territory in a little space with "Teaching the Concepts and Tools of Variation Using Body Temperature." John Petrie's "Pick a Card, Any Card" is a simplified version of the red bead experiment made popular by W. Edwards Deming.[1,2,3]

Knowledge of variation leads to the need for control charts. Robert D. Zaciewski examines the theoretical basis for control charts in "Versatile Visual Aids."[4]

The final three entries in this chapter are innovative methods to teach well-known quality tools:

- "Sticking with Flowcharts" by Leland R. Beaumont is quite clever because he has created an invaluable flowchart of the flowcharting process.[5]
- Jerry A. Fuller and Marisa W. Palkuti show how to "Use the Weather Page to Teach Histograms." (Both Thomas J. Cartin, in *Principles & Practices of TQM* and Nancy R. Tague in *The Quality Toolbox* do a nice job of further explaining histograms.[6,7])
- Joe Browne has a point to make and a devious way to make it in "Is Acceptance Sampling in the Bag?" (*Juran's Quality Control Handbook*, fourth edition, by J. M. Juran has a great deal of information about acceptance sampling.[8])

References

1. Deming, *Out of the Crisis*, pp. 110–12.
2. Walton, *The Deming Management Method*, Chapter 4.
3. Gabor, *The Man Who Discovered Quality*, Chapter 1.
4. The articles in this and the preceding paragraph might lead you to seek a broader understanding of variation. To do that, see the extended sections about the subject in Joiner, *Fourth Generation Management*, the December 1990 issue of *Quality Progress*, or any book by or about Deming.
5. It can be argued that the definitive text on the subject of flowcharting is Galloway, *Mapping Work Processes*.
6. Cartin, *Principles & Practices of TQM*.
7. Tague, *The Quality Toolbox*.
8. Juran, *Juran's Quality Control Handbook*.

Quality Quality Training

by Jill Ellis Feninger

Read J. M. Juran. Read Philip B. Crosby. Read W. Edwards Deming, Kaoru Ishikawa, Tom Peters, and Masaaki Imai. What are the components they agree are critical to any successful total quality management (TQM) program? "Top management," you'll probably answer. Of course, you'd be right. Another vital element they agree on is the importance of training—training in concepts, processes, and philosophies. "QC begins with education and ends with education," said Ishikawa.[1]

I'm sure your company has a quality improvement training program. I'm certain you could easily rattle off numbers of programs and trained employees. But how certain are you of what's going on in those classrooms?

Over the past two years, Colonial Penn Group, Inc. has been developing and implementing its TQM process. Colonial Penn is taking a three-dimensional approach that emphasizes quality planning (policy deployment), quality improvement (problem-solving teams), and quality maintenance (customer focus). It has designed a quality improvement training curriculum as part of this approach. Colonial Penn applies the same rigorous plan-do-check-act (PDCA) discipline to this training curriculum as it applies to its problem-solving process. PDCA helps ensure that those providing the training are meeting the needs of their customers: the employees. Here's what Colonial Penn has learned about problem-solving process training.

Train teams as teams

Don't simply develop a quarterly training schedule and weave individual team members into various classes. Instead, schedule all team members into class together. Train them together. Even seat them together around tables in the classroom. Because problem-solving process training is largely hands-on, you should schedule no more than three teams into each class.

The main benefit from training teams as teams is that, by the end of a day-and-a-half class, members will have already spent one-third to one-half of class time engaged in group activities. So the group's team development has already begun by the time the members actually participate in their first team meeting.

If group-dynamic and team-building skills are part of your training content, try the following: Conduct one team-building exercise with the team leader serving as an observer. This will provide probably the first and last opportunity for a team leader to sit back and observe the workings of the team. Past participants have been particularly grateful for this opportunity.

Train in chunks

Basic learning theory (and common sense) will tell you if you don't use what you've learned as soon as possible after formal training, you'll probably forget it. Peters said,

"If you don't do something practical with what you've learned within 72 hours, you won't do anything at all."[2]

With a process as complex as problem solving, it's unrealistic to assume trainees will remember all covered tools and techniques in the months following class. So why not provide training in modules? The initial module can establish the overall structure of the process and cover the tools and techniques needed to define the problem (e.g., brainstorming, data gathering, check sheets, and Pareto charts).

After team members have quantified and stratified their problem, they're ready for the next module. The trainer can conduct analysis training (e.g., cause-and-effect diagrams, verification, and scatter diagrams) at a team meeting. The team can then immediately apply these newly learned tools and techniques to its problem. Future modules can be offered in the same just-in-time manner.

Train in the real world

Experience has taught trainers that groups aren't nearly as interested in generic examples—such as the typical cause-and-effect diagram for why a car won't start—as they are in work-related examples. So if a team has been assigned a general problem area, you should use examples from this area when teaching the process.

From a training perspective, using work-related examples can be challenging. How can you go through the process using a real issue when you don't have accompanying data? After all, problem solving is nothing if not data driven. But you can research available data or even simulate data, if necessary.

If you train teams as teams, train in chunks, and train in the real world, teams will get off to a faster, more focused start while making the most efficient use of both training time and learning theory. Isn't that what training is supposed to be about?

References

1. Ishikawa, *What Is Total Quality Control? The Japanese Way.*
2. Tom Peters, from a speech presented at the Philadelphia Area Council for Excellence Conference, Sept. 23, 1988.

When this column was published in March 1989, Jill Ellis Feninger was the manager of quality improvement and planning at Colonial Penn Insurance Company, Philadelphia, PA. She received a bachelor's degree from The George Washington University. Feninger was a member of the American Society for Quality.

The Learn-Use-Train-Facilitate System
by Forrest Kessler

Effective communication of total quality management (TQM) principles and techniques is critical to TQM's successful implementation. You must communicate your commitment to TQM and educate your associates in the subject. The learn-use-train-facilitate (LUTF) system is a means to accomplishing both.

In the LUTF system, you study and apply TQM, then use the knowledge and experience you gain to help others learn to use the tools (see Figure 3.1). This system offers many benefits. Using the tools and then training others not only reinforces your learning, but also demonstrates your commitment to TQM. In addition, the assistance provided to others helps ensure successful TQM implementation. The system is extremely efficient because the number of people being educated increases exponentially.

The steps in the LUTF system are simple. First, you learn about TQM by:

- Attending training programs and seminars
- Studying books, videotapes, and other media
- Working with people knowledgeable in TQM principles, such as quality consultants

The best way to ensure comprehension of a subject is to either use or teach the material studied. With the LUTF system, you do both. After studying TQM, you put

Figure 3.1.
The LUTF System

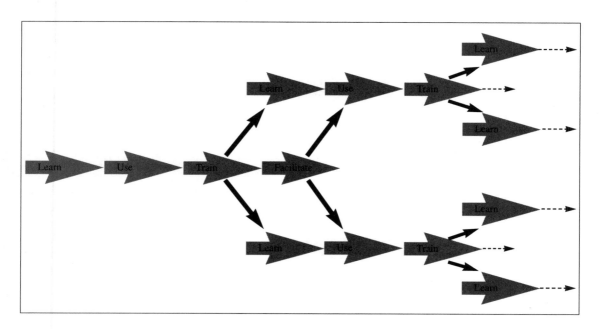

the principles to use so that they become your tools. You can either work on a simple individual project or become involved in a larger TQM project. If you select an individual project to work on, it should be one that has a high chance for success, can be completed in less than three months, and is within your area of responsibility. If you select a larger TQM project to work on, make sure that someone knowledgeable in TQM is leading it. The larger project can be multifunctional.

Once you are experienced, you can teach others, using training materials from an outside source or those you develop. For a less formal approach, you can simply get others involved in your TQM projects, training them as you work.

At this point in the LUTF system, it is a good idea to audit the accuracy of your understanding of TQM; you do not want to teach incorrect philosophies and techniques that might do more harm than good. The audit can be performed by returning to the source of your learning: your training materials, your instructor, or a quality consultant. You might even need an expert to help you train others and clarify issues you are not yet comfortable with.

Now it is time for you to facilitate a project. You will be coaching those you taught as they practice using TQM tools and techniques. This activity will ensure your understanding and further demonstrate your commitment. Once the individuals you trained are experienced, they will be ready to communicate with and train others.

The number of individuals involved in and committed to TQM will grow rapidly within the LUTF system. To make the system work even faster, the number of people you train and facilitate can be increased. For example, if you train four others rather than two, more than 1,300 people could be working within the LUTF system in five sequences (the first four you train would work with 16 others, who would train 64 people, who would help 256, who would assist 1,024). Of course, the number of people trained is never a constant number, but as the number of people each trainer works with increases, so does the efficiency of the LUTF system. In addition, the demonstrated commitment of each trained individual provides the encouragement needed to implement TQM throughout your organization.

The greater number of people who understand and are involved in the TQM effort, the greater its chance of success. Xerox Corporation demonstrates this relationship. Xerox implemented the Learn-Use-Train-Inspect (LUTI) process, which is similar to LUTF, to provide TQM training to its employees. In the LUTI model, managers first learn about TQM principles and tools; then they use the tools on projects in their work areas. Once they have finished their TQM projects, they train their staff on how to use the tools. As the staff members use the tools, the managers inspect to make sure the tools are being used correctly. David Kearns, then the chief executive officer of Xerox, began this cascading training process in 1983; by 1988, all Xerox employees worldwide received TQM training. In 1989, the Xerox Corporation Business Products and Systems won a Malcolm Baldrige National Quality Award.

Since the benefits of successful implementation far outweigh the pains associated with change, you will want to maximize your chance for success. You can increase the odds by using the LUTF system and encouraging others to do the same.

When this column was published in November 1992, Forrest Kessler was the president of Forrest A. Kessler & Associates in New Orleans, LA. He received a master's degree in engineering from the University of Louisville in Kentucky. Kessler was a member of the American Society for Quality.

In most fields, you can't get a job without experience, and you can't get experience without a job. Co-op programs were invented to solve this catch-22.

In co-op programs, colleges and businesses create formal arrangements that permit students to alternate between school and career-related work. Although it is called a program because it has a beginning, middle, and end, I have found it to be a process of human growth and professional development that needs to be effectively and efficiently structured.

Sometimes co-op students are left with busy supervisors, who, in turn, pass them on to others who are not prepared for the responsibility. Other times students are merely given odd jobs unrelated to their careers. Such co-op students become disappointed because they don't acquire meaningful knowledge and experience; thus, they form a bad opinion of work sponsors.

When working with engineering co-op students in the past decade, I found there are several steps that you can take to ensure they receive the proper training.

First, if possible, start them off in the inspection department—it's the best place to begin an engineering career. By training people in inspection methodology, you have an excellent opportunity to get them in the habit of always considering quality and reliability issues.

Second, since the shelf life of a modern technology degree is less than 10 years, you need to stress *how* to think, not *what* to think. To do this, you should create a structure that enhances the co-op students' human growth and professional development.

Human growth

To nurture human growth, you should stress:

- *Values.* Explain your corporate credo and quality policy. Give true-life examples. Include definitions for "businesslike" and "professional." I define "businesslike" as being organized, efficient, timely, and dependable. I define "professional" as being trustworthy, ethical, knowledgeable, and experienced.
- *Integrity.* Explain to the students that they should not give their word unless they intend to keep it. If failure is anticipated, they should inform those involved.
- *Teamwork.* Explain that, as the late Ray Kroc, entrepreneur of McDonald's fame, rightly said, "None of us is as good as all of us." Discuss the five C's of teamwork: coaching, consideration, communication, coordination, and cooperation.
- *Maturity.* Explain to the students that they need to think beyond "what I need" to "what customers need."
- *Thinking skills.* Provide exercises designed to enhance creativity, teach students how to ask proper questions, and build human relations skills.

Professional development

To help co-op students grow professionally, you should provide:

- *A syllabus.* Students look for structure. You can provide it by preparing and following a syllabus. The syllabus I used covered three months and included the fact that we would meet daily for 30 minutes to discuss such essentials as assembly, inspection, metrology, and installation.
- *Methodologies.* As with all people, students need to see the logic behind the way things are done.
- *A training package.* You should prepare a training package that includes checklists of items you need to cover and questions you should ask. The questions should test both the right side and left side of the students' brains; that is, ask down-to-earth questions to test comprehension (left side) and blue-sky questions to encourage creativity (right side).
- *Rewards.* After the students have completed a given task or exercise, they should be rewarded. Co-op students at my organization were rewarded with certificates at official ceremonies.

A long-term investment

Does this preparation sound like too much trouble? Does it require resources your company doesn't have? At least schedule co-op students to work in departments that parallel their curricula. For example, schedule their first semester in drafting, the next in assembly, and the last one assisting an engineer. Such structure will be an improvement to ad-hoc mentoring.

If you are thinking about including a co-op program in your organization, plan an efficient, effective structure. It is a long-term investment. You will help develop a pool of the type of people your company would want to hire.

When this column was published in October 1991, Henry Kling was retired from the U.S. government, for which he worked as an electronics technician. He received an associate degree in electronics from Capitol Radio Engineering Institute in Washington, DC. Kling was a member of the American Society for Quality.

The Quality Chain

by Tom Troczynski

The quality chain in Figure 3.2 synthesizes three important quality concepts involved in production activities: process performance, measurement, and product characteristics. It was developed at the University of British Columbia to help quality engineering students understand that these concepts are integrated and part of a larger system. Its application, however, is not limited to college students; it can be used to teach virtually anyone who is learning about quality concepts.

Measurement is at the center of the quality chain. This location emphasizes the importance of measurement, which links process performance (left) to product characteristics (right). Both the process and the measurement of it (which is a process in itself) are influenced by people (P), the environment (E), and materials, machines, methods, and money (the four M's). This is depicted by the fishbones pointing to the process and measurement links in the quality chain. The six influences of P, E, and the four M's clearly correlate with those in Kaoru Ishikawa's cause-and-effect diagram.[1]

Figure 3.2.

The Quality Chain for Production Activities

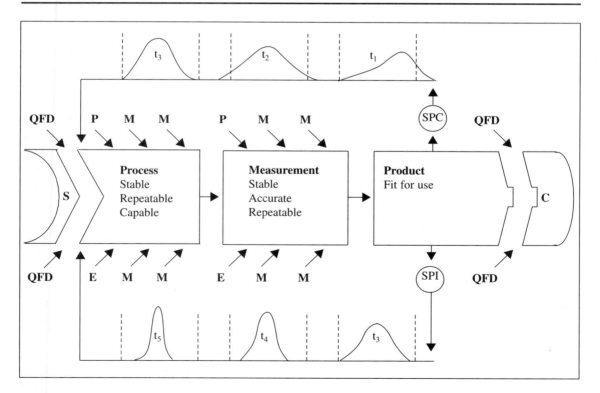

The desired performance of a process is high, sustained stability, repeatability, and capability. High, sustained stability and repeatability are also desirable in the measurement system. In addition, a good measurement system produces results that are accurate and precise.

If the desired performance for the process and its measurement are achieved, there is a good chance that the resulting product will be fit for use. If this is not the case (or if the fitness-for-use qualifications change due to competitive market conditions), two classes of statistical quality assurance tools can be used: statistical process control (SPC) and statistical process improvement (SPI).[2] SPC's primary goal is to monitor a process's outcome to identify early symptoms of special-cause variation that could shift the process into an out-of-control state. SPI's main objective is to improve in-control processes. SPI includes dozens of tools and methods, ranging from evolutionary incremental improvements (i.e., kaizen) to extensive changes suggested by statistically designed experiments.

SPC and SPI, however, can only be applied if reliable process-output data are available through stable, accurate, and repeatable measurements. Both should be implemented in feedback loops that compare the product's actual parameters to those desired, so that the process can be modified if needed. While SPC and SPI are complementary, SPC should always be introduced first since a process improvement would not even be noticed if the process were unstable and unrepeatable.

A change in the product due to the use of SPC tools (and the subsequent modification of P, E, or the 4 M's) appears along the upper feedback loop in Figure 3.2. Initially, at time 1 (t_1), the product characteristics might fall beyond the specification limits (as illustrated by the broken vertical lines), causing the distribution to be off center and nonsymmetrical. This indicates that the process is likely to significantly fluctuate with time—a feature of an out-of-control process under the influence of special-cause variation.

Corrective action should stabilize the process and center the process output. This is schematically indicated in the figure by the distribution at t_2. Eventually, the product variation range should fall within the specification limits to the distribution shown at t_3. Although the reduction in variation ensures process stability and repeatability, it does not guarantee high capability. This is schematically illustrated by the process outcome spread covering the whole specification range at t_3. Such a process is sensitive to minor changes in average and scatter and has a low process capability.[3]

At this point in time, wise organizations start SPI. This is the lower feedback loop connecting the product data to the process parameters in Figure 3.2. The SPI tools can be different from those used in SPC, but invariably they have to act again on P, E, and the 4 M's. Successful SPI actions will eventually increase process capability with time, as exemplified by progressively narrower distributions at t_4 and t_5. (Changing market conditions, however, might dictate adjusting the distributions to a new desired average and specification limits.)

Production activities are frequently only part of a larger customer-supplier chain. Thus, the process in Figure 3.2 is presented as such. To the left is the supplier (S) of the production activities, and to the right is the customer (C) of those activites. Both ends will join the larger chain, but only if the customer's expectations match the supplier's output. While the quality of the supplier's output is determined through extensive, constant use of SPC and SPI, a good match calls for something more: detailed, quantitative knowledge of the customer's expectations. This knowledge can be gained through quality deployment function (QFD).[4] QFD results in learning the customer's explicit expectations, present and future. Using QFD, a supplier must adjust its product characteristics to match the customer's expectations. This is illustrated with the puzzle-piece-like ends of the C and S links in the quality chain.

The quality chain synthesizes several important quality concepts in a compact, self-explanatory graphical representation. Although Figure 3.2 just addresses production activities, the quality chain can also be used to teach quality concepts in service activities. Whether for service or production activities, the quality chain helps integrate and systematize quality concepts that otherwise might seem unrelated.

References

1. Ishikawa, *Introduction to Quality Control.*
2. Beauregard, Mikulak, and Olson, *A Practical Guide to Statistical Quality Improvement.*
3. Ibid.
4. Akao, *Quality Function Deployment.*

When this column was published in September 1996, Tom Troczynski was an assistant professor in the Metals and Materials Engineering Department at the University of British Columbia in Vancouver. He received a doctorate in materials engineering from McMaster University in Hamilton, ON. Troczynski was a member of the American Society for Quality.

Idea 17

Training for Non-English-Speaking Employees
by Robert Smith

Imagine sitting in a classroom trying to learn the concepts and mechanics of a new program such as statistical process control (SPC) and not fully understanding the language in which it is being taught. For many, it is hard enough just to learn how to apply SPC techniques. Not only would it be frustrating and discouraging to be instructed in a language you don't fully grasp, but your understanding and effectiveness in applying what you have learned would be greatly diminished.

The fact is that many employees in the United States do not speak English or have a limited comprehension of it. Although these employees should be given every opportunity to learn or improve their English, the success of an SPC or similar quality effort depends on everyone's immediate involvement. Thus, they need to be given training in their own languages.

The advantages

The benefits of training employees in their native languages are obvious:

- Employees don't have to struggle to simply understand what is being said.
- Employees are better able to ask questions because they understand what is being said.
- Employees can identify and are more comfortable with their instructors and classmates.
- Employees don't have to be afraid of not being understood or speaking incorrectly.
- Employees can help teach each other.
- Employee involvement is maximized.

The tasks of learning SPC concepts and practicing the techniques still exist, but the employees have a much greater chance of success.

It works

To ensure the success of its SPC program, G & M Manufacturing Corporation hired an outside consulting company to provide training in Spanish for nine of its production personnel who did not speak English fluently. First, the employees received training in the math and statistical concepts they needed for SPC. Then they spent about eight weeks learning SPC basics.

As a result of the training in their native tongue, these employees grasped what they were being taught and asked questions when they didn't. Charts are now being meticulously tended on the production floor. Processes are being scrutinized when unusual patterns appear. These employees are able to answer questions about their processes during audits. I strongly believe that the levels of understanding and performance that have been reached at G & M Manufacturing wouldn't have occurred had the training been provided in English only.

In-house bilingual personnel have also proven to be a great asset in moving the SPC program forward. They will teach future training and refresher courses.

SPC and other quality efforts are hard to initiate, mature, and maintain. Training employees in their own languages offers the best possible chance for success.

When this column was published in June 1991, Robert Smith was a quality engineer and was responsible for SPC training at G & M Manufacturing Corporation in Palatine, IL. Smith was a member of the American Society for Quality.

<table>
<tr><td>Idea
18</td><td>**Get Quality Meetings Buzzing**
by Hedy G. Abromovitz</td></tr>
</table>

The average meeting has 594 buzzwords, unless, of course, it runs longer than an hour. In that instance, you'll probably lose track of the number.

When it's a meeting introducing employees to the concept of quality, the number of buzzwords can escalate. There will be dozens of words that will be familiar only to those who know quality terminology. Along with the buzzwords, there will be acronyms. Companies love acronyms that spell out something clever.

The problem

The problem is that most companies' buzzwords and acronyms continually change. For example, the performance review might be called the performance management system, or PMS, one year and the performance management appraisal, or PMA, the next.

Unfortunately, to those in your organization who've watched programs come and go, total quality management (TQM) might be just another buzzword and acronym. Although you might vow that your organization is committed to TQM, your employees will question this commitment, saying to themselves, "You'll be back next year with the NAITQM program: new and improved TQM."

The solution

There is a way to help avoid this problem and have fun at the same time: Give a buzzer to someone in the meeting. If that person or anyone else hears a buzzword or an acronym he or she doesn't understand, he or she is free to hit the buzzer.

Hokey? Sure. But it can be an effective way to get people's undivided attention—and you'll need it when you talk about quality. You will learn quickly that not everyone is as familiar with the quality language as you are. You will also realize that people get turned off if they hear "benchmarking," "baselining," or "paradigm" too many times. Using such concepts indiscriminately diminishes their importance.

When a person hits the buzzer, you must stop and define the quality term mentioned. Early in the meeting, you should purposely use terms that will prompt people to use the buzzer. After all quality terms have been explained at least twice, the buzzer can be put away.

Naturally, there are some potential problems in using the buzzer as an attention-getter. The person in control of the buzzer might begin using it indiscriminately, or the novelty of the buzzer might wear off quickly. Thus, the buzzer should only be used as an ice breaker to introduce TQM terminology.

When used in this limited fashion, the buzzer has proven to be an effective tool for introducing TQM concepts. It is a fun way to defuse the anger that some people might feel when they're being dragged to a TQM meeting against their will.

The buzzer can also help neutralize cynics who believe that TQM is a lot of jargon with no substance. It will help you convey the message that TQM isn't just another clever acronym.

When this column was published in August 1993, Hedy G. Abromovitz was a TQM consultant and author in Pittsburgh, PA. She received a bachelor's degree in chemistry from the University of Pittsburgh in Pennsylvania. Abromovitz was an American Society for Quality member.

Experiment Shows the Importance of Training
by John F. Thiele

At my company, I used a simple training experiment to illustrate the importance of operational definitions as well as the importance of several of W. Edwards Deming's 14 points. This experiment was performed on a group of five managers who were told they were participating as actors in an experiment resembling a movie script.

The script

The managers were to make believe that their present business went bankrupt. Because most were near retirement age, they received early retirement payoffs. Unfortunately, they were persuaded by a local financial adviser to invest their retirement funds in "safe" junk bonds. They lost everything. Thus, they needed to go back to work. The only employment available was at a quality book publishing company.

I was the supervisor of these five new employees. I needed them to display samples of two books—*Juran's Quality Control Handbook* and *Out of the Crisis*—for customers arriving the next day.[1,2] I instructed manager No. 1 to place the books on the southwest corner of the table for the customers. After he performed this task, I looked at the result (i.e., placement of the books) and made dramatic comments such as "Oh no, that's not right" and "We just don't get good employees nowadays."

Then I gave manager No. 2 the two books and asked him to place them on the southwest corner of the table. I gave him additional information on what manager No. 1 did wrong: He stacked them instead of separating them. I reviewed the job manager No. 2 performed, again making negative comments about the results.

Next, I went to manager No. 3 with the same request and additional information gained from the mistakes of managers No. 1 and 2. This process was repeated with the other managers until I finally gave them the operational definition: Take the books to the southwest corner of the table. Place Juran's book on the table with the front cover facing up. Put the book's bottom edge 6 inches from the south edge of the table. Put the book's bound edge 8 inches from the west edge of the table. Place Deming's book next to Juran's book, with the front cover facing up. Put the book's bound edge 10 inches from the open edge of Juran's book. Put the book's bottom edge 6 inches from the south edge of the table.

After I gave the managers the operational definition, I held a training session. A tool (tape measure) was used to place the books accurately on the table. This experiment could be expanded by taking measurements (distances) and making a run or control chart with them.

What was learned

After the experiment, I explained that most employees in U.S. companies are given vague instructions and very little training—then they are blamed for not doing the job right and for producing poor-quality products and services. The problem is not the employees, but the lack of an operational definition for the task and the lack of adequate training. There is an additional handicap—fear—created by supervisors' derogatory statements. Fear prevents employees from offering useful suggestions on how to improve their jobs and consequently the quality of service. These factors are a major part of the management system described in Deming's *Out of the Crisis.*

Subjective comments from the managers indicated that this experiment enhanced their understanding of operational definitions far more than a theoretical discussion on the topic would have.

References

1. Juran, *Juran's Quality Control Handbook.*
2. Deming, *Out of the Crisis.*

When this column was published in December 1991, John F. Thiele was the maintenance manager at the NASA Ames Operation of Arvin/Calspan Corporation in Moffett Field, CA. He received a master's degree in psychology from Loyola Marymount University in Los Angeles, CA. He was an American Society for Quality member and certified quality engineer.

TQ Scramble: A Participatory Process That Works for Teams
by Dolly Berthelot

Too often teams are thrown together without proper training or experience and expected to perform perfectly. Experiential training can nurture involvement, commitment, and cooperation. An activity called TQ Scramble offers a useful introduction to teamwork and shows the value of high-involvement cooperation.[1] It also can stimulate a lethargic or resistant team, reinforce familiar team concepts, and enhance productivity and working relationships within a team.

The activity succeeds with people of diverse ages, cultures, education, and experience in almost any work or classroom setting. A skilled facilitator should monitor the activity and prompt discussion to explain and emphasize the principles of teamwork.

How it works

TQ Scramble is an anagram game using the words "total quality." First, ask 15 to 20 participants to individually scramble the letters and form new words for one or two minutes, without discussing or sharing information. Afterward, through a show of hands, ask the participants to share how many words they made. Some will have as few as three words while others might have as many as 30; most will have fewer than 10. Expect the best results from those who are highly articulate, creative, and quick-witted or who excel at working alone and under pressure.

Before those who didn't come up with many words feel too bad, ask how the results would have differed if the exercise were based on other, nonverbal skills, such as mathematics, music, visual arts, sciences, or construction. Explore who would be more outstanding in those contrasting activities and why. If the participants don't know, the group needs more instruction on individual and group analysis and sharing. If the variation is minimal, the group needs participants with more varied backgrounds. If participants seem reluctant to openly discuss it, the group needs to further examine interpersonal relations and prevailing cultural norms. With good facilitation, the potential for revelation in this portion of the activity is profound, no matter what the participants' reactions.

Next, divide the participants into teams of five to seven people. Within each team, ask each person to share any two words. Repeat this exercise until all the participants' words are listed. Team members can freely add to their lists as ideas are spurred by input from others, but get at least two words from each team member before a free-for-all exchange. Each team should have a recorder (perhaps an observer) who lists the cumulative words and later shares them with the entire group.

As the teams work, observe and note procedures and interactions. How did everyone contribute, question, clarify, determine standards and rules, set parameters, support or antagonize each other, use disparate inclinations, use skills and talents, and reach decisions? Discuss these observations with the entire group, exploring challenges and conflicts. How might similar challenges or conflicts arise in any group trying to achieve a common goal? Who made special contributions? Did these relate to the task itself (task expertise) or to group processes and relationships (relational expertise)? Were there any surprises?

Note how the dearth of certain skills on any team can be as debilitating as the absence of a critical "e" or "s" in an anagram. Likewise, note that the addition of certain skills can exponentially multiply a team's potential. Of course, it must be the right addition. The letter "z," for example, will add little value to an anagram unless "zoo" or "zebra" are required. Similarly, team composition matters.

Finally, compare the teams' scores not only to one another but also to individuals' scores. Although the teams' scores might be similar, they will be significantly higher than any one individual's score. Even the most skeptical person can't deny this benefit of teamwork.

With 15 to 20 participants, TQ Scramble can be squeezed into an intensive hour; if given two or three hours, however, teams can further strengthen their cohesiveness and their understanding of teamwork.

The activity can be adapted endlessly to meet participants' and organizations' needs. To demonstrate the value of originality, for example, count only those words with more than four letters or those words that only one person came up with.

Important lessons

TQ Scramble teaches teams about themselves and demonstrates the relationship between teamwork and total quality. Participants are enlightened, energized, and enticed toward effective team performance. They learn from experience and from one another. Most important, participants see indisputably that total quality teams must attend to tasks and relationships, that every individual has something to offer, and that a well-functioning team can achieve far more than any one individual.

TQ Scramble illustrates that productive teamwork occurs when diverse, active participants enjoy appropriate, well-planned processes and sensitive, effective facilitation. If one of these factors is missing, it is like a "q" without a "u"—you get little use out of it.

Reference

1. The TQ Scramble process was designed and copyrighted by the author, but may be used by readers as long as proper credit is given.

When this column was published in April 1993, Dolly Berthelot was a communication and training consultant in the human side of quality at Berthelot's Consulting E.T.C. Inc. in Pensacola, FL. She received a doctorate in adult educational curriculum and instruction from the University of Tennessee at Knoxville.

Cheese Isn't Just for Eating Anymore:
Use It to Introduce Basic Quality Concepts
by John J. Lawrence and John S. Morris

Education tends to be more effective when students are active classroom participants. We have developed an activity that has proved both fun for the students and effective at introducing basic quality concepts. It helps students understand the basic definitions of quality, the importance of process variation, the need for product specifications and work instructions, and the power of group quality improvement efforts. We have successfully used this activity in both freshman- and junior-level college classes; it is also suitable for use in organizations' quality training programs.

The activity involves slicing cheese; thus, a block of cheese, a cheese slicer, and a cutting board are needed. The activity works best if the block of cheese is frozen and then thawed prior to use. For a cheese slicer, we use the spatula type with the cutting edge in the middle of the spatula surface. This type of slicer makes it virtually impossible for the students to injure themselves, particularly if they are required to wear gloves.

Let the slicing begin

Begin the activity by asking for a volunteer. Ask this person to slice the cheese, providing no further instructions. The combination of freezing the cheese and the type of cheese slicer used guarantees that the person will be unable to produce nice looking, consistent slices. The remaining students in the class usually find humor in their classmate's inability to perform such a simple task. Try to create an atmosphere that encourages both the volunteer and the other students to openly express their reactions as the activity proceeds, and allow some good-natured ribbing of the volunteer's effort. Someone almost always suggests firing the person or docking his or her pay.

Next, present the finished product to the class and ask if it is of high quality. The answer is invariably "No." Probe the class for why it is not. A laughing "Look at it" is typically the first response. After several students have argued that its appearance makes it low quality, raise the issue of how they intend to use the cheese by asking, "Suppose we intend to make nachos or cheese sauce. Is the cheese still of low quality?" Through the follow-up discussion, introduce the fitness-for-use definition of quality and the importance of understanding the customer's needs and desires in determining quality levels.

More quality concepts can be presented by asking students to assume that the cheese is for the president's luncheon buffet. Using this scenario, reinforce the need to understand customer requirements and then talk about the need to translate these requirements into specifications so that employees know exactly what to produce. At this point, formally discuss the concept of process variation and the desire to minimize slice-to-slice variation. Present the conformance-to-specifications definition of quality and the concept of quality control.

Next, ask the students how the cheese-slicing process could be improved so that variation is reduced and a higher-quality product is obtained for the president's luncheon. After some discussion, introduce the concept of a fishbone diagram and suggest that a systematic group effort to identify the causes of a problem is often more effective than a haphazard, individual effort. This part of the activity can lead to a conversation on how standard procedures (e.g., how the cheese is held), written work instructions, employee training, employee incentives, equipment, equipment maintenance (e.g., the sharpness of the cheese cutter's blade), raw materials, and suppliers influence product variation and quality.

Most students recognize that they would not have thought of as many sources of variation as the group identified. Typically, the volunteer who slices the cheese raises several concerns that most other students miss (such as the need for a fixture to hold the cheese). Use this opportunity to stress the benefit of including the person who performs the work in the improvement effort. If desired, discuss how cost trade-offs can arise in quality improvement efforts when the issue of equipment choice is raised (e.g., the cost of the supermarket cheese slicer vs. that of an industrial cheese slicer).

Conclude the cheese-slicing activity by pointing out that most of the problems identified by the students are system related and traceable back to decisions made by management (i.e., the instructors). Remind the students that most of them initially blamed the volunteer, and stress that care must be taken to avoid holding people accountable for what they cannot control.

Informational and fun

Because students discover these concepts through active participation, they tend to understand the concepts better, remember them longer, and better appreciate their importance. In addition, both the students and the instructors have a lot more fun in the process.

When this column was published in February 1996, John J. Lawrence was an assistant professor of production/operations management in the Department of Business at the University of Idaho in Moscow. He received a doctorate in production/operations management from Pennsylvania State University in State College. Lawrence was a member of the American Society for Quality. John S. Morris was a professor of production/operations management in the Department of Business at the University of Idaho in Moscow. He received a doctorate in production/operations management from the University of Oklahoma in Norman.

Idea 22	**Companies Need to Help Employees Cross the Grand Canyon**
	by Richard Yingling

Problem solving is a core competency of continuous improvement. Many progressive companies have developed or adapted some type of structured problem-solving process that usually involves five to 10 steps, including problem definition, process understanding, cause analysis, solution brainstorming, and project design and implementation. Individuals or teams are then provided with such tools as flowcharting, cause-and-effect analysis, statistical analysis, and charting methods so that they can uncover the root causes of problems and permanently eliminate or control them.

Borden Packaging and Industrial Products, a division of Borden, Inc., introduced a problem-solving process a few years ago, but many managers and employees had questions about when to use highly structured tools to solve problems. Some people believed that they should be used for nearly every problem; others believed they should be tried only when other methods failed.

To help its future problem solvers, the division developed the Grand Canyon metaphor to explain how they should think about problem solving and how to determine when to use structured tools. The metaphor also helps management understand why a cultural change is needed for employees to become effective problem solvers. Understanding these key concepts has helped the division's teams become better at solving problems and more willing to tackle difficult and potentially risky opportunities.

The canyon

A problem exists when there is a difference between what is desired and the current state—in other words, a gap between where you are and where you want to be. Picture the Grand Canyon. You are standing on one side and you want to be on the other side. The objective is to develop and implement a plan that will get you safely to the other side.

The width, or span, of the canyon represents the difficulty of the problem; the wider the span, the more difficult the problem. Small canyons (small problems) can be easily crossed. Some might be so narrow that you could jump across without developing a formal plan of attack. In other words, some problems do not require structured methods. It makes no sense to organize a team and engage in structured problem solving to solve the many minor roadblocks encountered daily.

Wide canyons (difficult or big problems) can't be easily traversed. The wider the canyon, the more structured the tools that are needed. One problem might only require a team using a well-drawn process flowchart. Another more difficult problem might require more complex tools, such as statistical analysis. In the latter case, structure is important to ensure that progress is made without wasting time and resources, that potential causes are fully analyzed, and that solutions are fully debated. It is the problem-solving team's responsibility to reduce the chances of failure by using structured problem-solving tools.

The depth of the canyon represents the risk to the problem solver for a particular problem or opportunity. The deeper the canyon, the greater the chance of disappointment or disaster should a solution fail or a promising opportunity be lost. Imagine looking over the edge of a canyon wall. The longer the potential drop, the more intense the emotions and the need to ensure a successful canyon crossing. Not even the best and bravest problem solver is going to attempt to cross a canyon if he or she fears a fatal fall.

Problem-solving paralysis can result in a company because of the fear of failing. Every company has a culture in which an inherent level of risk aversion exists. Risk aversion can stifle creative and opportunistic problem solving because people try to blame others when an attempt to solve a problem fails. In cultures with high risk aversion levels, avoidance of problem-solving opportunities is the norm. Progressive companies, however, have a risk-taking culture, in which employees spend their energy on learning from their failures instead of on finding someone to blame.

Symbolically speaking, management can reduce the fear of failure by giving employees parachutes, first-aid kits, crash pads, or other tools to help survive a possible fall. In other words, management needs to make it safe to take a risk. Problem solvers must know that management supports risk taking and will expect them to try again if they fail. If a problem-solving effort fails, those involved need to learn what went wrong by asking such questions as: Did the problem occur in analysis, planning, or implementation? What could have been done better?

In a risk-taking culture, more employees will try to solve problems and take advantage of opportunities—the result of which is more successful projects. In many ways, continual improvement is a numbers game: More attempts result in more successes, which leads to progress.

Everyone has an important role

Both management and employees are responsible for creating a problem-solving culture. Employees must determine when they should use structured problem solving and to what extent. Too much structure is wasteful, while not enough structure might result in failure. Management must create a culture that allows risk taking. Although these responsibilities are different, they can both be better understood with the help of the Grand Canyon metaphor.

When this column was published in June 1995, Richard Yingling was the plant manager at Borden Packaging and Industrial Products in Kent, WA. He received a bachelor's degree in chemical engineering from the University of Washington in Seattle. Yingling was a member of the American Society for Quality.

Teaching the Concepts and Tools of Variation Using Body Temperature

by Carolyn K. Amy and Ann Strong

Teaching the concepts and tools of variation can be accomplished effectively by using examples and classroom demonstrations. To make the subject of variation more interesting and meaningful, you can use body temperature as a data source.

Normal body temperature varies from individual to individual by up to 4.8° F and in the same individual over time by as much as 1.09° F.[1] This information can be used in training sessions, especially in health care settings, to illustrate the concept of variation and to demonstrate the development of a histogram.

Several education centers run by the Department of Veterans Affairs use the following exercise in train-the-trainer sessions to teach participants about total quality improvement tools. About 30 participants attend a session, which is taught by two instructors. A digital electronic thermometer with disposable thermometer covers (like the ones used by the Red Cross for screening blood donors) is used to aseptically take participants' temperatures.

During the training session, the instructors ask whether the participants would be willing to provide data. Then, while one instructor continues the training, the other walks around the room, measuring and recording each person's temperature. When it is time to discuss histograms, the instructors refer to the recorded temperatures and use the data to develop a histogram. Figure 3.3 shows the data from a training session, both in raw form and displayed in a histogram.

Figure 3.3.
Body Temperature Data

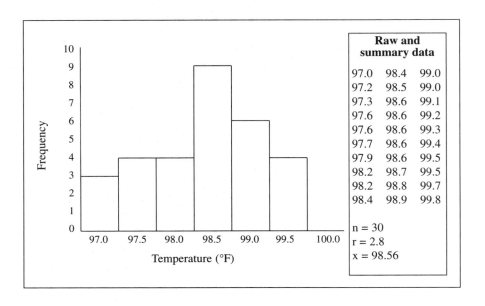

Raw and summary data		
97.0	98.4	99.0
97.2	98.5	99.0
97.3	98.6	99.1
97.6	98.6	99.2
97.6	98.6	99.3
97.7	98.6	99.4
97.9	98.6	99.5
98.2	98.7	99.5
98.2	98.8	99.7
98.4	98.9	99.8

n = 30
r = 2.8
x = 98.56

In their discussion, the instructors focus on a few key points:

1. *The fact that variation happens.* Even in the seemingly most simple or regulated of systems, a range of acceptable or normal values occurs. Using data that have just been collected effectively illustrates this concept to the group.

2. *What is meant by normal or average and how it is determined.* Most people believe that the normal body temperature is 98.6° F. This measure, determined in 1868 by Carl Wunderlich, actually represents an average of more than 1 million body temperature measurements.[2] The students learn that this is the average temperature because someone, at some time, has taken the time to take measurements and determine the expected variation. The participants can predict, within limits, what their temperatures would be because of normal variation. At this point, the concepts of average and variation can be translated into how to measure and track work process characteristics.

3. *How process variation is effectively illustrated.* After learning how to create a histogram, participants can identify whether their temperatures conform to expectations. Developing a histogram based on group-generated data reinforces the effectiveness, ease, and usefulness of this quality improvement tool.

With a little adaptation, this temperature-taking exercise can be used in any type of training session with any number of instructors. Using group-generated data heightens participants' interest and fosters involvement in the learning process.

References

1. Raoff, "Body Temperature: Don't Look for 98.6° F."
2. Mackowiak, Wasserman, and Levine, "A Critical Appraisal of 98.6° F, the Upper Limit of the Normal Body Temperature, and Other Legacies of Carl Reinhold August Wunderlich."

When this column was published in March 1995, Carolyn K. Amy was the educational project manager, National Decision Support System, Education Office, at the Department of Veterans Affairs in Brecksville, OH, Formerly, she was a total quality improvement master trainer and project manager at the Cleveland Regional Medical Education Center, Department of Veterans Affairs. Amy received a master's degree in health sciences education from Case Western Reserve University in Cleveland, OH. She was a member of the American Society for Quality. Ann Strong was a training coordinator and program director at the St. Louis Continuing Education Center, Department of Veterans Affairs, in Missouri. She received a master's degree in community mental health from Southern Illinois University in Edwardsville.

Pick a Card, Any Card

by John Petrie

A bead box is a classic training tool to demonstrate variability and to get people involved in developing run charts. The different colored beads graphically represent various kinds of nonconformances.

One time, however, I was leading an introductory statistical process control workshop and did not have a bead box. I realized that a deck of ordinary playing cards could do the job. I found several identical decks in a local discount department store for about a dollar each. (Several decks were needed because of the size of the group.)

The demonstration

I introduced the variability demonstration by telling the workshop participants, "We are a high-quality manufacturer of playing cards; customer satisfaction is our only objective. One of our largest accounts has invented a new game that only uses three suits of cards. Clubs are unacceptable. We are certainly not going to change our whole manufacturing operation, so we'll just have to remove the clubs and inspect the resulting decks to make sure no clubs are sent to this customer."

I then thoroughly shuffled the decks and gave each participant a sample of eight consecutive cards, face down. I told the participants that their objective was zero defects and that I was relying on them to uphold the company's high standards.

I asked the participants to inspect their samples for nonconformities (i.e., clubs). I then asked participants to indicate the number of nonconformities they found so that I could plot the data on a run chart.

When a participant had zero nonconformities, I lavished him or her with praise, pointing out to the others what can be achieved with effort and dedication. When a participant found one or two clubs, I reviewed the company's objectives with that person and suggested that he or she should concentrate more on the job. If a participant had three or more clubs, I fired him or her on the spot to teach the others an important lesson. Finally, I had the participants calculate control limits to show that the process was in statistical control.

The lesson

This lesson leads to a discussion of:

- How people can be appraised, rewarded, and punished for results over which they have no control.
- How results vary from one sample to another, but with a long-term average approximating the expected value of, in this example, two nonconformities.
- How a stable process does not necessarily meet customer requirements.
- How the only solution to the problem of nonconformances (clubs) is to change the process so they are not produced.

Participants usually comment that their companies operate in much the same way. Participants also learn that inspecting out nonconformities is never the way to achieve what the customer wants.

When this column was published in May 1989, John Petrie was president of Quadrex Resources Ltd., a consulting firm in Mississauga, ON. Petrie received degrees in engineering and business administration. He was an American Society for Quality member.

Versatile Visual Aids

by Robert D. Zaciewski

As a certified adult education teacher in statistical process control (SPC), I have found that my students have difficulty understanding the relationship between control and capability while still maintaining each as a separate entity. To help my students, I use transparencies whose original purpose was to explain the central limit theorem. The main advantage of transparencies is their ability to concisely portray many concepts.

I use two transparencies to explain the control-capability relationship:

- The slide transparency
- The base transparency

As shown in Figure 3.4, the slide transparency displays the distribution of individuals. The natural limits (6 standard deviations) are listed next to the distribution. The distribution of averages is then depicted, followed by the corresponding points for the distribution of averages. Note that the pictorial representation of the distribution of averages is not mathematically portrayed as having the same area as the distribution of individuals. This situation did not prevent my students from accomplishing the two course objectives for the target population:

- To be able to define process stability and process capability
- To identify the tools, data, and parameters used to measure process stability and process capability.

Figure 3.5 shows the base transparency. The specification limits at the top are equal to 16 gauge increments (zero to ± 8). The control limits at the bottom are from the distribution of averages. The $\overline{\overline{X}}$ and the upper and lower control limits are labeled. The control limits are divided into the 6 standard deviations of the distribution of averages.

Figure 3.4.

The Slide Transparency

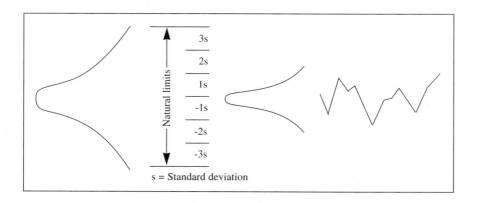

Figure 3.6 shows what occurs when the slide transparency is laid on top of the base transparency. The process is now centered on the nominal (target) value of zero. If the process remains centered, the plotted averages will indicate statistical control. (The range portion of the control chart should be looked at first.) As shown in Figure 3.6, only common cause variation is present. With control (i.e., stability) established, capability can be determined. In this case, a C_p value of 1.33 is depicted (i.e., 75 percent of the specification tolerance is used). With the process centered on nominal, the C_{pk} value is also 1.33.

As shown in Figure 3.7, moving the slide transparency toward the upper specification limit causes a shift in the central tendency of the process. This introduction of special-cause variation into the process results in an out-of-control condition on the $\bar{X}$ portion of the control chart. This part of the exercise can be used to effectively illustrate the fallacy of imposing specification limits on a control chart.

After this exercise is complete, I show my students one more transparency that compares the data, tools, parameters, and evaluation of capability and control (Figure 3.8).

To maximize the value of these visual aids, the instructor should be a skillful presenter and knowledgeable technician. If the topic is not skillfully covered, students might infer that capability can be determined just by analyzing the control chart. Only by practicing with a peer group will the instructor become proficient and confident in using these visual aids. As with all processes, instruction becomes stable and capable only when variation is minimized.

Figure 3.5.
The Base Transparency

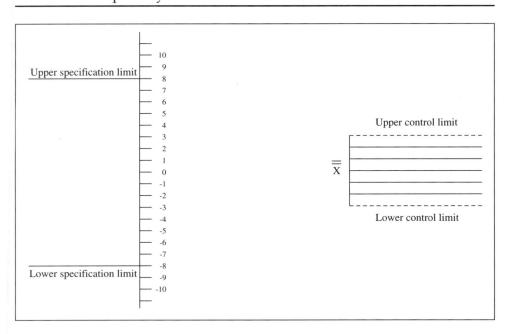

Figure 3.6.

Slide Transparency on Top of Base Transparency

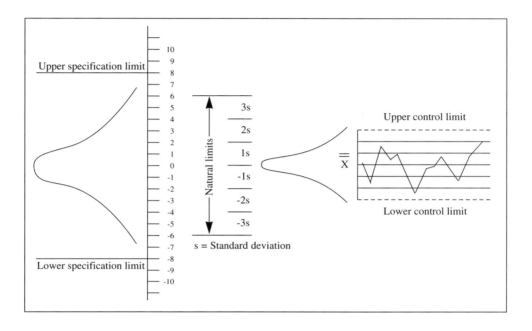

Figure 3.7.

Moving Slide Transparency Toward Upper Specification Limit

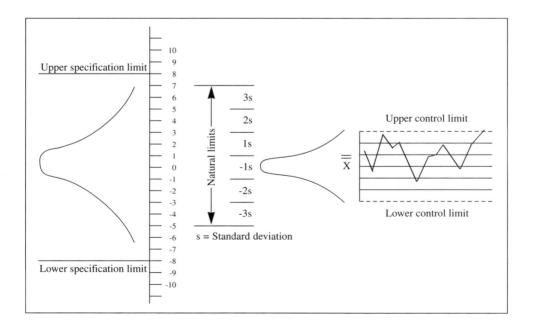

Figure 3.8.

Comparison of Data, Tools, and Parameters

CONTROL		CAPABILITY
If control has been established, <u>then</u> capability can be assessed		
Averages ($\overline{X}$) and ranges (R)	*Data*	Individuals (X)
Control chart ($\overline{X}$ – R), $\overline{X}$, and R	*Tool*	Histograms and normal curves (6-sigma spread)
Control limits	*Parameters*	Specification limits
Stability of the process over time	*Evaluation*	Ability of the process to produce parts within specification limits

When this column was published in January 1993, Robert D. Zaciewski was a quality control instructor and implementer at UAW-GM Quality Network Implementation Support Team in Detroit, MI. He received an industrial engineering certificate from Owens Technical College in Oregon, OH. Zaciewski was an American Society for Quality member, certified quality engineer, certified quality auditor, certified quality technician, and certified mechanical inspector.

Sticking with Flowcharts
by Leland R. Beaumont

The importance of flowcharts in quality improvement efforts is well known. Teams, however, still seem to struggle with using this tool, often facing the following difficulties:

- Team members are unsure of where to begin drawing the flowchart.
- The first few drawings quickly become a tangled mess of lines as process steps are added, moved, and reconnected.
- Work activities are often confused with work products; thus, work activities and work products are inconsistently applied in the flowchart.
- Team members disagree on the level of detail needed.
- Team members question the lasting value of a flowchart.
- Employees often do not use the completed flowchart effectively in their daily work.

In working with many teams creating flowcharts, I have developed a technique that is useful in solving these problems (see Figure 3.9).

First, hand out packs of self-stick removable notes to each team member. Have each person write on a self-stick note one activity he or she performs or an item he or she handles in the process being flowcharted. Have the team members continue writing activities and items on separate notes until they slow down or stop.

Have one team member offer a note that seems central to the process. Place that note in the middle of a large sheet of paper hanging from an easel or wall. Discuss whether the note describes an activity (verb) or an object (noun). If it describes an activity, draw a bold rectangular border around the note. Next, ask for other notes that describe activities preceding or following the activity on the sheet. Place the preceding activities above the note with the rectangular border, and place the following activities below the note. Draw connecting lines to indicate the flow of control.

If the note describes an object, draw a parallelogram-shaped border. Have the team decide whether it is an input to the process, an output from the process, or an intermediate work product. Ask for other notes that describe inputs, outputs, and intermediate products. Place them in their appropriate positions, moving the notes around to provide space for new ones. Work forward from inputs, backward from outputs, and both ways from intermediate products. When the team is confident of the notes' placement, connect them with lines.

Review the final flowchart for completeness and level of detail. Ask the team:

- Are all process steps simple enough so that operators can perform them?
- Are all inputs and outputs shown and connected?
- Are the decision blocks defined using unambiguous and objective criteria so that employees can evaluate whether the criteria are met?

Have the team modify the flowchart to satisfy these needs. Assign a team member to draw the flowchart neatly.

Figure 3.9.

A Flowchart of the Flowcharting Process

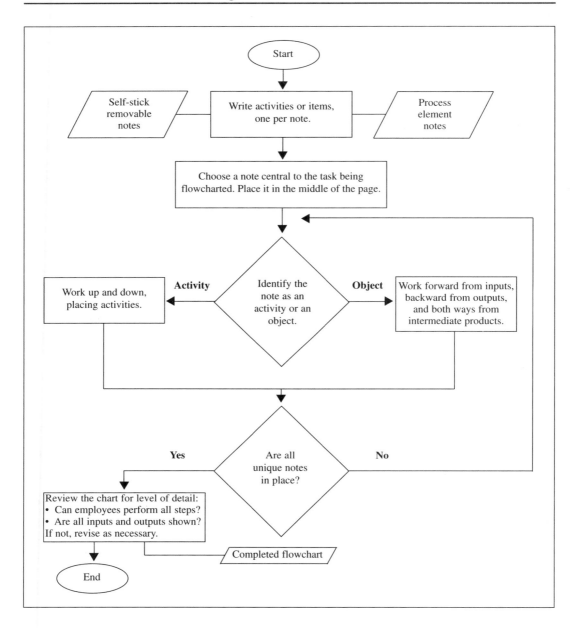

Next, get feedback. Post the flowchart in work areas, inviting co-workers to suggest improvements. If necessary, redraw it based on their suggestions. Then show the flowchart to customers and suppliers, inviting their improvement suggestions. Once again, revise the flowchart if necessary.

Now it is time to put the flowchart to work:

- Mark process measurement points on the flowchart. These might be measures of transit time, defects, or rework. Use this information to simplify and improve the process.

- Use the flowchart to discuss or report the status of projects. Ask employees to indicate on the flowchart at which point they are in their specific projects.
- Use the flowchart as the basis for procedures documentation as part of compliance efforts to standards such as ISO 9000.

With this flowcharting technique, teams can quickly produce accurate flowcharts and use them effectively in improvement efforts.

When this column was published in July 1993, Leland R. Beaumont was the head of the Engineering Process Improvement Department at AT&T Bell Laboratories in Middletown, NJ. He received a master's degree in electrical engineering from Purdue University in West Lafayette, IN. Beaumont was an American Society for Quality member.

Idea 27	**Use the Weather Page to Teach Histograms**
	by Jerry A. Fuller and Marisa W. Palkuti

As quality instructors, we constantly receive pleas from our students to demonstrate the concepts being taught with practical, real-life examples. The students' cry for examples underscores a basic principle of adult learning: adults quickly grasp concepts related to their previous knowledge and experience. With this in mind, we combined the weather report with histograms and discovered a unique way to present the concept of process variation.

The only tools you will need are a flip chart, the *USA Today* weather page, and a marker. Prior to class, review the weather page to determine the highest temperature, the lowest temperature, the temperature range, the number of temperature classes to include in the histogram, and how wide those classes should be (e.g., 5° span or 7° span). On the flip chart, draw and label your x and y axes. The temperature scale should be consistent with the range for the high temperatures reported for all 50 states.

When class starts, tell the students that they will be driving to the airport, catching a plane, and flying to an undetermined location in the United States. Not knowing their exact destination, they will need to pack appropriately for a range of temperatures. To keep their bags light, they will need to construct a histogram to analyze variations in temperatures across the nation.

Next, hand the weather page to one student and ask him or her to call out the highest temperature recorded for each state. As the numbers are read aloud, mark an "X" in each appropriate class until the 50 temperatures have been recorded (see Figure 3.10).

Then ask the students to make general observations about the range and shape of the distribution. To facilitate discussion, you might ask them: Why does the distribution look this way? Are there any extreme points on the histogram? If so, what might account for these readings? How can other unique characteristics of the histogram be explained? The students might notice a bell-shaped distribution or perhaps a bimodal or skewed distribution of temperatures.

At this point, expand the discussion generated by the weather map example into the details of constructing, interpreting, and applying histograms to the improvement process.

This is a quick, fun introduction to histograms. It is easy to picture the concept of variation and relate it to personal experience. After all, everyone can relate to the weather. More important, it simplifies the concept of process variation, reduces some of the students' anxiety about using this statistical tool, and creates an environment for learning.

We have used this method of teaching process variation and histograms in numerous consulting assignments, training projects, and histogram training sessions. In addition, total quality improvement master trainers in the Department of Veteran Affairs were taught this technique as part of their master trainer training and have the option to use the technique during team leader/facilitator and team member training sessions in Veteran Affairs medical centers. We find the technique to be well received because it helps students understand averages, shapes, and types of distributions of histograms and it uses available data.

Figure 3.10.

The Histogram

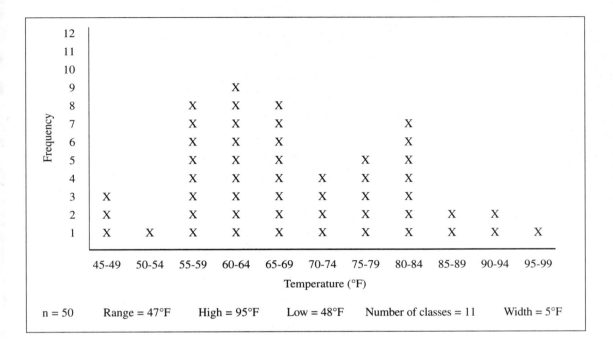

When this column was published in September 1993, Jerry A. Fuller was the vice president of operations for APQC Consulting, a subsidiary of the American Productivity and Quality Center in Houston, TX. He received a bachelor's degree in operations research from Franklin University in Columbus, OH. Marisa W. Palkuti was an education project manager for the Department of Veteran Affairs at the Cleveland Regional Medical Education Center in Ohio. She received a bachelor's degree in education from the University of Kentucky in Lexington. Palkuti was an American Society for Quality member.

One of the most common sources of confusion among employees at all levels is the error found in attributes acceptance sampling. It is commonly believed that a constant sample size taken repeatedly on a single lot of product should yield the same percentage of errors. When a certain entity is sampled and found to be defective, the call goes out to take another sample. If this sample is taken (but it shouldn't be taken), there is a chance that the second sample will pass. The immediate reaction is "How can we find 2 percent defective one time and 0 percent the next? Obviously, the sampling procedure is defective."

I have found an exercise that clearly illustrates the problem with sample-based acceptance sampling. To conduct this exercise, all you need are marbles, paper lunch bags, and an empty box that is 1 foot wide by 2 feet long by 1 foot tall.

The sampling exercise

Prior to class, put a series of 12 or more lunch bags inside the box. Put 20 marbles—16 of the accepted color and four of the rejected color—in one bag. Keeping possession of the box of bags is key to the lesson.

When class starts, announce to the class that an exercise is being done to accept or reject bags of marbles based on the presence of a certain color marble that will be called defective. With the box behind the podium or held high to conceal the trick, choose the bag with the marbles and take a sample of five. With the class's help, calculate the percent defective and make a disposition on the bag. If there are no defective marbles, the bag is good for shipment to the customer. If defective marbles are found, the bag must be rejected and scrapped. In either case, return the marbles to the bag and place the bag back in the box.

Repeat the process of "choosing" and sampling a bag about a dozen times. Invariably, there will be some good bags and some bad ones. When you get a bad bag, pledge to do better next time.

After you get a several bad bags in a row, ask for a volunteer to take over sampling the bags. When this person opens all the bags and finds all but one empty, the class will realize that they have been making decisions on the same bag and arriving at different conclusions about the quality of that one bag.

The truths of the matter

The lessons to be learned from this quick exercise apply to all types of sampling inspections, from receiving inspection to final acceptance sampling. The following truths should be stated to the class:

- A constant sample size does not guarantee constant results.
- It is possible and indeed probable that different conclusions can result on a single lot of material if sampled repeatedly.

- A single sample does not reveal the quality of the lot, but rather merely suggests it. A single sample might allow defective products to be shipped to a valued customer.

When a class member asks the obvious questions—"If this is not the way to be certain about products, what is?"—then the most important lesson of all will surface. The only way to make certain that defectives do not reach the customer is to make the manufacturing process incapable of making them.

When this column was published in August 1989, Joe Browne was a quality engineer for Rockwell International Automotive Division, New Castle, PA. He received an engineering degree from Tennessee Technology University in Cookeville.

How to Get Feedback

Brian L. Joiner writes that organizations should do their best to increase customer complaints. "The trick," he writes, "is to increase complaints while improving the quality of your products and services."[1] His underlying point is that organizations must make it easy for customers to provide feedback.

George R. Bateman and Harry V. Roberts suggest that this process should start early. Their article, "Two-Way Fast Feedback for Continuous Improvement of Teaching and Learning," shows how instructors can use a simple form to learn more about both themselves and their students. While designed for classroom use, broader application is clearly possible. (We're familiar with one professional group that used a variation of this process. It was unclear, however, whether the participants took it seriously. Their frequent answer to the question "What one item could the facilitator have done to improve this meeting?" was "Next time, bring doughnuts.")

A frequent frustration for people attempting to improve operations is that they understand the task at hand, but they believe their manager doesn't. Gerard R. Tuttle and Richard I. Lester tackle that dilemma in "Employers Provide Supervisors with Feedback." Their plan includes thoughtful ways to protect the innocent (that is, respondents).

This chapter's three final entries focus on different approaches to gathering feedback related to customers:

- "Using QFD to Identify Customer Needs" by Gregg D. Stocker is a quick examination of how quality function deployment (QFD) can be used to identify and prioritize internal improvement opportunities.[2]
- "Executive Calls: A Jump Start for Your Quality Program" reminds organizations that they must not allow their top executives to lose touch with customers. The process described by author Robert N. Robertson could have easily served as the inspiration for a memorable television commercial for a major U.S. airline from several years ago. After being fired by its best customer, the boss announces that the staff needs to immediately reacquaint itself with its other customers. An assistant distributes airline tickets to everyone gathered in the room.

- "Listening to the Behavior of Customers" argues that customer feedback is inconsistent and frequently inadequate. To learn about customers, one must observe them in their surroundings. Author Michael E. Smith shares an unusual experience to reinforce his opinion.

References

1. Joiner, *Fourth Generation Management*, p. 85.
2. Readers seeking a more complete QFD explanation could examine the concise chapter on the subject in Cartin, *Principles & Practices of TQM*.

Two-Way Fast Feedback for Continuous Improvement of Teaching and Learning

by George R. Bateman and Harry V. Roberts

Two-way fast feedback is springing up at colleges and universities nationwide. The key idea is for instructors to use simple surveys to get fast feedback from students at all or most class meetings and then, in return, give students prompt, detailed feedback (oral or written) on their feedback.

Although many instructors use a "minute paper" that asks only one or two questions (such as "What was the muddiest point in the lecture?" and "What was the most important thing learned?"), a more formal survey, still typically only one page long, can also be used (see Figure 4.1). The key requirements are that the process be systematic and sustained and that instructors provide prompt, reverse feedback to students, not only by changing the manner of teaching (when necessary), but also by clearing up confusion and answering questions that were not raised during class. If these requirements are not met, the feedback effort might fail.

Two-way fast feedback leads to never-ending improvement of teaching and learning via correction of teaching flaws reported by the students. It also opens up a second channel of communication between the instructor and students. For example, if a student indicates that a point was

Figure 4.1.

Fast Feedback Survey

This particular survey was used for a three-hour session in a course on statistics and quality management. The computing question was understandable to students because a major goal of the course was to give students hands-on experience in using statistical computer software to perform interactive statistical analysis of quality data.

If you are having problems with the course, please get in touch with me!

	Little or nothing	A fair amount		A great deal
Overall, how much did you get out of today's class?	1	2	3	4	5

What was the muddiest point?

What single change by the instructor would have most improved this class?

	Much too slow	About right		Much too fast
On balance, how did you find the pace of today's class?	1	2	3	4	5

Comments?

	Inadequate	Adequate		Ample
How do you assess your preparation for today's class?	1	2	3	4	5

Comments?

	Little or nothing	A fair amount		A great deal
How much did you get out of the readings for today's class?	1	2	3	4	5

Comments?

	Very insecure	Moderately secure		Very secure
Overall, how secure is your understanding of computing?	1	2	3	4	5

Comments?

Do you have any other feedback about any aspect of the course, including questions about where we're going or topics that you would like to hear more about?

muddy, the instructor can quickly clear it up by giving that student written feedback, without spending more time on the topic in the next class.

Students need and value fast, reverse feedback. Through time, the frequency of teaching flaws is gradually but steadily reduced. Many flaws are obvious (such as illegible writing on the blackboard or overhead or not talking loudly or clearly enough) but seem to require student feedback to be brought to the attention of even the most experienced teachers. Other flaws are more deep-seated, such as muddy points in a presentation. Through time, instructors learn general lessons about teaching:

- Students can never get too many concrete examples to illustrate theories.
- Students are frustrated by course reading packets that contain more material than they can possibly read.
- Students are often inherently skeptical about the value of course material; a little "marketing" by the instructors can reduce this skepticism.
- Constant vigilance is needed to adjust a class's pace to accommodate the needs of all students.

Two-way fast feedback does not encourage students to dictate what should be taught. Although students can offer useful suggestions that should be considered, the instructors must ultimately decide what to teach because they usually know more about the topic than the students. But students have a unique insight into which topics are confusing, boring, or of dubious importance to them. This information does not come automatically; it must be consciously sought and acted on by instructors through the use of fast feedback.

At first, it would appear that two-way fast feedback applies only to college and university courses with repeated class meetings during an academic term. But it also applies to short training courses in business, as we learned recently from Robert F. Anderson, vice president of quality and productivity at UOP. Anderson made a very successful presentation on total quality during one session of a course. (The fast feedback survey showed that his presentation was the most effective module of the entire course.) He obtained his own real-time feedback during this presentation. From this feedback, he prepared a 16-page follow-up handout that included, among other things, a background document on team chartering—a topic that had elicited great interest during the presentation. Needless to say, Anderson's reverse feedback was greatly appreciated by the students. So, whether for short- or long-term courses, two-way fast feedback can be beneficial.

When this column was published in October 1995, George R. Bateman was a senior lecturer of statistics and quality management in the Graduate School of Business and the Graduate Program in Health Administration and Policy at the University of Chicago in Illinois. He received a master's degree in business from the University of Chicago. Bateman was a member of the American Society for Quality. Harry V. Roberts was the Sigmund E. Edelstone professor emeritus of statistics and quality management in the Graduate School of Business at the University of Chicago in Illinois. He received a doctorate in business from the University of Chicago. Roberts was a member of the American Society for Quality.

Employees Provide Supervisors with Feedback
by Gerard R. Tuttle and Richard I. Lester

Total quality management (TQM) requires feedback. In most organizations, only downward feedback is given—in other words, the supervisor tells the employees what they need to do to improve their TQM performance. With the Supervisor's TQM Behaviors Evaluation Instrument, however, employees can provide feedback to the supervisor. The combination of downward and upward feedback will help ensure a thriving TQM effort.

The Supervisor's TQM Behaviors Evaluation Instrument resulted from the feedback of students taking TQM classes at the Center for Quality Education at Wright-Patterson Air Force Base in Ohio. The students expressed concern that their immediate supervisors did not understand and therefore did not implement TQM. Realizing that TQM efforts have to be actively endorsed and practiced from the top down, the students suggested that the class instructors send specific feedback to their supervisors' boss to ensure direction from above in the implementation of TQM.

The students' suggestion made the instructors realize the value that could be gained if employees were able to speak directly and freely to their supervisor about his or her TQM performance. To facilitate this type of feedback, the instructors developed the Supervisor's TQM Behaviors Evaluation Instrument (Figure 4.2).

This instrument examines TQM behaviors identified in the Supervisory Code of Professionalism. The code—developed jointly by managers, employees, and union representatives at the Sacramento Air

Figure 4.2.

Evaluation Instrument

You have been asked to assist your supervisor in the continuous improvement process of his/her total quality management (TQM) skills. Your supervisor will receive only aggregate data so there is no danger of you being identified by your response. There are 21 items to rate. Please rank your supervisor using the following point/value scale:

1 = Never applies   4 = Usually applies
2 = Rarely applies   5 = Always applies
3 = Sometimes applies

1. What is your supervisor's name? _____

2. Provides effective management of TQM processes
   a. Focuses on mission needs _____
   b. Provides vision _____
   c. Defines objectives to develop and executes planning _____
   d. Fosters trust at all levels by exercising loyalty _____
   e. Encourages people to take smart risks _____
   f. Fosters a positive labor-management climate _____

3. Demonstrates followership
   a. Is willing to speak up or speaks up when playing the role of follower _____
   b. Runs the play the team has called _____
   c. Follows through until the job is complete _____

4. Communicates understanding
   a. Fosters open lines of communication to keep information flowing _____
   b. Encourages constructive questions and feedback _____
   c. Listens without stereotyping _____

5. Demonstrates integrity
   a. Is honest _____
   b. Keeps promises _____
   c. Accepts responsibility for success or failure _____

6. Fosters team participation
   a. Is committed to team success _____
   b. Works with team to set and achieve goals _____
   c. Compromises _____
   d. Is willing to accept consensus _____

7. Technical competence and commitment
   a. Has technical competence in TQM _____
   b. Demonstrates commitment to TQM principles _____

Logistic Center in California in 1989—identifies the TQM behaviors that an effective manager should demonstrate.

With this list of behaviors as a guide, any person in a supervisory position can easily ask employees for direct feedback. Employees rate the supervisor using a five-point scale.

To ensure that employees answer truthfully, the feedback must be compiled in a group report. Working under the principle of group consensus, a designated employee should collect and aggregate the data and calculate a median evaluation response for each behavior listed. Individual responses should then be discarded, and the supervisor should be given a scored sheet listing the medians.

Using the employees' feedback, the supervisor can develop a self-improvement plan. If needed, the supervisor can get even more detailed feedback by asking employees: What should I do to improve my TQM skills in these areas? Two methods can be used to collect this information, both of which ensure employee anonymity. The first is the Crawford Slip method, in which employees write their responses on slips of paper.[1] The second is a brainstorming session in which employees provide their responses verbally. (The brainstorming session can also be conducted with the supervisor present. With everyone participating, no one employee can be identified as being more critical of the boss.)

After the responses have been gathered, employees should come to a consensus on a prioritized list of actions that the supervisor should take to improve his or her TQM performance. Units of measure can also be included to identify progress made.

Reference

1. Fiero, "The Crawford Slip Method."

When this column was published in November 1993, Col. Gerard R. Tuttle was the director of academic plans and policy at the National Defense University at Fort McNair in Washington, DC. He received a doctorate in social work from Florida State University in Tallahassee. Tuttle was an American Society for Quality member and certified quality auditor. Richard I. Lester was the educational advisor at the Ira C. Eaker Center for Professional Development at Maxwell Air Force Base in Alabama. He received a doctorate in economic history from the University of Manchester in the United Kingdom.

Using QFD to Identify Internal Customer Needs
by Gregg D. Stocker

Quality function deployment (QFD) is used to organize the needs of external customers. However, many work groups perform functions targeted to meeting the needs of internal customers. Fortunately, they can use the QFD matrix diagram in Figure 4.3 to identify the needs of their internal customers. Here's how to construct and use the QFD matrix.

Step 1. Identify work group functions

In a brainstorming session, have the work group members list the activities they perform regularly in the far left column of the matrix. Across the top of the matrix, have them list the work groups with which they interact. Include a column labeled "External customer" to ensure their needs are considered.

Figure 4.3.
Inspection Department Customers

What / Who	Production control	Purchasing	Engineering	Stores	Manufacturing	Executive committee	External customer	Subtotal	How well?	Total
Design feedback			◎					5	1/5	1
Quality results feedback		◎			◎	◎		15	1/3	5
Quality records	△						○	4	1/5	0.8
Calibrated gages					◎		○	8	1/4	2
Packaging	△	△		◎	△		△	9	1/2	4.5
Final acceptance	○		△			○	◎	12	1/1	12
Material movement information	◎				△			6	1/2	3
Inventory documents	○	○		◎				11	1/2	5.5
Material handling	◎	△		○	◎			14	1/1	14

◎ = Strong (5)   ○ = Moderate (3)   △ = Weak (1)

Step 2. Survey customer needs

Based on the items listed in the far left column, develop a survey for internal customers. Three important questions are:

- On a scale of 1 (weak) to 5 (strong), how important is the task to your function?
- Using the same scale, how well is the task being performed?
- Are there any needs not currently being met by the work group?

The survey results can be summarized and added to the matrix as importance values and success ratings.

Step 3. Determine relationships

Using the survey results, place the corresponding symbols in the appropriate intersecting box. Translating the survey results into symbols lets users easily review the matrix. The group must agree on the symbols' assigned values. In this example, the survey results were averaged to the nearest 0.5 and classified as:

$$0 \text{ to } 2 = \triangle \, , 2.5 \text{ to } 3.5 = \bigcirc \, , \text{ and } 4 \text{ to } 5 = \circledcirc \, .$$

Since it is difficult for many groups to effectively reach the external customer, the group will need to act as the voice of the customer for the matrix.

Step 4. Calculate row values

Add the symbols across each row to arrive at a subtotal for each function. (Use the values listed at the top of the matrix for totals.) Multiply this score by the inverse of the "How well?" column (an average of the results to survey question 2) to get a total score.

The finished chart will show which functions are most important and which need improvement. This will help the work group prioritize improvement projects. Remember to use common sense when interpreting the results (avoid blind faith). In Figure 4.3, it is fairly obvious that the final acceptance and material handling processes need the most improvement.

If the chart is used correctly, a small amount of work will result in a sophisticated Pareto chart for translating subjective ideas into objective data.

When this column was published in January 1991, Gregg D. Stocker was the quality manager at Ruska Instrument Corporation in Houston, TX. He received a bachelor's degree in materials and logistics management from Michigan State University. Stocker was an American Society for Quality member.

<table>
<tr><td>

Idea
32

</td><td>

Executive Calls: A Jump Start for Your Quality Program
by Robert N. Robertson

</td></tr>
</table>

Ask anyone who has tried it—building a quality culture focused on keeping customers happy is not an overnight job. It is a long-term process, but time is precious. Fortunately, you don't have to wait until all the pieces of the quality puzzle are in place to start your quality journey. The executive call program can get you up and running tomorrow.

The executive call program requires no additional personnel or expense, no reorganization, no committee meetings, and no inch-thick procedure manuals. Its purpose is to ensure the satisfaction of important customers, thereby retaining their business and helping the company grow. Here is how you can put it to work at your company.

Make every executive a service rep

Make every senior executive responsible for five of the company's key customers, as measured by revenue or other important criteria; in effect, make him or her a customer service representative. The executive's job is to call each of the assigned customers whenever necessary, but no less than once a year. The executive performs all the duties of any service representative or manager. He or she discusses overall levels of satisfaction or dissatisfaction, assigns the resources to solve specific problems, and learns about the customer's long-term needs so that plans are in place to meet them. The executive doesn't displace the regular customer service representative who deals with the customer regularly. Rather, the two work as a team and keep in touch throughout the year, with the executive being the senior team member.

Most executives profess that customer satisfaction is essential to beat the competition. However, I recall a seminar at Stanford University in which more than 80 executives were asked, "How many of you called a customer in the past 12 months?" Six hands went up, and most of them belonged to marketing executives. It is important not to restrict the executive call program to sales, marketing, and service executives. Senior executives from every department—including legal, human resources, development, finance, production, and plant management—should be involved.

What can you expect?

Ceridian Employer Services in Bloomington, MN, began using this simple but effective program six years ago when it was beginning its quality journey. The company's experience suggests that you can expect these benefits:

- Giving an executive ultimate responsibility for a customer helps ensure that the appropriate resources are assigned to resolve problems. After all, if a senior member of the management team can't mobilize the troops, who can?
- Executives become customer-driven, more sensitive to competitive issues, and more productive leaders. As they receive direct feedback unfiltered through the corporate lens, the executives gain greater appreciation of the real world that

lies outside headquarters. They also learn more about their organization and its strengths and weaknesses.

- A well-publicized executive call program produces forceful evidence that the executives mean business when they say, "Quality and customer satisfaction is everybody's job." When executives become role models for employees, the odds of building a successful, lasting quality culture improve dramatically.
- Most important, the company's strategic and operating plans will be on target and realistic because the executives are armed with direct input from customers. In effect, the customers become partners in determining which direction the company should be heading—and that is the only way to succeed.

You might be thinking, "Great idea, but how do I find the time?" The real question is, "How can you *not* find the time?" Customer satisfaction is the most important job of every employee in your organization. It directly affects profitability. If executives put off calling customers because other activities get in the way, your company has a culture problem.

An executive call program is just one strand in the fabric of a thriving quality culture. It complements rather than replaces existing feedback tools such as surveys and formal research. Executives who regularly move into the front lines will have a marked effect on customer satisfaction and quality throughout your entire organization. So jump-start your quality effort. Get your executives out of the office and in front of the customers, where their time and skills really count.

When this column was published in September 1992, Robert N. Robertson was the general manager of quality and strategic planning for Ceridian Employer Services in Bloomington, MN. He received a bachelor's degree in industrial engineering from the University of Maryland in College Park. Robertson was a member of the American Society for Quality.

<table>
<tr><td>Idea
33</td><td><h1>Listening to the Behavior of Customers</h1> by Michael E. Smith </td></tr>
</table>

You likely have heard about customer-driven companies and how they listen to the voice of their customers. Often, this strategy is put forward as the panacea for all quality ills and as the sustenance of competitive superiority.

Clearly, satisfying the needs and desires of customers is critical to an organization's success. However, just attending to what customers say or write is not enough. Usually, dissatisfied customers don't tell companies about their lack of pleasure; instead, they speak with their actions by obtaining goods and services elsewhere. When customers do tell companies their needs and desires, the information is often inadequate for the companies' needs.

Don't believe what they say

Psychology literature is replete with examples indicating that people often inaccurately report the reasons for changing their behavior. This inaccurate introspection has long been known, and it's been frequently demonstrated by experimental subjects attributing changes in their behavior to any number of seemingly likely causes while failing to detect the experimental manipulations that caused their behavior to change.

There is considerable debate about why inaccurate introspection occurs. However, what is clear is that such inaccuracies could spell disaster for companies relying only on what customers tell them. Even if a company gets feedback from its customers—and that information might not even be from those who have critical concerns—it will probably not learn the cause of discontent or unsatisfied needs.

What can companies do to overcome these concerns? First, they need to continue listening to the voice of their customers. But listening to the customers' voice is not enough. A second action is needed: Companies must listen to the behavior of their customers. In other words, companies must observe their customers to see how they act when using their products or services. Does the observed behavior suggest satisfaction or dissatisfaction? Does the behavior indicate how the product or service can be improved? Does the behavior indicate any new products or services that might be developed to delight them?

Two cases in point

I work at a large government institution for developmentally delayed adults. It has become almost second nature to use these clients' behavior as communication about their wants and needs.

For example, at one point the clients were displaying a high incidence of pica, which is the eating of nonfood items. This behavior most frequently occurred immediately after a meal. The frequency tapered off as the time for the next meal approached. (To the clients, the end of a meal signaled that the probability of immediately eating again was nearly zero; the probability increased as they progressed through the inter-meal interval.)

To some extent, the frequency of pica communicated that the meal times were unsatisfactory to the customers. Thus, several changes were made. One major change was to install client-accessible refrigerators and snack areas stocked with a variety of preferred (again determined by observing the clients' behavior) and appropriate snacks in living and work areas. As a result of these changes, the frequency of pica was substantially reduced. For instance, there were 124 incidents of pica in July 1990 (prior to changes) and only 25 incidents in January 1992 (after the changes).

Such attention seems obvious when dealing with people who lack well-developed communication skills. However, how many restaurants, for example, are observing their customers' behavior?

Another example of the benefits of observing customer behavior is the experience of a manufacturer of cutting chains for chain saws. In spite of mechanisms for listening to its customers (including surveys and interviews), this manufacturer's market share continued to drop in comparison to that of foreign competitors. By spending time with the loggers out in the woods, the company officials were considerably enlightened. While all the loggers said that the chains were excellent, the officials discovered they did not use the chains in the out-of-the-package condition. Instead, they were sharpening the chains before using them. As a result of talking with and observing the loggers, the production sharpening specifications were changed.

By observing customers' behavior and attempting to determine what that behavior might be saying about its product or service, a company can answer questions that it might never have thought to ask and thereby clarify customers' needs and desires. Try observing your customers' behavior—you will like the results.

When this column was published in July 1992, Michael E. Smith was the quality assurance information director at the Fairview Training Center in Salem, OR. He received a master's degree in experimental psychology at the State University of New York at Stony Brook and a master's degree in general psychology at Hollins College in Roanoke, VA. Smith was an American Society for Quality member and certified quality auditor.

How to Get People Involved

There is a rule commonly used at the American Society for Quality called the 20-60-20. We aren't sure where it originated, but it goes like this: For every initiative undertaken, you can expect 20 percent of the people to be supportive, 60 percent to be uncommitted, and 20 percent to be dead set against it.

The latter group can't be convinced to support the project no matter what. They are a modern-day version of Professor Wagstaff, the Groucho Marx character in the 1932 movie "Horse Feathers," who sang, "Whatever it is, I'm against it."

The challenge is to not let that negative 20 percent influence the uncommitted 60 percent. In fact, the major challenge that initiative supporters face is influencing the central block to follow their lead rather than that of the naysayers.

The authors in this chapter offer several suggestions on how to face the challenge of getting as many people involved as possible. For example, Ricky M. Watson involves people by giving them responsibility. The title of his article is self-explanatory: "How Do You Get Everyone to Accept SPC? Try the Adopt-a-Graph Program."

"Get Employees in the Game with Catchball" is an excellent introduction to an underused Japanese data collection process that requires employee involvement. Author Joe Bowman covers what catchball is and is not. He also provides a step-by-step look at how the technique has been used at Dow Chemical Company.

Charlie W. Alexander provides an honest assessment of how involving the right employee can be overlooked. In his case, he was the one who wasn't getting involved. "SPC—Why Not the Quality Department?" shows how a solution can be right under your nose.

Borrowing from a popular television show helped Vera K. Pang. In the "Quantum Leap" show, the main character was forever taking the place of another person. In "Onan Division Takes a Quantum Leap," employees exchanged jobs with others to get a better appreciation of what co-workers did. In the process, the employees gained a better understanding of where their own work fit into the organization.

How Do You Get Everyone to Accept SPC?
Try the Adopt-a-Graph Program
by Ricky M. Watson

One of the challenges that any organization trying to implement statistical process control (SPC) faces is getting all employees to use SPC. Often, SPC is accepted in small, isolated pockets, and the remainder of the organization aimlessly goes about its business.

The Texas Instruments circuit board facility in Austin, TX, was experiencing this very phenomenon. SPC was firmly grasped by some teams; these teams did an excellent job of using SPC in their daily work of building circuit boards. Other teams, however, were having difficulty crossing over from the old way of doing things to the new way of using SPC as a tool for improvement.

The single most compelling cause of this problem was a lack of ownership of the process by some team members. They continued to view the implementation of SPC in their area as something added by management or engineering. In 1990, Ledi Trutna and I developed a solution to the problem: the Adopt-A-Graph program.

Give a graph a good home

The concept behind the Adopt-A-Graph program was to have team members adopt at least one graph from the more than 1,000 graphs in the facility's computer SPC system. The requirements and expectations for adoption were:

1. The adopter must have successfully completed the SPC Tools 1 course. This ensured that he or she could understand the charts.
2. Each person must adopt at least one graph.
3. The adopter is responsible for reviewing the charts daily.
4. The adopter looks for out-of-control situations that have not been corrected, data that are not updated properly or often enough, and insufficient attention to corrective action.
5. The adopter is responsible for alerting the responsible person if the process changes.
6. The adopter is not responsible for fixing the problem; his or her purpose is to oversee and help the team stay focused. It is the responsibility of the persons operating the equipment to resolve all problems.

A popular program

Since the implementation of this program, it has become very popular with all of the teams. As team members change, adopters also change. In most cases, the adopter is one of the people on the team. In some cases, the adopter is outside the manufacturing function (for example, from the quality control or engineering function), but he or she takes the responsibility just as seriously as if operating the equipment.

We chose to highlight the names of the adopters by putting their names next to the titles of their charts. For example, the SPC computer screen might show:

Process: Plating line
Group: Line temperatures
Variable: Sulfuric acid, John
or
Process: Layer line
Group: Etch solution
Variable: Etch concentration, Mary

The program has been so successful that many companies have come to our facility to learn about SPC and have implemented their own Adopt-A-Graph programs. It is a good way to get everyone to own a piece of the SPC strategy and to ensure real process control.

When this column was published in September 1994, Ricky M. Watson was the SPC manager at Texas Instruments in Austin, TX. He received a bachelor's degree in biochemistry from the University of Texas at Austin. Watson was a member of the American Society for Quality.

<table>
<tr><td>

Idea 35

</td><td>

Get Employees in the Game with Catchball

by Joe Bowman

</td></tr>
</table>

Employee commitment in the implementation of a new plan is a key element in that plan's success. Preparing and delivering a presentation about a predetermined plan to employees and asking for their input seldom creates the necessary buy-in from them.

The catchball process, however, can help facilitate employee buy-in. In catchball, management involves employees in developing the plan before any decisions are made. Their involvement is obtained through sessions in which they are free to provide their thoughts and ideas.

How to play catchball

Here are the steps in the catchball process that has been used at Dow Chemical Company:

1. Identify the issue (e.g., a plan or problem) to be discussed.
2. Define the context (environmental conditions) surrounding the issue.
3. Identify the stakeholders (employees affected by the issue).
4. Select a facilitator (usually a manager; skipping a management level—i.e., selecting the boss's boss—works well).
5. Hold a preliminary session for the stakeholders. In this meeting, the facilitator explains the catchball process, the issue and context to be discussed at the upcoming catchball session, and what the stakeholders need to do to prepare for it. Once the catchball process is used several times, this session might not be needed. In such cases, the information on the issue and context is given at the beginning of the catchball session.
6. Send an agenda for the catchball session to all stakeholders. Ideally, there should be about eight to 10 stakeholders per session. The agenda should include a purpose statement, a statement describing the session's desired outcome, and when the session is scheduled.
7. Hold the catchball session. To begin the meeting, the facilitator should state the issue and context and ask if any clarifications are needed. After all questions are answered, participants are asked to share their ideas and give their perceptions on the issue. Participants respond better if a creative technique is used to attract their interest and to demonstrate that honest, innovate ideas are wanted. One technique is to pass a ball (sponge ball or tennis ball) between participants, with the ground rule that only the person with the ball can speak. The person with the ball shares an idea and then tosses the ball to another person. That person restates the previous person's idea and then builds on it with his or her own thoughts. When finished, he or she tosses the ball to a new person. The process continues until everyone has had an opportunity to share his or her ideas. The facilitator can record the ideas on a flipchart.

8. Use the results. The ideas recorded on the flipchart can be used for a variety of purposes, such as to develop plans or evaluate actions. Sometimes more than one session is needed to yield useful results.

What catchball is and is not

Unfortunately, catchball is often improperly applied. Limited session time, fear of retribution, and lack of understanding of an issue and context can limit employees' input. To apply catchball effectively, it is helpful to understand what catchball is and is not:

- *Catchball is a data collection process, not a communication process.* It is used to gain the insights of participants, not to communicate a message to them.
- *Catchball provides a forum in which ideas are shared, not presented.* During catchball, participants don't listen to a presentation and then react to it. Rather, each person is expected to share his or her ideas and listen to those of others. More insight can be gained through effective dialogue than through the traditional approach of presentation and follow-up discussion.
- *Catchball consists of multidirectional communication, not just two-way communication.* Two-way communication requires a predetermined message and order that limits the process. In catchball, ideas are communicated among participants without a prearranged message or order.
- *Catchball is expressive and creative, not structured and analytical.* Although the session is planned and includes an agenda, common meeting rules, and procedures, the flow of ideas is unstructured with minimum direction from the facilitator. Participants are encouraged to think creatively and not be restricted by known conditions and restraints. Catchball is a management tool for gathering abstract concepts and rarely lends itself to structured analysis.

Through catchball, employees can share their ideas on an issue. If those ideas are effectively used, a company can implement a new plan or process that will have their buy-in. Thus, both the company and the employees benefit from catchball.

When this column was published in April 1995, Joe Bowman was a quality process leader at Dow Chemical Co. in Freeport, TX. He received a master's degree in business from Butler University in Indianapolis, IN. Bowman was an American Society for Quality senior member and certified quality engineer.

SPC—Why Not the Quality Department?

by Charlie W. Alexander

Sometimes the solution to a problem can be right under your nose, if you only take the time to look for it. My experience is a perfect example of this.

Shortly after moving into the quality department, I became interested in statistical process control. My interest developed from discussions I had with quality engineers who had received American Society for Quality certification. I was inspired; I would get my certification, too.

I went through the nine months of classes, passed the examination, and was ready. But for what? On my own, I did some studies on the variability of manufactured parts and charted nonconformances of end items. But that was it. The way my organization was set up, there was nothing else I could do.

I talked to the resident SPC expert about doing other projects. He said, "Even though we study SPC in the quality department, SPC is for manufacturing." I thought, that's great, I study for nine months, take a test, and now I find SPC is nice to know, but it's for manufacturing.

A new job, a new situation

Eventually, I changed jobs. The director of quality told me he was in charge of getting SPC implemented. The people in manufacturing had heard about SPC and wanted to give it a try but needed someone to train them. This was my opportunity to get more involved in SPC: I would be a trainer.

First, a steering committee—consisting of the manufacturing superintendent, the manufacturing engineering manager, the director of quality, and several quality engineers—was formed. Then I started a training program and conducted several pilot programs. These projects were successful, but one day the manufacturing superintendent asked the question, "What is the quality department going to do? Manufacturing is now making and inspecting the parts. We did not sign up for SPC to do someone else's job."

The director and I tried to explain to him that SPC was really a manufacturing function and that the quality department's role was simply to provide training. But he was not buying it. About every two weeks, he would again raise the question. He was losing his interest in SPC.

His reaction got me thinking. If I didn't come up with some way to get the quality department actively involved in SPC, the program was going to fail. Then it hit me: When I first became involved with SPC, all I could do was complain that I had done all my SPC training for nothing. Now someone was asking me to get involved and I was fighting the idea. The solution was, quite literally, under my nose the whole time: I was the solution.

I became determined to get the quality department actively involved, but I still had to find a way. If the quality department was going to collect variable data for control charts, who would collect the attribute data for product acceptance? Prior to the Taylor system (creation of specialized departments) in large companies, the machinists inspected their own work. If I could get manufacturing to do some inspection, inspectors would have time to do SPC. I proposed the idea at the next meeting. I told them that if they would document their inspection, the quality department could use this information for product acceptance and could take over collecting and charting SPC data. The manufacturing superintendent agreed, saying that machinists were already inspecting their work informally.

The arrangement

Under this new arrangement, there is one full-time SPC inspector and about one-third of the shop under SPC control. All of the machinist's tools are certified, and manufacturing has agreed to tag all the nonconforming hardware found during inspection. This is proceduralized. The quality department still inspects the first piece and the dimensions the operator can't or doesn't have time to check. The quality department has stressed to the manufacturing superintendent that it doesn't want to interfere with productivity. If the machinist's inspection slows the product flow, then the inspection can be done by the quality department. Seeing that the quality department is concerned with productivity has made the manufacturing supervisor think more about quality. He is asking us to add dimensions to his operators' inspection sheets. He says, "See how much more they can inspect."

The results have been great. Not only has the quality department gotten involved with SPC, but the manufacturing and quality departments are no longer adversaries. Manufacturing is being held responsible for the quality of the hardware, and the quality department is a more productive member of the organization. Everyone is working together to make good parts.

When this column was published in May 1990, Charlie W. Alexander was the manager of quality engineering for J. C. Carter Co. Inc. in Costa Mesa, CA. He was a member of the American Society for Quality.

<table>
<tr><td>Idea
37</td><td># Onan Division Takes a Quantum Leap
by Vera K. Pang</td></tr>
</table>

Idea 37	**Onan Division Takes a Quantum Leap**
	by Vera K. Pang

Part of total quality control is having everyone in the organization feeling responsible for the entire manufacturing process. Participative management can make everyone conscious of costs and quality. This can motivate employees to explore the causes of poor quality and carry out improvements voluntarily. Many companies that have successfully implemented participative management have used some sort of mechanism to promote companywide employee involvement. Onan Corporation Power/Electronics Division borrowed the concept and title of a television series: "Quantum Leap." For two days, employees quantum leaped into different people's jobs.

The quantum leap

The objectives of Quantum Leap Days were to:

- Make employees appreciate each others' jobs
- Understand the problem areas in different work stations
- Boost employee morale
- Demonstrate management's sincerity in committing to employee involvement

Quantum Leap Days worked as follows. Two consecutive work days were divided into four-hour segments. For each segment, about a quarter of each department's employees exchanged jobs with people elsewhere in the division. All job titles, along with the name of the person who holds the job and that person's workstation location, were written down on slips of paper. These slips of paper were divided into four different boxes corresponding to shifts. All 361 Onan employees, from the director of manufacturing operations to the operators, drew from their designated boxes. Once a job title was drawn, the person was obliged to do this job on Quantum Leap Days. People who happened to select their own job were allowed to choose a different slip of paper.

The experiences of Don Shircliff and Tom Johnson provide two examples of how quantum leaping worked. Shircliff, the director of manufacturing operations, spent a shift inserting diodes, capacitors, IC chips, LEDs, and resistors into printed circuit boards. Johnson, a quality worker in the transformer area, spent a morning as manufacturing manager.

The process was set up so that, when a person quantum leaped into the other person's job, the other person would remain at his or her work station for the entire four-hour shift to answer all questions about the job, demonstrate the job, and help quantum leapers do the job.

How does it go together?

The Power/Electronics Division of Onan Corporation manufactures power supplies for the computer and communications industries. Employees were familiar with the division's final products, but were not familiar with what preceded and followed their own positions in the manufacturing process. Many did not know how the parts they made were being used. When Quantum Leap Days were over, many employees said that it was interesting to see what happens to the parts they work on. Most said Quantum Leap Days improved the working relationships among employees.

The division strongly believes that, to achieve maximum quality and productivity, a change process must take place to involve more and more employees and managers in joint problem-solving and decision-making activities. The division hopes that by having all employees quantum leap two days of their lives, they will better understand the importance of employee involvement.

When this column was published in April 1990, Vera K. Pang was a member of the worldwide operations management training program for Onan Corporation Power/Electronics Division in St. Peter, MN.

How to Manage Meetings

Recently, one of us sat through a meeting that was a genuine train wreck. The manager in charge had a long tenure at the organization. But his days were spent in a corner of the organization that was, for whatever reason, routinely overlooked by top management.

Suddenly, business trends shifted and his area was on display. He was called on to take charge of a brand new initiative directly related to his work. He was asked to lead a meeting involving people who were almost all at or above his management level.

The meeting started shakily when he walked over to the only lower-ranking person at the table, placed a pen and pad of paper in front of her, and dubbed her the session's note-taker. Taken by surprise, the woman only stared at him. She thought better of making a scene in favor of going along for the good of the meeting.

The manager then launched into a 10-minute monologue that covered a wide range of subjects. Unfortunately, none were about the matter at hand. Other meeting participants repeatedly tried to steer the conversation toward the subject matter, but were successful for only for short periods of time. The leader was very good at regaining control and delivering more passionate soliloquies.

When the scheduled hour for the meeting expired, most participants explained that they had previous engagements (a few probably did) and bid farewell. Nothing had been accomplished.

This example is extreme, but the fact remains that many people struggle with the task of running meetings and making them valuable for participants. How can such situations be avoided? Frederick Kolano urges leaders to take charge of meetings at the outset with "Kick Off Your Meetings with Flair." He has a sound game plan with ideas that can be adapted to many situations.

Charles Cook says being in mismanaged meetings ranks right up there with being in a traffic jam. He creates the metaphor of a meeting being a vehicle, then shows how to steer clear of congestion in "Trains, Planes, and Automobiles—and Meetings."

In "Take a Gamble: Play Poker at Your Next Training Session," David H. Willis encourages people to arrive at and return to meetings on time. With ordinary playing cards and a few prizes, Willis says participants can stay interested in material all day long.

Brainstorming is a wonderful quality improvement technique, unless the participants in the session don't get along, or don't trust each other, or already think they know the solution before they define the problem, or, well, you get the idea. Henry Kling has a measured, neutral approach in mind in "Get More out of Group Projects by Using Structured Brainstorming."

Idea	**Kick off Your Meetings with Flair**
38	*by Frederick Kolano*

One key to successful meetings is grabbing the attention of the participants. Using energetic, quick, eye-opening exercises to kick off a meeting can go a long way in helping participants view the meeting in a different light and have some fun at the same time. I have successfully used the following approach during my eight years of experience in facilitating groups.

Begin the meeting by discussing active listening, facts vs. perceptions, roles of meeting members, and the meeting agenda.

Active listening

Start the meeting by talking about good human relations etiquette. Tell the meeting participants that they should:[1]

- Focus on the process or product, not people.
- Raise questions for clarification, not for objection or criticism.
- Let another participant finish speaking before they speak.
- Be brief, clear, and to the point.

Facts vs. perceptions

Sometimes groups spend too much time discussing perceptions rather than factual information. The following short exercises can help demonstrate the difference between facts and perceptions.[2]

Tell participants that you will be conducting a short exercise to demonstrate how facts and perceptions can sometimes be confused with each other. Write the numbers 1,000, 1,000, and 40 in a column on a flip chart. Ask the participants to add the column of numbers together and say the total aloud as a group (2,040). Then write another 1,000 in the column. Again ask the group for the sum (3,040). Write 30 in the column and ask for the total (3,070). Add another 1,000 to the column and ask for the sum (4,070). Continue to encourage the group to give answers in unison. Write 20 in the column and ask for the sum (4,090). Add another 1,000 to the column and ask for the sum (5,090). Finally, write 10 in the column and ask for the sum. They should say "5,100" but the majority of the participants will likely respond "6,000."

Your question to the group is: "Why did this happen?" Typical responses are "You tricked us," "We got into a rut," "You led us to the answer," and "It was groupthink" (i.e., conformity to group values, whether accurate or not). After a short discussion, point out that they have just experienced the facts vs. perceptions paradox. Then discuss the following elements of facts vs. perceptions:[3]

- Both exist.
- Both are OK.
- How to distinguish between them.

Another attention grabber that demonstrates the facts vs. perceptions concept is to have participants read the following sentence, which is given to each person on a small piece of paper: "Fantastic fortunes are the result of years of confident pursuit combined with the effort of many people."[4] After one minute, ask the participants to count the number of f's in the sentence. Using a show of hands, ask participants if they counted one f, two f's, three f's, four f's, and so on until everyone has raised his or her hand. Record the answers on a flip chart. Mention that it seems strange that the individual responses are so varied, especially since everyone is working with the same sentence. Ask participants to switch pieces of paper among themselves and recount the f's to ensure that they are all working with the same sentence. Record these answers next to the first responses. Compliment the group if the numbers have improved (i.e., more people have higher numbers).

Now inform the group that the correct answer is eight. Those who did not find all eight probably missed the "f" in the word "of," which is found three times in the sentence. Again, ask why this happened. The reason is that the "f" in "of" is pronounced with a "vee" sound. Many people's minds lead them to find only those words in which the "f" sounds like the "f" in fish.

Later in the meeting, help participants distinguish between facts and perceptions by asking them if points made are fact or perception and why. Encourage participants to ask the same question of others when they suspect that a perception might exist. A few minutes spent on distinguishing fact from perception can save significant discussion time. Just knowing the difference will help participants feel their time is being spent in the most productive manner.

Do not use the two exercises consecutively. Use the second one at another meeting or later in the day to re-emphasize the point. Although both exercises are eye openers and fun to conduct, their real purpose is to make people aware that first impressions are not always true. These exercises will help the group enter discussions with open minds and will most likely improve meeting results.

Roles of meeting members

Discuss team members' roles in a successful meeting. The object is to ensure that each participant's knowledge, expertise, and viewpoints are valued. The following role descriptions can be customized or expanded to fit the meeting's goals:

- Facilitator: Keeps the meeting on track and intervenes to maximize synergy.
- Leader: Ensures that the group does not stray from the topical content of the meeting, contributes information, and breaks deadlocks.
- Participant: Contributes information and makes decisions.
- Scribe: Records important information during discussions and distributes notes.
- Timekeeper: Ensures that the group follows the agenda and calls for breaks and lunch.

The meeting agenda

The last item to cover before the group begins its deliberations is to review the meeting agenda. With the agenda on the flip chart, go through each item, adding a few explanatory words about the major focus of each bullet. Let the team know that the agenda is not cast in concrete; if the energy of the group's discussion peaks on one or more areas, adjustments in the agenda might be needed. Also, put a little humor into the agenda review by telling the group that the "important times" are written in red, with the important times being time off, such as breaks, lunch, and adjournment.

Covering all four of these areas—active listening, facts vs. perceptions, roles of meeting members, and the meeting agenda—generally work well for workshop and interactive team settings. Some activities, however, might not be appropriate for every meeting. For example, business meetings in which financial or proprietary topics are discussed would not be a good time to use the facts vs. perception exercises. Use your judgment. Review the purpose of the meeting and the type of participants and tailor the activities to optimize group synergy. An ideal application for all four activities would be when a group of individuals who do not know each other get together for the first time.

References

1. Janecke, "Upside Down VE, Study Analysis Sessions."
2. AVATAR International Inc., Training Activities.
3. Parker, "Applying Understanding of Individual Behavior and Team Dynamics Within the Value Engineering Process."
4. *Triggers—Skill-Building Exercises for Teams.*

When this column was published in December 1995, Frederick Kolano was a senior value engineering specialist for Rust Geotech, U.S. Department of Energy, Grand Junction Projects Office in Grand Junction, CO. He received a master's degree in business administration from West Virginia University in Morgantown.

Trains, Planes, and Automobiles—and Meetings

by Charles Cook

My two pet peeves are being stuck in traffic jams and being stuck in mismanaged meetings. Traffic jams are often unavoidable, but ineffective meetings are particularly irksome since it is simple to plan and manage successful meetings. Using the necessary tools to create dynamic and inspirational meetings doesn't require a doctorate or months of training. Why, then, are these simple tools so often ignored?

Meetings are too often seen as an end unto themselves. I've attended more than my share of meetings where the object was to get to the meeting. Once there, the participants dutifully filled the allotted time while producing only a minimum of new ideas, plans, and actions.

An effective meeting starts with the understanding that the meeting is not the destination, but the vehicle for reaching a strategic objective or organizational destination. With this in mind, the meeting can move forward.

Thinking of a meeting as a vehicle—i.e., the means to an end—clarifies objectives and itineraries (see Figure 6.1). It lets the participants get in the driver's seat and focus their attention on the results they want to achieve and the means to achieve them. This requires selecting the appropriate type and structure of meeting, picking a competent leader and facilitator, determining the key participants, and identifying the critical steps in making the best use of participants' time and energy.

With a clear destination in mind and way stations noted, it is possible to map the route and determine whether a bike, bus,

Figure 6.1.

Meetings as Vehicles

Meetings	Vehicles
Desired results	Destination
Structure	Route
Critical steps in moving forward	Way stations
Key participants	Passengers
Leader	Driver
Facilitator	Navigator
Type of meeting (informational, problem solving, or team building)	Car, plane, or train
Time and energy spent	Time and fuel consumed

plane, chariot, or truck is the most appropriate vehicle. With a clear idea of the objectives, the participants can determine how each part of the meeting should be structured and managed to achieve the desired results.

Despite how fast, fuel-efficient, or comfortable a vehicle might be, it can still get caught in a traffic gridlock. Fortunately, participants can avoid a meeting gridlock by understanding the purpose of the meeting and effectively planning and managing it.

Increasing meeting productivity requires effectively using leadership, operating systems, measurements, and rewards to motivate people to learn and apply available knowledge. The participants will then be able to use the meeting not as a destination, but as a vehicle to efficiently and strategically achieve their objectives.

When this column was published in June 1992, Charles Cook was the principal of Cook Associates in Old Greenwich, CT. He received a master's degree in psychology from the City University of New York and a master's degree in education from Tufts University in Medford, MA. Cook was an American Society for Quality member.

Take a Gamble: Play Poker at Your Next Training Session

by David H. Willis

Every trainer, whether teaching quality principles or another business subject, is familiar with a problem that plagues all classes: tardiness. Most classes start between 10 and 20 minutes late because of participants' tardy arrivals. In addition, five- and 10-minute breaks stretch into 20 minutes, and hour lunches end up being 75 to 80 minutes long. Before long, an instructor can easily lose up to an hour in a daylong training session. This hour can never be regained—unless, that is, you play poker.

How to play

Poker is a simple technique that can keep participants keenly aware of starting and return times. It also adds an element of fun and competitiveness to training sessions.

To begin, simply purchase two decks of regular playing cards for about every 20 participants. Remove the jokers and shuffle the decks together thoroughly. At the precise minute when your training session is scheduled to begin, deal a card to those participants who are sitting in their seats. Do not explain why you have given them a card. Refuse to give cards to anyone who arrives late.

Once the session begins, review the following rules. These rules should be posted on a flip chart and tied into your discussion of the session's schedule:

- The wall clock is the official clock.
- Participants in their seats when the session begins will get a card.
- At each break and at lunch, participants will be given an exact time when the session will resume. Participants in their seats at that time will be given another card.
- If the instructor is late, all participants get two cards.
- Participants can look at their cards.
- Card trading is not allowed.
- If more than five opportunities are given to receive a card, participants must discard a card before receiving a new one. In other words, participants can have no more than five cards in their hands at a time.
- Aces can be played high or low.
- There are no wild cards.
- At the end of each day, a hand of poker will be played. The participants with the highest and lowest hands will receive a prize.
- Participants must have five cards to play a low hand.

At this point, do not tell the participants what the prizes are. Instead, briefly explain the rank order of hands with the help of a flip chart. The following ranking should be used:

- Five of a kind (highest possible hand)
- Straight flush
- Four of a kind

- Full house
- Flush
- Straight
- Three of a kind
- Two pair
- One pair
- High card
  -
  -
  -

- A, 2, 3, 4, 5 (lowest possible hand)

When the time comes for your first break, tell the group that it is, say, a 10-minute break and that they must be in their seats at 10 a.m. to receive a card. Write the time clearly on a flip chart or post it in another highly visible place. When the designated time arrives, pass cards out to everyone in his or her seat. Repeat this process for each break and lunch.

At the end of the day, give each participant another card. Make sure that you have given them at least five opportunities to earn a card. Ask those participants who have a good (i.e., high) hand to stand up. Using the flip chart containing the cards' ranking order as a visual, ask those who do not have at least one pair in their poker hand to sit down. Then ask everyone who doesn't have at least two pairs to sit down and so on, until only one person is left standing. Award that person a prize. (Make sure you have extra prizes available in case of a tie.)

Next, ask participants with lousy (i.e., low) hands to stand. Ask those who have one pair or better to sit down. Then ask those with a king to sit down and so on, until only one person is left standing. Award that person a prize.

Finally, congratulate the winners, collect the cards, and, if the class continues the next day, remind them of the session's starting time and that they'll play poker again.

About the prizes

Prizes can be anything you want, but don't spend more than $15 on each prize. Company T-shirts and golf balls are usually well received. Books or audiotapes by well-known quality experts or on topics discussed that day are particularly relative and reinforce the importance of the topic. Toys, such as Slinkys and Koosh balls, are also fun. Letting the winners choose from a mix of prizes is always a good idea.

Save time and money

Losing an hour a day due to tardiness is costly in terms of the participants' and the instructor's lost productivity. By initiating this simple activity, the company can actually save money by eliminating lost productivity; this savings more than offsets the cost of the prizes. In addition, playing poker can add a lot of spice to your training. So take a gamble—play poker. Both the company and the participants will win.

When this column was published in October 1996, David H. Willis was a consultant at Salem Continuous Learning, a division of the Salem Co., in Charlotte, NC. He received a bachelor's degree in construction management from Clemson University in South Carolina. Willis was an American Society for Quality member and certified quality manager.

Get More out of Group Projects by Using Structured Brainstorming

by Henry Kling

Committee work can be disappointing. Although people get together for a constructive, creative exercise, they often fall back on basic tactics—politics, rhetoric, demagoguery, and ad hominem—that generate more heat than light unless the leader provides structure. One such structure that I've found helpful when dealing with extraordinary problems is formal brainstorming. Formal brainstorming generates possible causes of and solutions to problems for later analysis and action.

A four- or five-day process

Before beginning the process, volunteers must be recruited and briefed on the agenda. The next step is securing a meeting room that is conducive to creativity. A remote, comfortable room with good lighting and, if possible, a window with a nice view is ideal. The room should be reserved for the same one-hour period every day for a week. With this accomplished, the following schedule should be used:

Day 1: Discuss the problem. Don't consider solutions, just become familiar with the problem. Fuss and discuss, but don't bother with solutions yet. Just get a clear picture of where the group is going.

Day 2: After the problem is thoroughly understood, think about how to solve it. Jump in and ask for solutions—any solutions. Write the possible solutions on a large flip chart that everyone can see. As the sheets become full, tape them to the wall. Just two rules apply at this point: there should be no negative remarks ("That's stupid" or "That won't work") and the group's direction should be closely monitored. Aimless bull sessions, private agendas, and petty politics have no place in brainstorming sessions. Otherwise, there should be no constraints on creativity. Free the minds to fly anywhere.

Day 3: When the group has exhausted its supply of ideas, come down to earth and screen the contributions according to the following criteria:

- Will this idea solve the problem or does it get in the way?
- Is this idea rational, reasonable, and responsible (the three R's)?
- Can the group do a PMI (i.e., can the group evaluate whether the idea is a plus, a minus, or interesting)?

Coming down to earth means implemeting the right solution for the right reason. Ask these questions:

- If this is the right solution, what is the right reason for implementing it?
- How will this solution affect the customers?
- What is important to the company?

Candid answers reveal where the group is going and how it will get there.

Day 4: Decide who's going to do what (including follow-up). Because only a few hard-core volunteers will remain, this final phase is not hard. Be sure to ask for realistic commitments.

Day 5: The room is reserved for a fifth day as a safety valve. If earlier sessions took longer than a day, throwing off the timetable, use this extra day to catch up.

One problem to be aware of is the natural, face-saving, go-along-to-get-along tendency of typical committee work. This occurs during votes, when people raise their hands simply to go along with the majority. To overcome the natural group-think tendency, the committee chairperson might instead ask committee members to submit their votes anonymously by writing them on individual slips of paper.

Two examples

I used this structured exercise on two occasions in a Pentagon laboratory shortly before I had retired. The first was with engineering co-op students who, because of their status as students, were not being given tools. They progressed through all four days, then went back to school. Although none of these co-ops had returned, the supervisor assured me that the tool shortage problem has improved.

The second occasion was with scientists, engineers, and technicians. They determined there was a need for design standards. As a result of the structured brainstorming, they found the need to first learn about designing. They decided to query their respective professional societies for knowledge on this subject. Unfortunately, my recent calls revealed that these apparent hard-core professionals have not done any further work on this subject. Both experiences prove that you need a prime mover to follow through on intentions.

Despite these results, I contend that people should not endure the mediocrity that too often comes out of committee work. If you have extraordinary requirements (which are implicit in quality assurance) but are limited by ordinary resources (the five M's: money, man-hours, materials, machinery, and management), put your human resources into an extraordinary environment: a structured operation conducive to creativity.

When this column was published in March 1990, Henry Kling had retired from the U.S. government. He received an associate degree in electronics from Capitol Radio Engineering Institute, Washington, D.C. Kling was a member of American Society for Quality.

How to Promote and Celebrate Quality

There is nothing easy about rewarding and recognizing individuals' contributions in hopes of raising the profile of improvement efforts. In fact, former Xerox chief executive officer David Kearns once told *Quality Progress* magazine that promoting a person perceived by others as being unworthy was just about the worst action management could take.

There's also the sincerity factor. Do a lame job of recognizing people or celebrating quality and a manager might actually do more harm than good. So then, how does one go about reinforcing positive actions, rewarding good contributions, and seeking more of the same? Ron Baltz calls for "An Alliterative Approach to Recognition and Reward." In other words, he wants to see a consistent and constructive approach. Baltz also has a feeling for common sense. If employees save the organization money, don't hesitate to share the wealth.

Of course, not everyone might have wealth to share. "Celebrating Quality the Cheap Way" by Frederick Kolano shows what a little innovation can do when the organization is containing costs.

Recognition doesn't have to be limited to the workplace. Dale G. Sauers endorses the use of businesslike incentives at college. In "Quality Awards Raise Quality Awareness in the Classroom," he offers examples of appropriate actions to recognize and awards to bestow. Our favorite, of course, was sending a worthy recipient a year's worth of *Quality Progress*.

There are other ways to promote and celebrate quality besides reward and recognition. You can always turn to entertainment, as Herman Senter did. He used the red bead experiment to focus people's attention on quality. How entertaining is the red bead experiment? In the hands of W. Edwards Deming, it was a show-stopper.[1] Herman Senter sounds like he wasn't too bad with it either in "Quality Entertainment." Of course, giving away a television, microwave oven, and food processor will always get folks' attention.

Cheryl L. DeMeuse and Carol L. Jamrosz have a lot of nerve—and a fair amount of imagination. They took the old road map cliche and made it something meaningful in "On the Road to ISO 9000." This is one of the more clever quality promotion and celebration efforts we have seen.

Reference

1. Deming, *The New Economics for Industry, Government, Education,* pp. 158–75.

<table>
<tr><td>Idea
42</td><td>An Alliterative Approach to Recognition and Reward
by Ron Baltz</td></tr>
</table>

Everyone in your company has been trained, teams have been formed, and they are now continuously working to improve process, product, and service quality. In fact, the teams have already begun to see some results. That's great, but to keep the ball rolling in the right direction, you need to recognize and reward quality achievements.

Your recognition-and-reward system must be properly structured, communicated, and understood by everyone in the company. Alliteration—the repetition of initial sounds in neighboring words—can help you remember the important recognition attributes and types of rewards to consider when recognizing and rewarding teams and individuals.

Recognition attributes

A structured approach to recognition allows little room for ambiguity when selecting deserving candidates. To be considered for recognition of a quality activity, a team or individual should have the following attributes:

- An aggressive *attitude toward quality*. Some indicators of aggressiveness are enthusiasm, persistence, and a desire to improve. The team or individual should create a contagious atmosphere that positively affects others. Be on the lookout for people with a good outlook; they will have a lasting effect on everyone they contact.
- *Aptitude and ability*. Training and natural ability together are a valuable combination that doesn't occur by coincidence. Instead, training and natural ability feed off each other in teams and individuals demonstrating above-average performance. French scientist Louis Pasteur once said that chance favors the prepared mind. When quality training and initiative come together enabling a team or individual to succeed, it's time for recognition.
- *Activity in application*. Success comes from doing more than just reading and talking about quality improvement. Look for teams and individuals who, instead of just complaining about problems, are starting their own initiatives to solve them. Preparation is important, but sometimes persistence is the only way to get a job done right.
- *Accomplishments and achievements*. When a team or individual produces the kinds of results that you want to see again, it's time to let everybody know about the team's or individual's accomplishment. Avoid the soft approach. It shouldn't be difficult to identify the tangible benefits of work that deserves recognition. Just remember that some improvements might have a longer payback than others and could amount to even more worthy achievements.

Types of rewards

Once candidates have been selected, you must show gratitude for accomplishments, big and small. The following rewards can be used individually or in combination:

- *Accolades.* Let everyone know what has been accomplished and which team or individual is responsible. Publish articles and photographs in the company newsletter, post announcements on bulletin boards, mention the accomplishments in memos, or put notes in personnel files. Accolades provide opportunities to communicate the importance of quality.
- *Acknowledgment.* A lunch with peers or family or an invitation to share success stories at top management meetings can go a long way in reinforcing the kind of thinking and action that benefits the company. Make it a formal affair and give the champions the respect they deserve for work well done.
- *Awards.* Some type of memento, such as a plaque, certificate, or trophy, can be awarded to those selected. Take the opportunity to reinforce the critical link between the company, the employees, and quality by making appropriate inscriptions on awards. These awards will serve as constant reminders of both the deeds done and the company's awareness and approval of those deeds.
- *Appreciation.* Money might not be a prime motivator, but it's probably the key measure in your business (and it sure makes a nice gift). If a team or individual saves the company money, share the wealth. A small bonus, augmentation of a raise, or preferential consideration for promotion will certainly send a clear message about the importance of participating in quality improvement activities.

A key part of any quality effort is making sure that strategic quality initiatives are translated into the daily activities that move an organization forward. A recognition-and-reward system with clearly defined criteria will reinforce the behaviors that lead to improvement. It will also send a clear message to others who want to get involved by providing them with a pattern to follow—in other words, providing them with training in disguise.

When this column was published in October 1993, Ron Baltz was the quality control manager at the Mauldin Plant of Henkel Organic Products Group in Mauldin, SC. He received a master's degree in analytical chemistry from Villanova University in Villanova, PA. Baltz was an American Society for Quality member, certified quality engineer, and certified quality auditor.

<table>
<tr><td>Idea
43</td><td><h1>Celebrating Quality the Cheap Way</h1>
by Frederick Kolano</td></tr>
</table>

Many companies promote quality awareness and celebrate quality successes through "quality day" or "quality month" activities. Such activities, however, need not be extravagant affairs—you can celebrate quality the cheap way.

Before you gasp and say that it's an abomination to use the words "quality" and "cheap" in the same sentence, think about the following. In those quality celebration activities that you have planned or participated in, what did you get for the money spent? Could the money have been better spent elsewhere? For companies experiencing a reduction in budget or work force, the question also becomes: How do you continue to effectively promote quality awareness while tightening your belt?

Rust Geotech (a contractor for the U.S. Department of Energy that assists in cleaning up contaminated waste and materials nationwide) and U.S. Department of Energy staff found themselves in this latter situation.[1] They wanted to promote quality awareness during Quality Month but had to keep spending to a minimum—or have no celebration at all—because of the well-publicized cost-cutting initiatives throughout the federal government.

The challenge was to promote quality as inexpensively as possible while still providing a quality experience for everyone. After several coordinating meetings, the following events were selected by the Quality Month committee and approved by senior management.

Slogan contest

While you might be thinking, "How arcane," the slogan contest got the ball rolling. The contest involved using the word "team" in a slogan. In all, 25 slogans were submitted. The winning entry, "Team endeavors achieve maximum quality," which was chosen by the Quality Month committee, was submitted by a team of three individuals, each of whom received a small prize, such as a pen set or flashlight. While the slogan contest got employees thinking about quality and teamwork, its total cost was less than a few dollars.

A poker walk for quality

While gambling on company time might seem inappropriate, this version isn't. At this facility in Grand Junction, CO, a walking trail is used by many employees during lunch and breaks. On a nice, sunny October day, five quality-awareness stations were placed along this trail. As a walker passed each station, he or she was given a sheet of paper that briefly described and showed the typical application of a well-known quality tool, such as a cause-and-effect diagram, run chart, or flowchart. Thus, the walkers learned about quality tools while strolling. On the back of each sheet was a printed playing card. As an incentive to walkers, the top poker hands were awarded with small prizes. While there was about a 15 percent participation rate, the cost was minimal—just a few dollars to pay for small prizes.

Peer recognition

Each employee was given the opportunity to recognize an individual, team, or group that exhibited quality in some fashion. Employees wishing to recognize their peers filled out a nomination form and sent it to the quality office. No approvals or reviews were required. The Quality Month committee printed the name and nomination wording on a blank certificate. The finished certificate was then sent to the nominator, who personally presented the certificate to the fellow employee or group. Many people were surprised by the recognition they received. About 20% of the employees participated in this monthlong activity, which cost about $100 to buy the blank certificates.

Puzzles

Some people might believe that puzzles are a waste of money and a waste of employees' time, but these puzzles were designed to spread the quality message. Each week during October, a puzzle was put on the local computer network. The puzzles included:

- A word search made up of quality words
- A list of scrambled quality words
- A puzzle in which you try to find the most words in the word "customer"
- An "Are You a Total Quality Person?" questionnaire[2]

The Quality Month committee randomly picked three winners from all correct submissions each week. In some cases, extra prizes were given for creative or innovative answers to the puzzles. Winners' names were posted on electronic bulletin boards and in other public display areas. Quality awareness and enthusiasm grew with each new puzzle. About 30 percent of the employees participated at a cost of around $50 for the small prizes.

Presentations on quality topics

Presentations were offered on cost-saving documentation, team building, quality tools, and meeting facilitation. Each presentation was about 45 minutes long, with time for questions and answers. Presenters who were not the regular company experts in these areas were sought. Unfortunately, attendance was scarce at these nonmandatory presentations. Perhaps a little more motivation for individuals—such as a suggestion to attend from a peer or manager—could have increased participation. The cost was low: only the time spent to prepare presentations.

An open house

The open house was not an extravagantly catered affair. Rather, cookies and punch were provided, and balloons added a festive atmosphere. At the open house, the winners of the various Quality Month activities received their prizes from senior management. The open house also gave individuals an opportunity to talk about quality and provide the recognition that their fellow employees deserve. A "Wall of Fame" featured job-well-done citations, commendation letters, thank-you letters, and other quality recognition documentation. All of the peer recognition nomination forms were also posted so that employees could read the nomination information. The cost for the open house was about $100 for refreshments, which was donated by the company's Employee Association. Attendance was around 15 percent.

The total cost for facility's month of activities was less than $500. (Some prizes were donated by in-house organizations.) You will have to judge for yourself whether it's worth it. While the goal of the Quality Month celebration was to promote quality awareness, its real value was the personal interaction between employees when they gave each other recognition—in other words, the warm, fuzzy feeling that you get when someone tells you that he or she appreciates what you have done. This unquantifiable benefit goes a long way to help employees work together as a team.

References

1. Rust Geotech's work is performed under Department of Energy Contract No. DE-AC04-94AL96907.
2. Nathanson, "Are You a Total Quality Person?"

When this column was published in July 1996, Frederick Kolano was a senior value engineering specialist for Rust Geotech at the U.S. Department of Energy Grand Junction Projects Office in Grand Junction, CO. He received a master's degree in business administration from West Virginia College of Graduate Studies in Charleston.

Quality Awards Raise Quality Awareness in the Classroom

by Dale G. Sauers

In the Business School at York College of Pennsylvania, quality management is discussed in a required course on production and operations management and covered in more detail in the optional production management concentration within the management major. But, since quality concerns all facets of business, the faculty realized that it must be addressed in a much broader base than factory management. As a result, one statistics professor has found a way to elevate quality awareness in business students and particularly in those students who enjoy statistics.

All business students at the college are required to take two statistics courses. The statistics professor uses this opportunity to introduce students to the relationship between statistics and quality. He uses the simple device of presenting Quality First Awards to outstanding students—i.e., those showing excellent ability and proficiency in statistics in the classroom.

Calling it the Quality First Award makes a nice connection between the award and the printed material on the prizes, providing a professional touch to the process. A student membership in the American Society for Quality is given as the first-place prize, and inexpensive American Society for Quality promotional items (e.g., pens, coffee mugs, and key chains) are given as second- and third-place prizes. Winners are also given brochures describing American Society for Quality's certified quality engineer program.

The advantages

Awarding prizes has a number of advantages:

- All business students—whether they are marketing, finance, accounting, management, or computer information systems majors—have quality brought to their attention in a dramatic way.
- For 12 months, the student with the greatest ability and proficiency in statistics gets monthly mailings from the local American Society for Quality section as well as mailings from American Society for Quality headquarters, including *Quality Progress.* Thus, for a year, he or she is reminded that quality management is a career possibility.
- Whether or not the winners remember the name "American Society for Quality," the phrase "Quality First" will be in front of them for as long as they have the pen, coffee mug, or key chain. It will continually remind them that quality needs to be considered in all business processes.
- Although the prizes are given for accomplishment in statistics, they also honor the quality of the individuals who win.
- When the students read the brochure on the certified quality engineer program, they are impressed by the fact that they already have learned many of the statistical techniques covered in the exam.

An adaptable program

The statistics professor currently picks up the low cost of the prizes; however, funds could be obtained from other sources, such as universities, local businesses, or local American Society for Quality sections. And, although the professor currently presents the awards in the classroom, the process could be expanded by having them presented during departmental functions or at a recognition dinner.

When this column was published in April 1992, Dale G. Sauers was the professor of management at York College of Pennsylvania in York, PA. He received an MBA from the University of Houston in Texas. Sauers was a member of the American Society for Quality.

Quality Entertainment

by Herman Senter

"Quality as family entertainment? How?" asked five quality facilitators assigned to prepare a quality booth for their company's annual fair, a daylong, outdoor event for employees and their families. Management wanted the booth to promote quality awareness and to emphasize its commitment to a recently implemented plantwide statistical process control program.

On the suggestion of a consultant, the staff decided to run a contest that required participants to guesstimate the percentage of defectives in a large population of items based on random sampling. A large plastic drum was filled with resin beads, some red, the others white. The precise mix was determined by weight, and only two staff members knew the exact proportion of "defective" red beads. Three attractive prizes—a TV, a microwave oven, and food processor—were purchased.

Let the entertainment begin

The quality contest was announced before the fair, prizes were displayed in the cafeteria, and reminders were broadcast during the fair. When the booth opened at 1 p.m., each contestant was given a small plastic tray and an entry form. Contestants could examine the mix as it was stirred. They were instructed to take a scoopful of beads at random and use the tray to count the number of red and white beads. They were asked to record their name, the counts of each color, the sample percentage of red beads, and their guess of the percentage of red beads in the entire barrel.

To make the contest interesting and instructive, the staff maintained a large wall chart (p chart), plotting the sample proportions of red beads. A patch covering the true percentage was securely taped at one corner of the chart. Contestants could use the chart to formulate their guesses. Staff members checked calculations prior to plotting points and returned the bead samples to the drum. Entry forms were kept only for the three current best guesses. Out of view of the contestants, staff members prepared two other wall charts using the same scale as the one that was posted. One showed the sequence of guesses; the other showed the combined sample percentage, which quickly converged to the true percentage.

The booth closed at 4 p.m., and an awards ceremony followed. The staff explained each of the three charts and revealed the true percentage of red beads.

A fun, informative experience for all

The staff worked hard all afternoon and learned a few things themselves. They saw some contestants try to "randomly" scoop more or fewer red beads, and they saw some players resample the mixture until they got a "random" scoop they liked. A few contestants who clearly understood percentages still made blatantly wild and inexplicable guesses. Others carefully computed the long-run sampling proportion from the wall chart and gave accurate estimates. Contestants had little trouble understanding the estimation objective, but their notions of how to gather and use sampling information varied.

How did the contestants and charts perform? Did the sequence of guesses exhibit bias, excessive variation, and/or convergence? I won't tell you, but rest assured that three contestants were very happy with the results! To learn more, try the experiment yourself!

When this column was published in December 1990, Herman Senter was an associate professor at Clemson University in South Carolina. He received a doctorate degree in applied mathematics from North Carolina State University. Senter was an American Society for Quality member.

The rigorous task of implementing a quality system that would comply with ISO 9000 and certification requirements inspired some creative thinking at PDQ Manufacturing. Knowing it was critical to get employees to buy into the effort early, we created teams to complete various clauses of the standards. We conducted training sessions to help the teams understand the certification process, and we brought in a motivational speaker to build enthusiasm for ISO 9001.

It was a beginning, but it wasn't enough. We needed a way to prove the commitment of senior management and empower the employees to take a leap of faith and begin the journey.

We knew we were on the right track, though, when a group of employees came up with a great idea: Paint a giant mural on the lunchroom wall that would serve as a daily reminder of what we were doing, who was doing it, and how far along we were in the process.

The employees designed a mural that had a theme in line with what the company manufactures: vehicle wash equipment. Sketched on the wall were three highways: Highway P, Highway D, and Highway Q (see photo), representing the company name, PDQ, and the road to certification. Cutouts of all types of vehicles were constructed from pressboard. Each vehicle represented a clause of the ISO 9001 standard. A photo of the person responsible for heading up that

clause was inserted into the driver's seat of each car. Photos of the others who worked closely to get the task accomplished were placed in the passengers' seats.

On the wall, various entrance ramps to the three highways were painted to represent the official starting goal for each element of the certification process. A way station was included for team vehicles that got sidetracked. Each highway led to a car wash, a preassessment building, and PDQ's new office building, now under construction. Above the future headquarters, a title was printed: "PDQ ISO 9001 Certified."

A time frame of the certification effort was outlined at the top of the wall. Vehicles were affixed to the wall and moved along the highways as progress was made. The route to certification led first to the car wash, which indicated that the element was ready for an internal audit. The car moved through the wash during the internal audit, and exited upon completion. If nonconformities were found, the vehicle would loop around a circular driveway and re-enter the wash. If the audit was free of noncomformities, the car would then proceed to the preassessment building. When all cars have reached the building, the company will be ready for an official preassessment.

In addition to the cars, a train was painted to represent the progress of the process control element. The engine represents the management representative, each boxcar represents a different production department, and the caboose holds photos of the company's owners.

PDQ employees now have a simple, visual representation of where they are in the process and how they measure up to the original scheduled time frame. The pictorial has increased tremendously the knowledge and interest throughout the company. It makes the process a fun, competitive game. Employees are eager to get their vehicles to the car wash and the preassessment building and are determined to keep them there.

Our colorful lunchroom mural represents a joint commitment by management and employees that helps keep the enthusiasm high during our journey to ISO 9000 certification.

When this column was published in December 1997, Cheryl L. DeMeuse was the quality assurance manager at PDQ Manufacturing Inc. in Green Bay, WI. She received associate degrees in manufacturing engineering and quality assurance from Northeast Wisconsin Technical College in Green Bay. DeMeuse was a member of the American Society for Quality. Carol L. Jamrosz was a quality engineering technician at PDQ Manufacturing Inc. She received associate degrees in quality assurance and manufacturing engineering from Midstate Technical College in Wisconsin Rapids, WI. Jamrosz was a member of the American Society for Quality.

How to Organize, Analyze, and Present Data

How often has the following happened? Pages laden with data—whether they be completed surveys, graphs charting machine activities, or something else—have been returned. The resulting information might have been entered into a spreadsheet or other data management tool. But now comes the difficult part: data analysis. What do you do with all this stuff?

This is no minor issue. In an extreme instance, writes Yale University professor Edward R. Tufte, proper data analysis can mean the difference between life and death. Tufte has created three immensely interesting books about how to present information: *The Visual Display of Quantitative Information, Envisioning Information,* and *Visual Explanations: Images and Quantities, Evidence and Narrative.*[1,2,3]

Tufte's latest book, *Visual Explanations,* has a section titled "The Decision to Launch the Space Shuttle Challenger." It is a horrifying explanation of data analysis gone catastrophically wrong. Tufte shows how a simple scatter plot or scatter diagram could have been used by NASA to decide against the January 28, 1986, launch that sent the seven crew members to their deaths. He provides other examples of poor data analysis and concludes, "There are right ways and wrong ways to show data; there are displays that reveal the truth and displays that do not. And, if the matter is an important one, then getting the displays of evidence right or wrong can possibly have momentous consequences."[4]

All data analysis does not carry such monumental implications, but all data analysis has at least some importance—why else go through the trouble of gathering the information? With that in mind, the articles in this chapter should be considered in four groups: organizing data, selecting the right analysis tool, striving toward 6-sigma quality, and effectively presenting information.

Organizing data

Rob Parsons' "The Fact Summary" is the lone entry in this section. Parsons endorses a simple matrix for classifying gathered data so that facts can be separated from opinions and relevance can be established.

Selecting the right analysis tool

To be honest, it could take an entire book to describe all the tools available for data analysis. In fact, Nancy R. Tague did just that in *The Quality Toolbox*.[5] The five entries in this segment, however, offer tools that help you make data-driven decisions:

- Douglas J. Wreath has more than office work in mind with "Make Fact-Based Decisions at Work and at Home."
- Bennett N. Underhill believes that to understand quality costs, you must be able to classify them. He provides a method to make proper classifications in "Decision Tree Helps Categorize Quality Costs."
- Glen D. Hoffherr and John W. Moran Jr. create a hybrid of force field analysis and the process decision program chart with "Contingency Force Analysis: Combining Quality Tools."
- Woody Santy was struggling with several response variables when he hit upon "The DOX Decision Tree."

Striving toward 6-sigma quality

Motorola made 6-sigma quality an industry buzzword in the late 1980s when it won a Malcolm Baldrige National Quality Award. Statistical purists have often argued against whether Motorola's definition of 6-sigma quality—3.4 defects per million—is accurate. We've often thought that the spirit of Motorola's drive for perfection was the real meaning of 6-sigma quality. Neither Wendell E. Carr nor Anton B. Usowski are arguing with the definition either. Carr is providing useful background about such calculations with "A New Process Capability Index: Parts Per Million." Usowski wants to help people determine sigma values in "Programs Perform Normal Curve Calculations."

Effectively presenting information

Christopher E. Olstead borrows from control room annunciator panels to create "The Annunciator Report: Transforming Data into Information." The chapter concludes with a favorite One Good Idea installment, "Eschew Obfuscatory Statistics" by John R. Miller. The language of people who analyze data can be deadly. Miller promotes clear, simple presentations and three rules to live by: look at the data, look at the data again, and test the data.

References

1. Tufte, *The Visual Display of Quantitative Information*.
2. Tufte, *Envisioning Information*.
3. Tufte, *Visual Explanations: Images and Quantities, Evidence and Narrative*.
4. Ibid., p. 45.
5. Tague, *The Quality Toolbox*.

The Fact Summary

by Rob Parsons

Gathering and analyzing data are critical steps in the problem-solving process. For many teams (and individuals), these two activities create considerable confusion and frustration. Some teams become overwhelmed by data, causing them to lose their focus or momentum. Either way, frustration typically follows. Many times, the problem is a team's inability to identify what it does and doesn't know—in other words, a team's inability to literally take inventory of what it has learned.

Some data are based on facts, while others are based on opinions. In some cases, data are tangential and not relevant to the task at hand. In other cases, there are gaps in teams' knowledge that need to be filled. Thus, the challenge for teams is to distinguish between what information is useful and what is not. They also need to know when to gather more information.

The tool

The Fact Summary is a simple tool that can help teams organize their knowledge. This tool helps classify information, which is expressed as statements, by rating the substantiation and relevance of each statement. Statements are classified by asking:

- Is the statement fact based (substantiated) or opinion based?
- Is the statement highly relevant or not highly relevant?

After answering these questions, the statement is placed in the appropriate quadrant of the matrix shown in Figure 8.1. For example, a highly substantiated, highly relevant statement is placed in the upper left quadrant. This graphical presentation lets teams see the strengths and weaknesses of their research more clearly.

Challenging each statement is an important part of the technique. Some teams will have difficulty separating fact from opinion and even more will be tempted to consider all information highly relevant. To determine whether a statement is fact based, teams need to explore the information and its analysis. Typically, to be considered fact based, there must be accurate data in sufficient quantities to make the conclusions of the analysis reasonable. If a statement doesn't pass this test, it should not be classified as fact based.

Classifying relevancy is generally more difficult. Teams tend to consider all information highly relevant. This logjam can be broken in two ways. One method is to have the team force-rank the statements and decide the breaking point between high relevance and low relevance. Another method is to set a limit on the number of statements that can be considered highly relevant. Setting the limit that only half of the statements can be classified highly relevant is a good starting point. From this point, the team can decide how to handle borderline statements.

After the statements are classified, the team should assess how strong its knowledge is of the process being studied. Strength comes from having important, relevant

Figure 8.1.

The Fact Summary Matrix

You can use this matrix to classify data. Here, a team was addressing customer returns for a given product line sold by a mail-order distributor.

	High Relevance		Low
Fact based	❑ There were 30,000 returns in 1997 (baseline). ❑ Misinformation is the largest cause of returns. ❑ Sales representatives have no financial accountability. ❑ Policies are inconsistent. ❑ No coaching is given on how to handle problems properly.		❑ Phone sales comprise 20 percent of returns. ❑ Fees are returned (not a root cause). ❑ Four-year rule is in effect (insignificant). ❑ No policy for recall exists (not the issue). ❑ Goodwill gestures are offered (insignificant). ❑ No complete/accurate policy manual exists (insignificant). ❑ Data processing errors account for 10 percent of returns (not the issue). ❑ Buyers change mind during calls (insignificant).
Substantiation **Opinion based**	❑ Catalog information is incorrect. ❑ The problem cost $100,000 in 1997 (verify).		❑ Policies are clear to buyers. ❑ Sales representatives' computer screens contribute to errors.

fact-based statements. Ideally, the upper left quadrant should be full. The other quadrants, however, are important, too. The statements in the lower left quadrant (high relevance, low substantiation) are knowledge gaps that need to be filled (converted to facts) or agreed upon as assumptions. The statements in the upper right quadrant (low relevance, high substantiation) might represent areas of wasted effort.

The results

Teams at two companies have successfully used the Fact Summary to sort their data. "Our team had been collecting data and interviewing and needed to sort it all out," said Bob Shenberger, the publications manager at Resort Condominiums International in Indianapolis, IN. "This tool acted like a 'data funnel' to channel our thoughts. It helped us gain focus and direction."

Steve Brummel, the customer service manager at Southern Indiana Gas & Electric Company in Evansville, told of a similar experience: "Using this tool really helped us pinpoint what we needed to work on and identify those subjects for which we needed to get our facts in order. We had a clearer picture of what we needed to do so we could spend our time wisely."

When this column was published in May 1993, Rob Parsons was a performance improvement consultant with Ernst & Young in Indianapolis, IN. He received a bachelor's degree in industrial management from Purdue University in West Lafayette, IN. Parsons was an American Society for Quality member and certified quality engineer.

<table>
<tr><td>Idea 48</td><td>**Make Fact-Based Decisions at Work and at Home**
by Douglas J. Wreath</td></tr>
</table>

Long considered a tool reserved for quality and reliability engineers, the decision matrix has found new life as an effective method for making fact-based decisions both inside and outside the workplace. More and more, managers and team members are using the tool as a simple way to systematically evaluate alternatives.

The grid format in Figure 8.2 illustrates the basic structure of a decision matrix. Seemingly complex, the evaluation process actually consists of the following simple steps:

1. List alternatives in the rows.
2. List evaluation criteria in the columns.
3. Rate each alternative based on its potential to satisfy the corresponding criteria.
4. Total the ratings for each alternative.
5. Identify and act on the highest-scoring alternative.

Generating alternatives and criteria is the key factor for success when using this tool. A variety of methods can be used to generate alternatives and criteria. The amount of time and expense dedicated to this task should be in proportion to the importance of the decision. In other words, a situation with severe consequences requires more extensive and detailed alternatives and criteria.

Examples show how to use the matrix at work and at home

The following two examples illustrate the use of the decision matrix in two dramatically different situations:

Example 1. When provided with an opportunity to upgrade the office computer system, an office manager quickly realized that there was a wide range of systems from

Figure 8.2.
The Decision Matrix

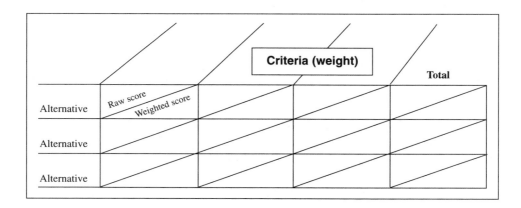

which to choose. In an attempt to proceed in a systematic fashion, she used the decision matrix shown in Figure 8.3. She started by limiting her alternatives to three computers that she believed represented the best range of options and capabilities while giving her the minimum performance she needed. (This can be viewed as evaluating the alternatives against constraints, or what the system must do, before moving to the criteria assessment.) Next, she created a list of specific criteria, keeping in mind that the criteria represented what she really wanted this system to do. Finally, she assigned a weight to each criterion in proportion to its importance. For instance, since she was on a limited budget, it was twice as important for the alternative to rate high for cost (10) than it was to rate high for central processing unit speed (5) or memory (5). She elected to use a 5-3-1 scoring system: an alternative was given a 5 if it best satisfied a criterion, 3 if it did an average job, and 1 if it did a poor job. As the matrix indicates, the 486SX featuring 25MHz, 2MB of RAM, and 210 HD was the best choice.

Example 2. Doug and Jen faced a tough relocation decision. Wanting to ensure that they made a logical and systematic evaluation of the alternatives, they decided to use the decision matrix in Figure 8.4. They generated a list of alternatives and evaluated

Figure 8.3.

Matrix for Computer System Decision

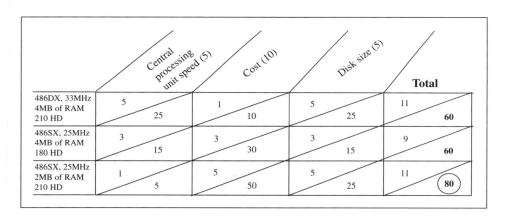

Figure 8.4.

Matrix for Relocation Decision

them against a set of constraints (i.e., what the alternative must do). Since they mutually agreed that at least one of them must remain on a steady career track, the alternative of touring and studying in Europe for a year was dropped. They then developed the criteria and gave them weights according to their respective importance. They also used a 5-3-1 scoring system. The procedure forced them to systematically evaluate the alternatives against stated criteria and not against their respective gut instincts. As the matrix indicates, the best alternative was for Doug and Jen to live in Virginia.

A word of caution

The decision matrix should not be viewed as a panacea when making decisions. The best decisions are those achieved through a more comprehensive systematic methodology, with the decision matrix perhaps being used at several points along the way. But when used as a vehicle for removing emotions and for considering various criteria in the decision-making process, the decision matrix is a powerful tool.

When this column was published in November 1994, Douglas J. Wreath was a consultant with Holmes-Tucker International, Inc. in Annandale, VA. He received a master's degree in systems management from the University of Denver in Colorado. Wreath was a member of the American Society for Quality.

Decision Tree Helps Categorize Quality Costs
by Bennett N. Underhill

Quality cost reporting, like most other measurement and analysis techniques in the field of quality management, has gone through the usual phases of intense short-term interest, lively controversy, frequent misunderstanding and misuse, and general disregard. But the fact remains that the proper identification and monitoring of quality costs can highlight major opportunities for system improvement.

Quality cost reporting provides a clear picture of the improvement opportunities that have always been accepted as legitimate operating costs. Without an understanding of the nature of quality costs, these opportunities will continue to be an unrecognized waste of organizational resources. (As with most other measurement and analysis techniques, however, quality cost reporting alone is not always adequate and must be used in conjunction with other techniques to ensure that improvement efforts do not benefit one aspect of the system to the detriment of the system as a whole.)

There are four basic categories of quality costs:[1]

- Prevention (costs of activities designed to prevent poor quality in a product or service)
- Appraisal (costs associated with measuring, evaluating, or auditing a product or service to ensure conformance to standards and requirements)
- Internal nonconformance (costs resulting from nonconformances found before the customer receives the product or service)
- External nonconformance (costs resulting from nonconformances found after the customer receives the product or service)

Although these categories seem simple enough, it isn't always easy to identify actual costs within a system and assign them to the appropriate category for analysis and monitoring. In the course of developing quality cost reporting systems for many organizations, I have found that the decision tree in Figure 8.5 helps people better recognize and properly classify quality costs. It lists the basic criteria for judging what is a quality cost and how it should be examined for improvement opportunities.

The decision tree helps with not only the first pass at defining the major costs, but also with refining the details of the quality costs report. The detail must be sufficient to identify the specific systemic source of the unwanted cost so corrective action can be effectively applied. Finally, the decision tree can be used to measure the progress made in implementing the corrective action.

Every cost in an entire operation can be examined with this decision tree and be properly classified in one of the four quality cost categories or as a cost of doing business outside the realm of quality cost concerns. Using this tree can significantly reduce the confusion usually encountered when establishing and maintaining quality cost reporting systems.

Figure 8.5.
The Cost-of-Quality Basic Decision Tree

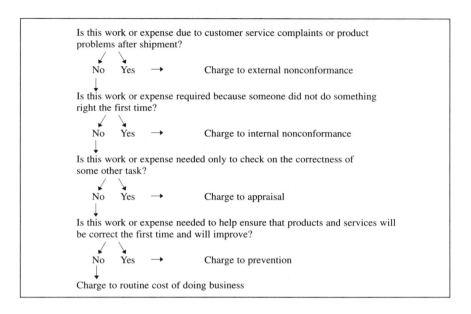

Reference

1. Campanella, *Principles of Quality Costs.*

When this column was published in August 1995, Bennett N. Underhill was a quality management consultant in Freeport, IL. He received a bachelor's degree in applied math and mechanics from the University of Wisconsin-Madison.

Contingency Force Analysis: Combining Quality Tools

by Glen D. Hoffherr and John W. Moran, Jr.

When planning teams make long-range plans, many factors with different levels of intensity come into play. There are also many possible unknown factors (uncertainties) that might have to be dealt with. Over the years, planning teams have used many tools to assess the certainty and uncertainty of successful plan implementation, including:

- Force field analysis, which is a graphic display of the positive and negative forces influencing progress toward a desired goal.[1]
- Process decision program chart (PDPC), which helps plan contingencies for possible conditions that might impede the implementation of a plan.[2] Teams often use this technique to identify obstacles to implementing solutions to problems.

Although helpful, these two tools have their drawbacks. Force field analysis only identifies what forces are present and does little to evaluate their strength or potential effect. In addition, this analysis doesn't prioritize the positive or negative forces or develop an action plan to overcome identified obstacles.

The PDPC is basically a negative analysis. It has the potential to turn a positive working session into a finger-pointing session because the PDPC's questioning process—which involves asking "Why won't the solution work?" and "What can go wrong?"—encourages team members to overlook a solution's positive aspects. With the PDPC, teams don't focus on developing breakthrough alternatives to solutions that have negative forces.

These two tools, however, can be combined into a graphical process called contingency force analysis (CFA), which provides a prioritized evaluation of positive and negative forces. The prioritized positive forces are used to show the solution's benefits to encourage its adoption. The prioritized negative forces are analyzed so that cost-effective alternatives can be developed.

The CFA approach encourages teams to adapt solutions as new information emerges at each stage of solution implementation. It is a dynamic process that must undergo periodic review.

Figure 8.6 shows an example of a constructed CFA on culture change. Its construction consists of five steps:

1. Brainstorm a list of positive and negative forces that might affect the solution under consideration. List these in the corresponding "Positive forces" and "Negative forces" columns.
2. Determine whether the identified forces are weak, moderate, or strong. Indicate the strength of the forces by the length of the arrow (the stronger the force, the longer the arrow).
3. Determine each force's occurrence probability using the scale of high, medium, or low. Put the ratings in the "Probability" column.

Figure 8.6.

Contingency Force Analysis

How	Why	Priority*	Probability**	Positive forces	Negative forces	Probability**	Priority*	Why	How
Increase sales	Overseas market	1	High	Implement ISO 9000 ⟶	Status quo is OK ◀	Medium	4	People are comfort-able	Explain need to change

WM S   S M W***

    * To obtain this number, use the prioritization table.
  ** Indicate the probability of occurrence using the scale of high, medium, or low.
*** S = Strong force, M = Moderate force, W = Weak force

4. Prioritize each force using the prioritization table in Figure 8.7. This table combines the probability of occurrence with the strength of the force. A force that has a high probability of occurrence and is strong has the highest priority (priority No. 1). Put the priority number for each force in the "Priority" column.

5. Analyze the forces, concentrating first on the forces that are classified as priority No. 1. For each negative force, analyze why it will occur and how it can be prevented. This analysis can lead to breakthrough solutions that do not even contain the negative force. For each positive force, analyze why it should occur and how it can best be used to reach the desired goal. Put this information in the corresponding "Why" and "How" columns in the CFA.

Figure 8.7.

Prioritization Table

		Strength		
		Strong	Moderate	Weak
Probability of occurrence	High	1	3	5
	Medium	2	4	6
	Low	7	8	9

By completing the CFA, a planning team can focus on actions that it must take to improve a solution's implementation. These improvements will reduce the risk of that solution failing. In addition, because the CFA shows problems with systems and not people, it will provide a positive environment for teamwork.

References

1. Moran, Talbot, and Benson, *A Guide to Graphical Problem-Solving Processes.*
2. Mizuno, *Management for Quality Improvement—The Seven New QC Tools.*

When this column was published in April 1994, Glen D. Hoffherr was the vice president of operations at Markon Inc. in Windham, NH. He received a bachelor's degree in electrical engineering. Hoffherr was an American Society for Quality member. John W. Moran Jr. was a director at Organizational Dynamics Inc. in Burlington, MA. He received a doctorate in operations research. Moran was an American Society for Quality senior member.

The DOX Decision Tree

by Woody Santy

I had just completed running a 2^{8-4} experiment with seven response variables. As an adjunct to multivariate analysis of variance, I was looking for a visual way to help sort the results from each response to communicate composite conclusions. Then an idea hit me to use a stem-and-leaf plot, with the stem designating the factors and the leaves representing the low- and high-level indicators for each factor. I called it the design of experiments (DOX) decision tree.

A DOX decision tree can help you visualize and select the best factor settings to use when many response variables are involved, such as in two-level screening experiments. Once you have determined which factors are important and the preferred operating level for each important factor using designed experiments, you are ready to plot the factors and responses in a DOX decision tree.

For example, suppose you just conducted an experiment with eight factors (A, B, C, D, E, F, G, and H) and nine responses (Y1, Y2, Y3, Y4, Y5, Y6, Y7, Y8, and Y9). After you analyze each response separately, you use normal probability (NP) and half normal probability (HNP) plots to select the important factors. Here's a summary of what you found and how you would plot this information in the DOX decision tree (see Figure 8.8):

- For response Y3, Y5, Y6, and Y9, no factors were found to be important (i.e., no factors fell off of the NP or HNP line). Thus, these responses are placed on either side of "None."
- For Y1, factor B was the only important factor. The high level was determined as the preferred operating level, so Y1 is listed beside B on the high-level side (i.e., at the B+ position).
- For Y2, factor C was the only important factor. The low level was determined as the preferred operating level, so Y2 is listed beside C on the low-level side (i.e., at the C− position).
- For Y4, the interaction (INT) between factors A and C was important, so it is placed on

Figure 8.8.

An Example of a DOX Decision Tree

Low (-) level		High (+) level
	A	Y4*
	B	Y1 Y7
Y4* Y2	C	
	D	Y7
Y8	E	Y7
	F	
	G	
	H	
	INT*	Y4* (A+ C−)
	Avoid #	
Y5	None	Y3 Y6 Y9

either side of INT and marked with an asterisk. The asterisk indicates that other factors might need to be considered should factor A or C be involved in a trade-off. Y4 is also placed at the C– and A+ positions, indicating the preferred level for each.

- For Y7, three factors are important: B, D, and E. Since each factor had a preferred high operating level, Y7 was put at the B+, D+, and E+ positions.
- For Y8, only factor E is important. Since it had a preferred low operating level, Y8 was positioned at E–.

Once constructed, the DOX decision tree tells you to set factors A, B, and D at the high level and factor C at the low level. For factor E, there is a tradeoff. Response Y7 prefers the high level, while Y8 prefers the low level. If a decision had to be made without more experimentation, you could set factor E to the low level, using the high level of factors D and B to recoup any loss to Y7. (At least you would know that there is a trade-off between Y7 and Y8 that is triggered by factor E.)

An additional situation that can arise when using the DOX decision tree is a type of interaction designated an "Avoid." An avoid is an interaction that is important, but there is only one situation that must be avoided. For example, if the interaction between factors A and C in Figure 8.8 had been an avoid, you would have avoided using the A+ level and C– level for Y4. Then, because Y2 wants factor C to be at the low level, factor A must also be set to the low level to avoid the A+ C– setting.

The DOX decision tree has helped me many times to visualize and select the best factor settings to use when many response variables are involved. It can help you, too.

When this column was published in September 1997, Woody Santy was the statistical consultant at John Deere Horicon Works in Horicon, WI. He received a master's degree in statistics from Iowa State University in Ames. Santy was a senior member of the American Society for Quality.

A New Process Capability Index: Parts per Million

by Wendell E. Carr

In his Statistics Corner column, Berton Gunter gives the process capability index C_{pk} for a measured product variable x as

$$C_{pk} = \frac{|\mu - \text{nearer spec}|}{3\sigma}$$

where μ is the process mean and σ is the process standard deviation.[1] Some people have trouble understanding what C_{pk} means. They wonder, "Is C_{pk} = 2.0 better than C_{pk} = 1.5, or is it the other way around? If C_{pk} = 1.5, what percent of my parts will be out of spec?"

People who have taken a statistics course recognize that C_{pk} is the standardized normal variable z divided by 3. In other words, $z = 3C_{pk}$.

If x follows a normal distribution, z can be converted to parts per million (ppm) out of spec with a z table or a computer program. For example, C_{pk} = 1.5 translates to z = 3(1.5) = 4.5. A computer program indicates that this means 0.00034 percent beyond the nearer spec for a normal distribution. To get the ppm, multiply the fraction out of spec by 10^6 (1 million) or, equivalently, multiply the percent out of spec by 10^4. Hence, 0.00034 percent becomes 3.4 ppm. Note that a higher C_{pk} is better because z is higher, so the ppm is lower.

For the overall ppm, both spec limits, not just the nearer spec limit, must be considered. To do this, calculate z and the ppm for the other spec limit and add the two ppm's to get the overall ppm. For example, Motorola's 6-sigma quality concept says that the distance from the target to the spec limit should be equal to 6σ, and μ should be no more than 1.5σ from the target.[2] In Figure 8.9, LSL = lower spec limit, USL = upper spec limit,

Figure 8.9.
Lower and Upper Spec Limits

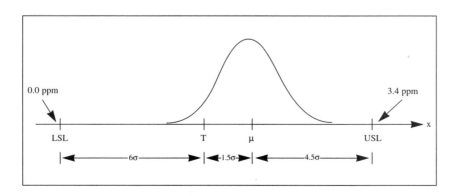

and T = target = (LSL + USL)/2. For this worst-case μ, $|\mu - \text{nearer spec}| = 6\sigma - 1.5\sigma$ = 4.5σ, so $C_{pk} = 1.5$, $z = 4.5$, and ppm = 3.4 for the nearer spec. For the other spec limit, $z = 1.5 + 6 = 7.5$, for which the ppm is 3.2×10^{-8}, or 0.0 to one decimal place. Hence, the total ppm is 3.4. This is a new process capability index that everyone can understand.

Now if people ask, "What is 6-sigma quality and $C_{pk} = 1.5$ all about?" tell them it is another way of saying 3.4 ppm. Tell them also if they want to achieve a low ppm, they should use control charts with statistically derived control limits. That's another story, and Acheson J. Duncan tells it quite well in *Quality Control and Industrial Statistics*.[3]

References

1. Gunter, "The Use and Abuse of C_{pk}," January 1989.
2. Harry, *The Nature of Six Sigma Quality*.
3. Duncan, *Quality Control and Industrial Statistics*.

When this column was published in August 1991, Wendell E. Carr was an advisory statistician at IBM Corporation in Essex Junction, VT. He received a bachelor's degree in mathematics from the University of Vermont in Burlington, VT. Carr was an American Society for Quality senior member.

Programs Perform Normal Curve Calculations
by Anton B. Usowski

A growing industry trend to achieve lower defect rates ultimately reaching 6-sigma quality and beyond piqued my curiosity: How were people determining the relationship between defect level and sigma at higher sigma values? The best I could do on any available table was 3.59 sigma, which led me to write three programs for personal computers (see Figures 8.10 to 8.12). Checking against published tables and other various reported points indicates that the programs are effective. Besides using them at high sigma values, you can use the programs as a substitute for standard tables.

The programs, written in BASIC, use the trapezoidal rule, performing an approximate integration to calculate the area under the normal curve. The term "DX" determines the size of the slices of areas under the curve that are summed to give the total

Figure 8.10.

Program 1

```
'This program calculates the areas
'under the normal curve from Z=0 to
'Z and from Z to infinity, given the
'value of the Z statistic.

twoPI=8*ATN(1)
200 PRINT: INPUT "The value of Z
   is"; Z
DX=.01
A=0: X1=0
X2=X1+DX
Y1=EXP(X1^2/(-2))SQR(twoPI)
100 Y2=EXP(X2^2/(-2))SQR(twoPI)
A=A+DX*(Y1+Y2)/2
Y1=Y2
X2=X2+DX
IF X2< =Z GOTO 100
PRINT "Area from Z=0 to"Z" is ";
   :PRINT USING"#.#####";A
PRINT "Area beyond Z="Z" is ";
   :PRINT USING"######.#######";
   (.5-A)*1000000#;:PRINT "ppm"
BEEP
GOTO 200
END
```

Figure 8.11.

Program 2

```
'This program calculates the Z
'statistic given the area under the
'normal curve from Z=0 to Z.

twoPI=8*ATN(1)
400 PRINT: INPUT "The area from
   Z=0 to Z is"; A1
IF A1 > = .5 GOTO 300
DX=.01
A=0: X1=0
X2=X1+DX
Y1=EXP(X1^2/(-2))SQR(twoPI)
100 Y2=EXP(X2^2/(-2))SQR(twoPI)
A=A+DX*(Y1+Y2)/2
IF A=A1 GOTO 200
IF A>A1 GOTO 500
Y1=Y2
X2=X2+DX
IF A<A1 GOTO 100
200 PRINT "The value of Z is";
   :PRINT USING"#.##";X2
BEEP
GOTO 400
END
300 PRINT "YOU MUST ENTER AN
   AREA OF LESS THAN 0.5000"
BEEP: BEEP: BEEP
GOTO 400
500 DX=DX/(-10)
600 Y1=Y2
X2=X2+DX
Y2=EXP(X2^2/(-2))SQR(twoPI)
A=A+DX*(Y1+Y2)/2
IF A>A1 GOTO 600 ELSE GOTO 200
```

Figure 8.12.

Program 3

```
'This program calculates the Z statistic
'given the area (in ppm) under the
'normal curve from Z to infinity.

twoPI=8*ATN(1)
400 PRINT: INPUT "The area in the
    tail beyond Z in ppm is"; A2
A1 =.5-A2/1000000#
IF A1=.5 GOTO 300
DX=.01
A=0: X1=0
X2=X1+DX
Y1=EXP(X1^2/(-2))SQR(twoPI)
100 Y2=EXP(X2^2/(-2))SQR(twoPI)
A=A+DX*(Y1+Y2)/2
IF A=A1 GOTO 200
IF A>A1 GOTO 500
Y1=Y2
X2=X2+DX
IF A<A1 GOTO 100
200 PRINT "The value of Z is";
    :PRINT USING"#.##";X2
BEEP
GOTO 400
END
300 PRINT "YOU MUST ENTER AN
    AREA GREATER THAN ZERO"
BEEP: BEEP: BEEP
GOTO 400
500 DX=DX/(-10)
600 Y1=Y2
X2=X2+DX
Y2=EXP(X2^2/(-2))SQR(twoPI)
A=A+DX*(Y1+Y2)/2
IF A>A1 GOTO 600 ELSE GOTO 200
```

Figure 8.13.

The Calculations

Area beyond Z in ppm	Z	Z	Area beyond Z in ppm
0.001	6.00	4.00	31.7
0.01	5.61	4.50	3.4
0.1	5.20	5.00	0.287
1.0	4.75	5.50	0.019
10	4.26	6.00	0.000987
100	3.72	6.50	0.0000401
1,000	3.09	7.00	0.0000012

area in the interval of interest. I have used DX equal to 0.01 sigma units. A larger DX would make the programs run faster but might give less accurate results. All programs perform the calculations on only the right half of the normal curve.

The first program (Figure 8.10) calculates the area under the normal curve from zero to the given multiple of sigma and the area beyond that point in parts per million (ppm). The second program (Figure 8.11) works in the other direction. From a given area, it calculates the distance from zero to the multiple of sigma that encloses the area. The third program (Figure 8.12) is similar to the second except that it uses the area beyond the sigma value of interest to calculate the value. You can, in effect, enter a defect rate in ppm to calculate sigma. Figure 8.13 shows some calculations made with these three programs.

When this column was published in August 1992, Anton B. Usowski was the quality assurance and reliability manager at Cera-Mite Corporation in Grafton, WI. He received a master's degree in material science/metallurgy from New York University in New York. Usowski was an American Society for Quality member and certified quality engineer.

The Annunciator Report: Transforming Data into Information

by Christopher E. Olstead

"The most valuable commodity I know of is information."

Even though this remark was made by a fictional character, Gordon Gekko, in the movie "Wall Street," it hits home in the real world. Today's business leaders need information, and they need it quickly. They need critical information in a simple, concise format—who has time to routinely read 30-page reports?

Process plant operators have similar information needs. They manage hundreds, often thousands, of production-related physical processes (e.g., flow, level, pressure, and temperature). As a result, many processing plants use annunciator panels similar to the one shown in Figure 8.14 to provide status information to control-room operators.

Figure 8.14.

Typical Annunciator Panel

R-101 High temperature	R-101 Low temperature	R-101 Low pressure
T-101 Low level	T-101 High level	T-101 High temperature
T-102 Low level	T-102 High level	T-102 High temperature

These annunciator panels can be adapted to provide management with a succinct format for reporting information critical to an organization's success.

How an annunciator panel works

Often, a critical process is represented by one or more dedicated windows on the annunciator panel. The annunciator panel window is not illuminated when the process is within normal operating parameters. When a critical process deviates more than a specified amount, however, the corresponding window is illuminated and an audible alarm alerts the operator. The visual portion of this process control methodology adapts easily to critical work processes in virtually any environment.

How the annunciator report works

Figure 8.15 shows a partial annunciator report taken from a materials management application. (The actual report contains more windows.) Like its control-room counterpart, the report provides status information at a glance. If an alarm results, the manager knows exactly where to investigate within seconds after receiving the report.

Figure 8.15.

The Annunciator Report

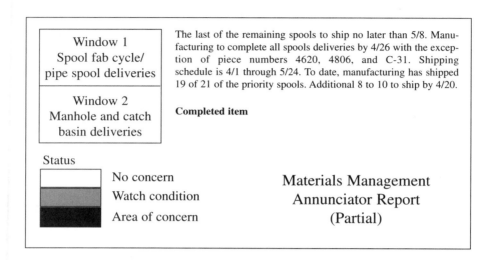

The annunciator report represents an aggregation of several windows, each corresponding to a critical work process. Each window provides the current process condition in one of three states:

- No concern (indicated by clear screen). The process is within operational targets, and there is no cause for concern.
- Watch condition (indicated by light shading). The process requires monitoring and possible corrective action at the natural work-group level.
- Area of concern (indicated by dark shading). The process requires senior management's attention.

Color coding can be substituted for the shading to increase the emphasis on out-of-control processes.

The annunciator report format aligns with the growing belief that reports in today's fast-paced business climate should be graphically oriented rather than text based. The annunciator report's graphics accelerate understanding, while the accompanying text provides additional information that people can read as needed. The report allows quick assimilation of critical information. Simply put, the annunciator report helps transform data into knowledge.

How to build the annunciator report

It is recommended that a computer spreadsheet program be used to create the annunciator report, but it is possible to create it manually. Here is how to construct it:

1. *Determine critical success factors.* These are the areas that must go well for a project to succeed. The focus should remain on the vital few areas rather than the useful many. Ideally, the critical success factors should represent a balanced perspective and provide a diverse list of variables for inclusion in the annunciator report (e.g., cost, schedule, quality, and innovation).

2. *Define operational set points for critical success factors.* The management team should determine the operational definitions and corresponding set points for each window (just as an engineer specifies alarm trip points for each physical process alarm). For example, the first window, "Spool fab cycle/pipe spool deliveries," in Figure 8.15 might contain the following parameters:

- No concern: less than 2 percent early or late
- Watch condition: 3 percent to 5 percent early or late
- Area of concern: more than 6 percent early or late

3. *Assign ownership of critical success factors.* Senior management assigns an owner to each critical success factor. The owner monitors the variable and takes corrective action as required.

An effective step

The primary objective of an information system is to get the right information into the hands of the right people at the right time. The annunciator report is a simple yet effective step in developing that system. The annunciator report provides relevant information at a glance and reduces comprehension time from minutes to seconds.

When this column was published in June 1994, Christopher E. Olstead was the project quality manager at Bechtel Corporation in Houston, TX. He received a master's degree in business administration from the University of St. Thomas in Houston, TX. Olstead was a member of the American Society for Quality.

Eschew Obfuscatory Statistics

by John R. Miller

Statistics is the science of making information out of data. Sadly, as with the rigors of any science, there is always the danger of trying to make the information so precise that it is as complicated and confusing as the data. Anyone discovering the tremendous power of statistics in analyzing a mountain of data and yielding a molehill of usable information can be easily seduced into believing that a good statistical test will solve all problems.

Unfortunately, analyzing the data is only the first step. You then have to sell the conclusions to management. The more powerful the statistical tool, the harder it is to explain and, thus, the less likely management is to embrace it. If you appreciate the usefulness of statistics, you must learn that a KISS is always better than a SMASH.

KISS

The familiar acronym KISS can be restated to: keep it statistically simple. This exhortation for simplicity is logical in any presentation. Sadly, all too often, statistical-application practitioners seem bent on using the most sophisticated technique available and then presenting the results using the most complicated terminology imaginable. The rationale is that sophistication yields power, robustness, precision, or some other measure of statistical "goodness." While often this is true, my experience leads me to believe that there might be two other reasons.

First, in any profession or science, there is usually a desire to develop a unique vocabulary. This vocabulary gives credibility to the field while providing an insulation that protects the current practitioners from "unqualified" newcomers. I'm not suggesting this is all bad. A specialized vocabulary is normally more efficient and precise at passing information within the profession. However, all you have to do is have a short conversation with the family doctor to see that passing information outside the group becomes very difficult with such vocabularies.

SMASH

The second reason is less defensible. As a young engineer, it became obvious to me that shoveling on the statistical mumbo jumbo scared even the most technical of managers. Thus, these managers didn't ask questions. Although this gave me a sense of security, those managers rarely made any decisions based on my analyses. This situation demonstrates what I call SMASH: stupefy management—apply statistics heavily.

In a world bewitched by a love for the latest management technique, statistics is a hot item. Managers seeking to show their commitment to the new way might tolerate or even encourage overcomplication. The zeal might even lead to them making decisions based on conclusions they don't understand. But what happens when the next fad hits?

Three rules to live by

To make a lasting impression on managers, you must present statistics clearly and simply. They must understand the statistics. Toward this end, I suggest that you follow three rules:

1. *Look at the data.* I know that this is a statistical sin equivalent to the groom seeing the bride in her dress before the wedding: a posteriori bias. Most statistical practitioners have the bias that the world is normal as they merrily apply the standard parametric tests to the data. But a quick look will at least show multimodality or skewness. A frequency distribution is also something management will understand.

2. *Look at the data again.* Change the scales. Change the intervals. The world is full of patterns that our eyes are well suited to discover. If a regression seems to work on the data, look at the residuals.

3. *Test the data.* Now apply statistics, but try to do so fairly. If in doubt, use the less powerful test. If the choice is one or two tail, use the two tail. Set a confidence level your managers will support, and stick with it. Remember, statistical tests are conservative and the world is full of random noise. In business, the picture you get from the data might tell a story that cannot be verified statistically at your level of confidence. If the picture can tell the story, management will draw a conclusion. A statistical test might give added confidence and spur action, but its failure does not disprove any apparent cause.

I have a sign in my office that sums up my belief about statistics. It reads, "Eschew Obfuscation." The way something is said can be as important as the message. Statistics should make the world less complicated. Sophisticated statistical techniques have many valid applications, such as finding needles in haystacks of data. The power of multiple regressions, pattern recognition, and all the other tricks of the trade are as close as your personal computer. But so is your ability to graph and manipulate graphs into a myriad of forms. If you use your computer to only generate more numbers, you might feel academically satisfied, but SMASH will not educate or convince your managers. KISS, on the other hand, will let managers experience the thrill of discovery with you—and that will change the way America does business.

When this column was published in October 1988, John R. Miller was the project manager at GTE in Taunton, MA. He received master's degrees from the University of Washington, Seattle, and from the Worcester Polytechnic Institute in Massachusetts. Miller was a member of the American Society for Quality.

How to Chart Data

Charting data is a subject One Good Idea writers returned to frequently. Jill A. Swift's "Flowchart Simplifies Decision about Which Control Chart to Use" indirectly explains the need for the frequency: gathering data isn't enough. One must know how to display the data. To that end, Swift presents a simple flowchart that can lead readers to the chart required. Some of the charts she mentions can be found in the remainder of this chapter. A good overall explanation of these charts can be found in both the *The Quality Toolbox* by Nancy Tague and *Statistical Quality Control,* the classic text by Eugene L. Grant and Richard S. Leavenworth.[1,2]

Four authors—Al Jaehn, Paul A. Kales, Gary Phillips, and Claude R. Superville—weigh in with variations on Walter A. Shewhart's control chart.[3] Their installments are "All-Purpose Chart Can Make SPC Easy," "Get More Out of Common Control Charts Using K-Limits," "Time-Saving Tips for Short-Run Average Charts," and "Monitoring Measurable Process Data: Why Not Use the EWMA Chart?"

This is followed by a nice combination of "The Dot Method C-Chart" by Glenn Roth and Nick Nocera, "The Dot Method C-Chart: The Next Generation" by Stephen Carty, and "How to Enhance Attribute Charts" by Alton Humphrey. All three articles seek to make process tracking simple enough for any operator to handle.

The remainder of the chapter is a collection of different charts that are often the products of the authors' knowledge of traditional tools multiplied by their need to create something specific for their organization.

John Buckfelder and Jon Powell use triangles to display C_{pk} ranges in "C_{pk} Dart Charts: An Easy Way to Track Continuous Improvement."[4]

Roger E. Duffy needed more than just a Pareto diagram when faced with recurring defects at his company. In "Pareto Analysis and Trend Charts: A Powerful Duo," he shows that months of personal experience can lead to the development of an even greater tool.

Richard (Coach) M. Carangelo was following a path similar to Duffy's during his benchmarking experiences. In Carangelo's case, he had several measurements but no easy way to display them. His solution can be found in "Clearly Illustrate Multiple Measurables with the Web Chart."

Finally, Raymond Goldstein shows what you should do when seeking to draw attention to information that might otherwise seem inconsequential: examine the negative instead of the positive. In "Get Management's Attention by Focusing on Rejects," Goldstein also advocates a powerful point: translate quality information into dollars. He effectively argues that cumulative cost will get management's attention much quicker than percent accepted.

References

1. Tague, *The Quality Toolbox*, pp. 84–116.
2. Grant and Leavenworth, *Statistical Quality Control*, pp. 31–390.
3. For background on control charts, see Shewhart, *Economic Control of Quality of Manufactured Product*, 50th anniversary commemorative reissue, pp. 275–347; Joiner, *Fourth Generation Management*; and Pitt, *SPC for the Rest of Us*.
4. There's no better explanation of C_{pk} than in Bert Gunter's very popular series titled "The Use and Abuse of C_{pk}," which appeared in his Statistics Corner column in *Quality Progress* magazine in January, March, May, and July of 1989.

Flowchart Simplifies Decision about Which Control Chart to Use

by Jill A. Swift

With the increased awareness of quality in the workplace, more and more people are being introduced to control charts. Many people want to use them but are uncertain about which one to use. In the past, the decision about which control chart to use was made by those experienced in such matters; now, however, those inexperienced in selecting control charts can make this decision themselves by using the flowchart in Figure 9.1.

Several different types of flowcharts currently exist to help people decide which control chart is appropriate for a particular situation, but the flowchart in Figure 9.1 has several distinguishing features:

- It is simple and easy to use.
- Only a basic understanding of statistics is required.
- All levels of personnel can use and, more important, understand it.

Figure 9.1.
The Flowchart

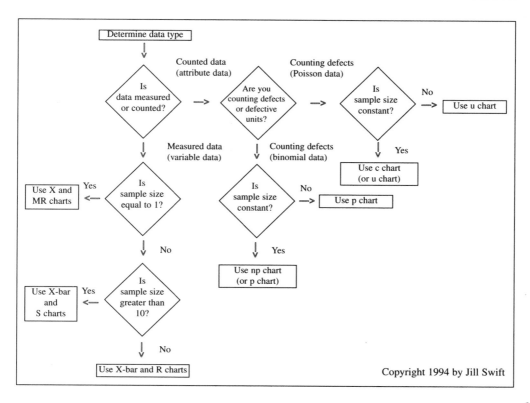

Copyright 1994 by Jill Swift

Here are three examples of how to use the flowchart:

Example 1: A manufacturer of crystal stemware wants to set up a control chart at the intermediate inspection station. Defects in workmanship and visual quality features are checked at this inspection station before the stemware is sent to the cutter station. The manufacturer wants charts prepared daily. The amount of stemware produced by the glassblowers per day varies.

Solution: Counted data → defects → sample size varies → u chart

Example 2: An independent contractor wants to track the number of bad and unusable products received from a particular supplier. Various sized shipments are received once a week.

Solution: Counted data → unusable (defective) → sample size varies → p chart

Example 3: A line foreman needs to keep track of the shaft lengths being cut to ensure that the customer's specifications are met. There are 250 shaft lengths cut per hour. Since one of the line workers will be responsible for collecting and measuring the hourly sample, the sample size needs to be kept below 8.

Solution: Measured data → sample size > 1 → sample size < 10 → X-bar and R charts

As the examples show, the flowchart is simple to use and understand. Many people have already successfully used it to integrate control charts into their work environments.

When this column was originally published in October 1994, Jill A. Swift was an assistant professor in the Industrial Engineering Department at the University of Miami in Florida. She received a doctorate in industrial engineering from Oklahoma State University in Stillwater. Swift was an American Society for Quality member and certified quality engineer.

All-Purpose Chart Can Make SPC Easy
by Al Jaehn

Efficiently applying control charts on the operating floor requires simplicity in construction, plotting, and interpretation. The conventional control chart has several drawbacks in these areas. These include the need for preparing differently scaled control charts for each different property, process, and product. Also, plotting points is often tedious and susceptible to errors. Finally, the decision of when to make a process adjustment depends not only on taking action when a point is outside the control limits, but also on the interpretation of unnatural patterns within the control limits. This would include runs above and below target and two consecutive points approaching the control limit.

The zone control chart simplifies the Shewhart control chart when applied to variables-type data. It is ideal for processes where single measurements are made periodically for control. It eliminates the drawbacks dealing with control chart construction, plotting, and interpretation. The zone chart is an all-purpose chart applicable to any data that approximate the normal curve. (However, this method might, at times, alter alpha risks.) Zone control charts can make statistical process control (SPC) easy.

I developed this control chart method in 1985. It has been successfully tested in production at Consolidated Papers, Inc. It has helped achieve reductions in variability and improved on-target performance.

A look at the procedure

Seven straight equally spaced lines serve as the nucleus of the zone control chart. They divide the chart into six zones that correspond to the intervals between the centerline and the 1-sigma limit, the 1- and 2-sigma limits, and the 2- and 3-sigma limits. A box is placed to the left of each line to record the target and the 1-, 2-, and 3-sigma values.

Each zone is assigned a numerical score. Between the target and 1-sigma limit, the score is 1. Between the 1- and 2-sigma limits, the score is 2. Between the 2- and 3-sigma limits, the score is 4. Anything beyond the 3-sigma limit is 8.

Figure 9.2 illustrates the zone control chart and an example of the procedure. The data are for a process whose target is 50 and standard deviation is 1.

Instead of plotting points at an exact location on the chart, the zone control chart procedure requires only drawing a circle in the appropriate zone. At the outset, the first circle representing the value of 50.2 is made in the zone between the target (50) and the 1-sigma limit (51). Based on the previously described zone scoring system, a score of 1 is assigned to this circle. The second test result, 51.8, is represented by a circle in the +1 to +2 sigma zone. In this case, a 3 is recorded in the circle. This is the sum of the score for this zone, 2, and the score of the previously circled number.

This summing procedure continues until a result falls on the opposite side of the centerline. At that time, the score accumulation process ends and a new one begins. This is illustrated by the third value, 49.3. A zone score of 1 is again assigned because this result is no longer on the same side of the centerline.

Figure 9.2.
Zone Control Chart Procedure

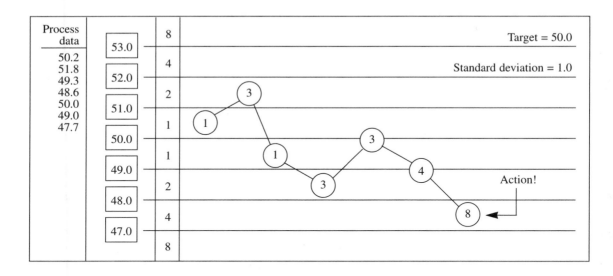

If the value falls exactly on the centerline, its zone score is zero and the previous cumulative score is recorded. This situation occurs for the fifth result in the example. In this case, the cumulative zone score of 3, assigned to the fourth result, appears again.

If a value falls exactly on one of the other zone lines, use the lowest score. The sixth result, 49.0, represents this situation. A zone score of 1 was added to the previous score to arrive at a cumulative score of 4.

A zone score of 8 or more is a signal that a process has shifted. This is illustrated by the last value of 47.7. The zone score of 4 assigned to this result, plus the previous zone score of 4 gives a cumulative score of 8. Following corrective action, the scoring process begins anew.

The statistical background

The zone control chart procedures uses the statistical tests for detecting process shifts described in the *AT&T Statistical Quality Control Handbook* (formerly the *Western Electrical Quality Control Handbook*).[1] These tests are:

- A single point falls outside of the 3-sigma limit.
- Two out of three successive points fall within the 2- and 3-sigma zone.
- Four out of five successive points fall within the 1- and 2-sigma zone.
- Eight successive points fall between the target and the 1-sigma zone.

These tests are applied separately to the upper and lower halves of the control chart, not in combination.

Figure 9.3 illustrates the results obtained when applying the zone control chart procedure to these four tests. Note that for each test, the cumulative zone score is either 8 or more. The selection of 8 as the action number is thus in complete agreement with established quality control practices.

Figure 9.3.

Applying the AT&T Statistical Tests for Instability

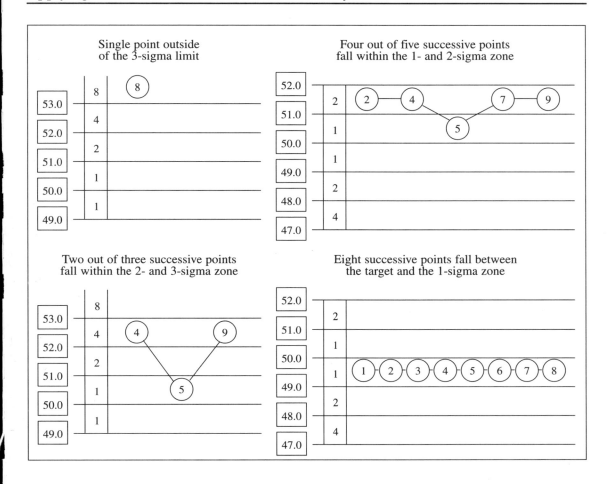

Reference

1. *AT&T Statistical Quality Control Handbook.*

When this column was originally published in February 1989, Al Jaehn was the quality systems manager for Consolidated Papers, Inc. in Wisconsin Rapids, WI. He was an American Society for Quality Fellow and certified quality engineer.

Get More out of Common Control Charts Using K-Limits
by Paul A. Kales

Quality control analysts have long been interested in finding more sensitive ways to interpret control charts and, in particular, to detect trends. The method most commonly available, provided by the *Statistical Quality Control Handbook,* divides the control chart into zones, using interpretive two-of-three, four-of-five, and eight-in-a-row rules.[1] The cusum (cumulative sum) control chart, introduced in the 1950s, also provides a trend-detecting capability, but it has not been widely accepted on the production floor because of its complexity. Here is a modification that will make the traditional Shewhart chart easy to use and able to reveal trends.

This method uses a series of K-limits as supplements to the control charts so that K-or-more points in sequence outside the UKL or LKL (the K limit on either side of the control chart) indicate an out-of-control condition. As an example, Figure 9.4 shows an X-bar control chart with upper and lower control limits ($UCL_{\overline{X}}$ and $LCL_{\overline{X}}$, respectively) as well as upper and lower K-limits ($U2L_{\overline{X}}$ and $L2L_{\overline{X}}$; $U3L_{\overline{X}}$ and $L3L_{\overline{X}}$; $U5L_{\overline{X}}$ and $L5L_{\overline{X}}$).

Figure 9.4.

Sample $\overline{X}$ Control Chart Showing Control Limits and K-Limits for K = 2,3,5

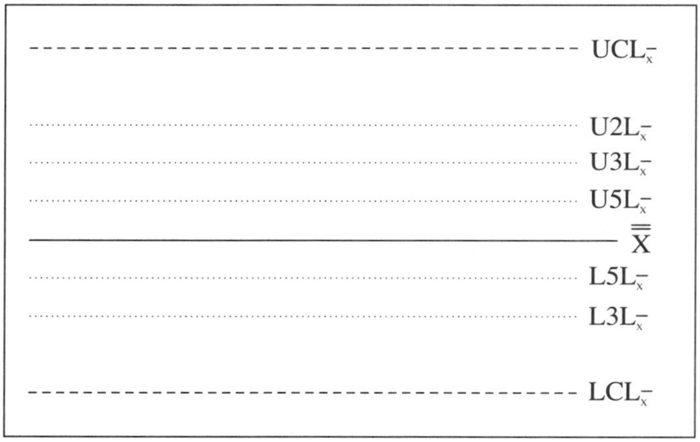

A single point above the $UCL_{\overline{X}}$ in Figure 9.4, or two points in a row above the $U2L_{\overline{X}}$, or three points in a row above the $U3L_{\overline{X}}$, or K points in a row above the $UKL_{\overline{X}}$, etc. are indications of an out-of-control condition. Similar conclusions can be drawn from the occurrence of points below the lower control or K-limits, i.e., $LCL_{\overline{X}}$.

For X-bar control charts, the K-limits are:

$$UKL_{\overline{X}} = \overline{\overline{X}} + MA_2\overline{R}$$

$$LKL_{\overline{X}} = \overline{\overline{X}} - MA_2\overline{R}$$

where $\overline{\overline{X}}$, $\overline{R}$, and A_2 are as defined for Shewhart $\overline{X}$ charts and M is determined in Figure 9.5.

Figure 9.5.

M Factors

K	M
2	0.60*
3	0.40*
4	0.30
5	0.20*
6	0.15
7	0.10
8	0.05
9	0.00

*Shown in Figure 9.4

For p, np, c, and u charts, the K-limits are:

$$UKL_p = \bar{p} + 3M\sqrt{\bar{p}(1-\bar{p})/n}$$

$$LKL_p = \bar{p} - 3M\sqrt{\bar{p}(1-\bar{p})/n}$$

$$UKL_{np} = n\bar{p} + 3M\sqrt{n\bar{p}(1-\bar{p})}$$

$$LKL_{np} = n\bar{p} - 3M\sqrt{n\bar{p}(1-\bar{p})}$$

$$UCL_c = \bar{c} + 3M\sqrt{\bar{c}}$$

$$LCL_c = \bar{c} - 3M\sqrt{\bar{c}}$$

$$UCL_u = \bar{u} + 3M\sqrt{\bar{u}/n}$$

$$LCL_u = \bar{u} - 3M\sqrt{\bar{u}/n}$$

where n, $\bar{p}$, $\bar{c}$, and $\bar{u}$ are defined for Shewhart $\bar{X}$ charts and M is determined in Figure 9.5.

The M factors in Figure 9.5 were derived from normal distribution probabilities such that the probability of having K points in a row above the UKL (or below the LKL) is the same as having a single point above the UCL (or below the LCL) for an in-control system. While the normal assumption is more valid for $\bar{X}$, p, and np charts, and less so for c and u charts, the K-limits provide a simple method for getting more information from common control charts.

For example, consider the data presented in the $\bar{X}$ control chart in Figure 9.6. These data were generated at a recent workshop from a process created to demonstrate control chart principles. The control chart parameters had previously been computed to be: $\bar{\bar{X}} = 20.9$, $\bar{R} = 9.5$, $UCL_{\bar{x}} = 26.4$, $U3L_{\bar{x}} = 23.1$, and $U5L_{\bar{x}} = 22$.

Figure 9.6.
$\bar{X}$ Control Chart with K-Limits Showing a Trend

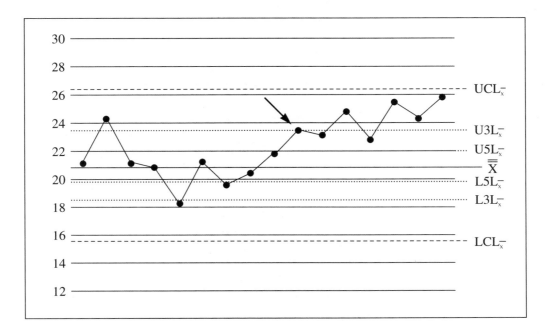

The process is deliberately destabilized by changing the source material at the 10th point on the plot (see arrow). By the fifth point, the change was detected by the U5L$_{\bar{x}}$ limit. By the seventh point, it was detected by the U3L$_{\bar{x}}$ limit. Western Electric's eight-in-a-row rule would also have detected it by the seventh point. It had not yet been detected by the upper control limit. Not shown is the U4L$_{\bar{x}}$ limit (22.6), which would have detected the change by the fourth point.

Reference

1. *AT&T Statistical Quality Control Handbook.*

When this column was originally published in July 1990, Paul A. Kales was an assistant professor of industrial technology and faculty adviser of the student American Society for Quality branch at the University of Lowell, Lowell, MA. He was a member of the American Society for Quality.

Time-Saving Tips for Short-Run Average Charts
by Gary Phillips

If you use stabilized or semi-standardized average charts in your job, you might be able to save some time by taking two shortcuts. These time-saving tips can be used for charting the following types of processes:

- Those with a variety of part numbers, characteristics, or target values that are plotted on the same chart. Items within a subgroup, however, must be homogeneous.
- Those with an anticipated range, $\hat{R}_j$, that varies for each subgroup but is predictable based on previous short-run capability studies using common elements, such as size, material, or tools.
- Those in which the data are recorded as x = deviation from target. This permits a common target central line of zero for all subgroups and simplifies notation.

Tip No. 1

Figure 9.7 contains five different part numbers made by the same process and represented on the same chart by five different subgroups. Each part has its own anticipated range, which is generally not equal to the actual range of a subgroup. In this type of short-run situation, an overall average range is not used and would be meaningless.

The usual procedure for preparing a stabilized average chart is to calculate the sum Σx for each subgroup, divide by the subgroup size n, and then take the extra step of dividing by the anticipated range.[1] The resulting unitless values are $(\Sigma x/n)/\hat{R}_j = \bar{X}/\hat{R}_j$. They have limits of $0 \pm A_2$, where A_2 is taken from a table of control chart factors.

To save time, however, you can skip the step of dividing by the subgroup size. Instead, simply divide the subgroup sum by the anticipated range. This saves a step for every point plotted. The unitless values will be $\Sigma x/\hat{R}_j$ with limits of $0 \pm nA_2$. This time-saving tip is illustrated in Figure 9.7 by omission because the extra arithmetic is, of course, not there.

In addition to saving time, the chart's unitless limits are easier to relate to because the 3-sigma limits will be approximately ± 3 instead of an arbitrary number. For example, the limits for a subgroup size of five would be $\pm A_2 = \pm 5(0.58) = \pm 2.9$. Limits for other subgroup sizes are given in Figure 9.8.

The semi-standardized average chart is robust enough to accommodate an occasional point with a slightly different subgroup size because the limits won't change much, as long as you use an anticipated range appropriate for the actual subgroup size. (Small runs of one to 10 items are often 100 percent inspected, resulting in subgroup sizes that are inconsistent. If that happens frequently, consider the next tip.)

Tip No. 2

If the subgroup size of a process varies frequently but stays between three and 15, you could use a chart like that shown in Figure 9.7, with rounded-off limits of 0 ± 3. This

Figure 9.7.

A Semi-Standardized Chart for a Short-Run Process

Part number		Q	Y	Z	D	A
Target	T	220	385	410	325	200
Anticipated range	$\hat{R}_j$	3.3	5.7	6.1	4.9	3.0

Deviation	x_1	0	1	-5	3	1
from	x_2	-1	-4	-2	1	0
target	x_3	-2	0	1	6	-3

Plot value	$\Sigma x/\hat{R}_j$	-0.9	-0.5	-1.0	2.0	-0.7
Actual range	R	2	5	6	5	4

Semi-standardized

average

chart

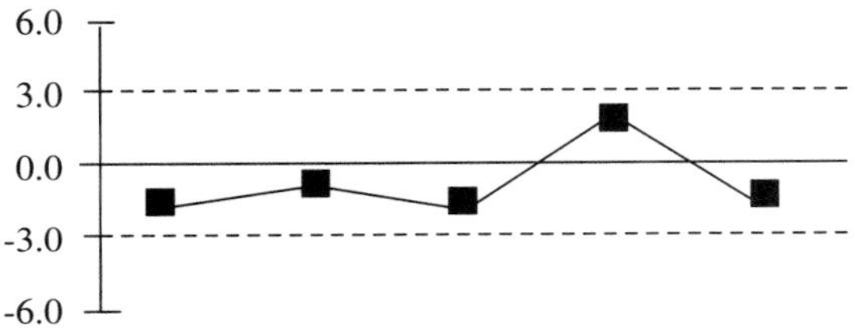

Figure 9.8.

Limits for the Semi-Standardized Short-Run Average Chart

n	2	3	4	5	6	7	8	9	10	11	12	13	14	15
$\pm nA_2$	±3.8	±3.1	±2.9	±2.9	±2.9	±2.9	±3.0	±3.0	±3.1	±3.1	±3.2	±3.2	±3.3	±3.4

practice is much easier than manually plotting a fully standardized chart—but only if you can easily look up anticipated ranges $\hat{R}_j = (\hat{\sigma}_j d_2)$ for the various subgroup sizes. If you have to manually recalculate the anticipated ranges for unpredictable subgroup sizes, you might as well plot the fully standardized short-run average statistic $\Sigma x/(\hat{\sigma}_j \sqrt{n})$, which has exact limits of 0 ±3 regardless of the subgroup size.[2]

For any of the short-run average charts mentioned, you should also plot a range chart. When preparing the range chart, you should plot $R/\hat{R}_j$ and use an upper control limit of D_4, a lower control limit of D_3, and a central line of 1. Fully standardized charts for range or sample standard deviation (with exact limits of 0 ±3) can also be prepared.[3]

Save time

If your processes are similar to those described here, save yourself some time by taking advantage of these two simple tips.

References

1. Pyzdek, "Process Control for Short and Small Runs," p. 56.
2. Phillips, *SPC for Low Volume Manufacturing*, p. 6–2.
3. Ibid.

When this column was originally published in December 1994, Gary Phillips was the director of the Customer-Focused Engineering Unit of Productivity Action Associates, Inc. in Northville, MI. He received a bachelor's degree in industrial engineering from Wayne State University in Detroit, MI. Phillips was a member of ASQ.

Monitoring Measurable Process Data: Why Not Use the EWMA Chart?

by Claude R. Superville

The exponentially weighted moving average (EWMA) control chart has been in existence since the 1960s. While it is well known by academicians, it seems to be underutilized in the business world, even though a number of statistical software programs will produce EWMA charts as easily as $\overline{X}$ charts.

There are several reasons why companies should use the EWMA chart:

- Small process disturbances can be detected more quickly by the EWMA chart than the $\overline{X}$ chart. This can be useful, for example, in chemical process operations in which small changes in the value of an ingredient can have a large effect on the final product.
- Unlike the $\overline{X}$ chart, the EWMA chart works well when the process data are not normal.
- The EWMA chart can be used in conjunction with an $\overline{X}$ chart to provide greater effectiveness in detecting small and large process disturbances.
- The EWMA chart can be used as an alternative to the individuals chart for monitoring individual observations (samples of one observation each) when small process observations are of interest.

The EWMA statistic

The EWMA control chart is a weighted average of all previous and current sample means. The chart requires the calculation of:

$$W_t = \alpha \overline{X}_t + (1 - \alpha)W_{t-1}, \ 0 < \alpha \leq 1$$

In this equation, α is the weight assigned to the present sample means and $1 - \alpha$ is the weight assigned to earlier sample means. Smaller α values increase the chart's sensitivity to small process disturbances, while larger α values increase the chart's sensitivity to larger disturbances.

Values of α in the interval $0.05 \leq \alpha \leq 0.3$ are usually recommended, with $\alpha = 0.1$ or 0.15 being commonly used values. The initial EWMA value, W_0, is set equal to the grand mean, $\overline{\overline{X}}$, from preliminary samples of observations. The centerline is $\overline{\overline{X}}$, and the 3-sigma control limits are:

Lower control limit

$$(\text{LCL}) = \overline{\overline{X}} - (A_2 \, \overline{R}\sqrt{[\alpha/(2 - \alpha)]})$$

Upper control limit

$$(\text{UCL}) = \overline{\overline{X}} + (A_2 \, \overline{R}\sqrt{[\alpha/(2 - \alpha)]})$$

with a minor adjustment when the number of samples is small. The average range, $\overline{R}$, can be obtained from preliminary samples, and the chart constant, A_2, can be found in most quality textbooks.

An example

A fertilizer manufacturer was concerned that small changes in the level of ammonia in the product was affecting its granularity. The small changes were not easily detectable using an $\overline{X}$ chart. Having heard that the EWMA chart effectively detects small process disturbances, the company used it to monitor the data.

From 20 preliminary samples of four observations each, the process mean was estimated to be $\overline{\overline{X}} = 12$ and $\overline{R} = 4.03$. Calculation of the EWMA values with $\alpha = 0.1$ is shown in Figure 9.9. For samples of four observations each, $A_2 = 0.729$. The control limits were:

$$LCL = 12 - [0.729(4.03) \sqrt{(0.1/1.9)}] = 11.326$$

$$UCL = 12 + [0.729(4.03) \sqrt{(0.1/1.9)}] = 12.674$$

The EWMA control chart is shown in Figure 9.10. The chart confirmed the manufacturer's suspicions that the small changes in ammonia levels did affect the fertilizer's granularity. As this manufacturer discovered, the EWMA control chart can be used as an alternative to the $\overline{X}$ chart when greater chart sensitivity to small process disturbances is required.

Figure 9.9.
EWMA Values

Sample number	Sample mean ($\overline{X}_t$)	EWMA value (W_t)
	$\overline{\overline{X}} = 12$	
1	11.64	0.1(11.64) + 0.9(12.00) = 11.96
2	11.41	0.1(11.41) + 0.9(11.96) = 11.91
3	10.81	0.1(10.81) + 0.9(11.91) = 11.80
4	12.74	0.1(12.74) + 0.9(11.80) = 11.89
5	11.42	0.1(11.42) + 0.9(11.89) = 11.84
6	12.66	11.93
7	11.52	11.89

Figure 9.10.
EWMA Control Chart with $\alpha = 0.1$

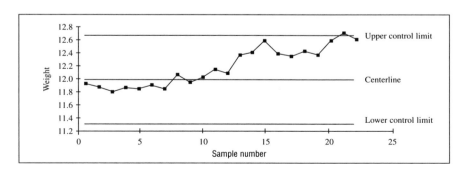

When this column was originally published in July 1995, Claude R. Superville was an assistant professor of management and information systems at Valdosta State University in Valdosta, GA. He received a doctorate in applied statistics from the University of Alabama in Tuscaloosa. Superville was an American Society for Quality member and certified quality engineer.

The Dot Method C-Chart
by Glenn Roth and Nick Nocera

The dot method C-chart was developed to be easy on the operator. The chart is universal. It does not matter what type of product is being charted as long as attribute data are being plotted.

The X axis of the chart represents the time that the subgroup sample will be taken. The Y axis represents the subgroup sample size to be taken. Subgroup sizes can vary.

Figure 9.11 shows the dot method C-chart. Suppose the operator takes the first sample at 7:45 A.M. and finds no nonconformities. The operator then colors in the zero and continues to run the job. If the operator finds one nonconformity in the subgroup sample taken at the second check at 8:45 A.M., he or she colors in the "one" and stops the job for corrective action. Similarly, if the operator finds two, three, four, or five nonconformities, he or she colors in the corresponding quantity of nonconformities and

Figure 9.11.
The Dot Method C-Chart

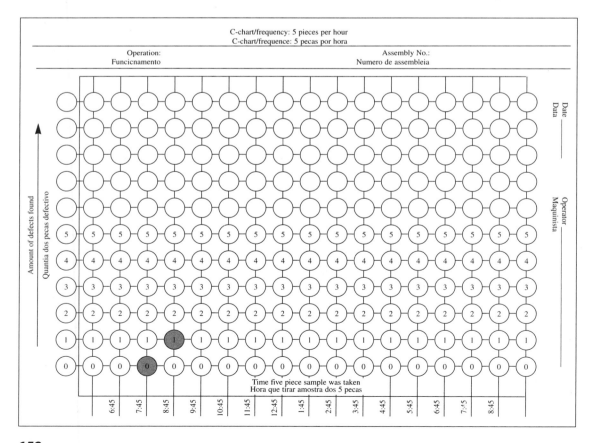

stops the job. Standard statistical calculations are then used to compute the upper control limit, lower control limit, C-bar chart, and C-chart.

Each C-chart acts as a run chart and is kept at the operation for the entire day's production. A new chart is issued each day or production run.

Usage of the C-chart can be expanded if a second language, such as Spanish, is added (see headings in Figure 9.11). The top portion or heading section of the C-chart contains the operation, part number, frequency of sample, and required sample size. The right side of the chart includes an area for the operator's name and date.

On the back side of the chart (Figure 9.12) is space to make notes on any machine adjustments or corrective actions.

This chart method was developed in 1983 and was tested in production during 1983 and 1984 at Joseph Pollack Corporation. It has now become a standard control chart at the company.

Figure 9.12.
The Dot Method C-Chart (Back Side)

Time	Corrective action	Signature

When this column was originally published in July 1988, Glenn Roth and Nick Nocera worked for Joseph Pollack Corporation in Boston, MA. Roth, an American Society for Quality member, was the director of quality assurance. Nocera, an American Society for Quality member, was the senior quality assurance engineer.

The Dot Method C-Chart: The Next Generation

by Stephen Carty

The control chart described and illustrated here is a variation of the Glenn Roth and Nick Nocera's dot method C-chart. It follows the same general rules for use, but can be applied more directly to assemblies requiring control of more than one attribute characteristic.

As Figure 9.13 shows, the revised chart includes a grid in which you plot the number of nonconformances found (Y axis) vs. the time the sample was taken (X axis). Sample assemblies are selected at the specified time, and the individual characteristics are checked. Nonconformances are recorded with a solid dot at the intersection of the vertical and horizontal lines.

When a nonconformance is discovered, the operator stops the job and performs corrective action. (In some processes, however, it might be impractical to stop the process.) A corrective action summary is provided on the back of the chart. The operator gives a brief description of the nonconformance, the corrective action performed, and the initials of the individual responsible for implementing corrective action.

The chart can be modified to accommodate varying frequencies of inspection (see Figure 9.14). In this chart, audits are conducted twice daily, with the time the audit is performed entered under each grid. Control limits for the chart are calculated using standard techniques. The benefits of this combination chart include using less paper and maintaining and tracking fewer documents. Also, combining charts lessens the possibility of overlooking a scheduled audit. Total nonconformances and nonconformances-per-unit information is available in a clear, concise form, and a running history of corrective action maintenance is easily referenced.

When this column was originally published in July 1989, Stephen Carty was a quality assurance engineer at Joseph Pollak Corporation in Boston, MA. He was a member of the American Society for Quality.

Figure 9.13.

The Next Generation

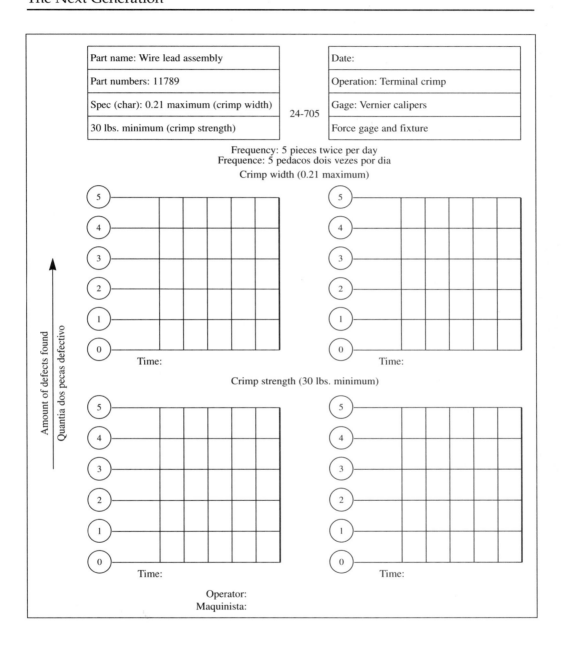

Figure 9.14.

Modifying the Chart to Accommodate Varying Frequencies

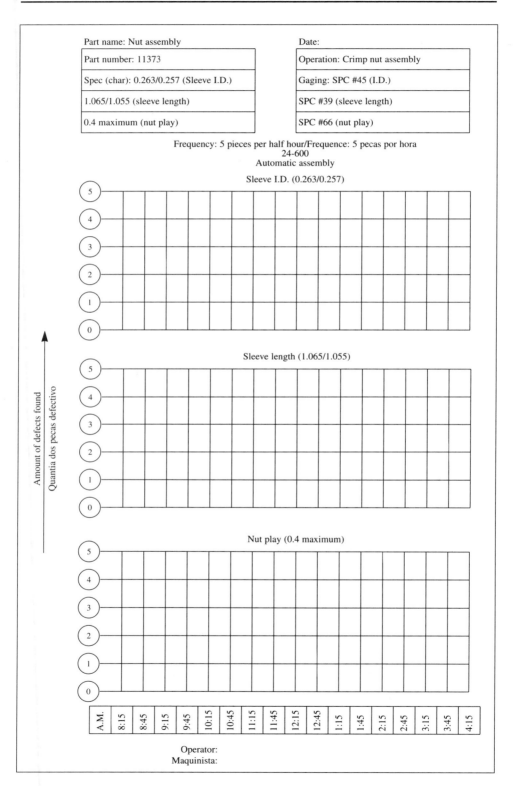

How to Enhance Attribute Charts

by Alton Humphrey

Attribute charts continue to be very effective in tracking defects in the Mid-South Electrics, Inc., manufacturing facility at Gadsden, AL. I have, however, found a method that will enhance the data being recorded on the attribute charts. This technique, called the Quality DataGram, has proven to be an excellent tool for improving overall quality performance.

The Quality DataGram

The Quality DataGram contributes to the quality effort by:

- Identifying problem areas
- Tracking quality trends
- Evaluating the quality awareness and understanding of quality standards of both the manufacturing and quality work forces
- Giving real-time feedback to departmental supervisors, enabling prompt corrective action.

Use of the Quality DataGram in Figure 9.15 to plot attribute data on a characteristic-for-characteristic basis is similar to plotting variable data using the frequency distribution format. Manufacturing operators plot each failure or defect at their station as they are detected, providing real-time information for immediate analysis. The symbol "X" is used to indicate a single occurrence of a failure or defect for a particular characteristic. Similarly, the quality auditor plots failure or defects he has found on the same Quality DataGram using the symbol "O" plotted alongside the X's previously recorded by the operator.

A simple, effective tool

This system has proven to be very helpful in correlating understanding of acceptance criteria, particularly those that are subjective such as color standards and plating quality. The same principle can be applied by adding other symbols to indicate the results of different elements, such as different customers or shifts.

Customers who visit our facility have been very complimentary of the Quality DataGram because it gives a pictorial assessment of problem areas requiring corrective action. The real advantage is its simplicity. Because computer software is not required, the Quality DataGram can be readily adapted to any quality assurance program.

When this column was published in June 1988, Alton Humphrey was the quality assurance manager for Mid-South Electrics, Inc. He was an American Society for Quality senior member and certified quality engineer.

Figure 9.15.
The Quality Diagram

Mid-South Electrics, Inc.   Product: HSG   Station: Final test   Date: 12-5 through 12-10   Sheet 1 of 2

Item No.	Method	Quantity of defects (5 · 10 · 15 · 20 · 25)	Description	Item total	% of total
1	Fixture		Location of R.R.		
	Go/no-go		pivot arm		
2	Fixture		Location of F.R.		
	Go/no-go		pivot arm		
3	Fixture		Location of R.R.		
	Go/no-go		plate		
4	Fixture		Location of F.R.		
	Go/no-go		plate		
5	Fixture	X X X X X X X X X X X X X X	Alignment of right	18	15.0
	Go/no-go	O O O O	gray seal		
6	Fixture	X X X X X X X X X X X X X X X X	Alignment of left	17	14.3
	Go/no-go	O	gray seal		
7	Fixture	X X X X X X X X X X X X X X X X X X	Alignment of	19	16.0
	Go/no-go	O	gate housing		
8	Fixture	X X X X X X X X X	Alignment of	10	
	Go/no-go	O	lower seal		
9	Fixture	X X	Baffle - check for	3	
	Go/no-go	O	bends, damage, etc.		
10	Fixture		Space between		
	Go/no-go		pivot arm and end plates (audit)		
11	Visual		Bent pivot arms	2	
		O O	R.R. and F.R.		
12	Visual	X X X X X	Chipped	5	
			paint		
13	Visual	X	Rod and cam	1	
			missing		
14	Visual	X	High screw	3	
		O O	(end plate)		
15	Visual	X X X	Cam	8	
		O O O O O	cracked		
16	Visual	X X	Thumper won't	2	
			turn		

X = Manufacturing   O = Quality control   Total produced __800__   Total | 88 | 11.0

C_{pk} Dart Charts: An Easy Way to Track Continuous Improvement

by John Buckfelder and Jon Powell

Would you like to present C_{pk} values to your customers using a simple tool that clearly sums up quality improvements? Could you use a tool that turns C_{pk} into a measure of continuous improvement? If you answered "yes" to either question, the C_{pk} dart chart is for you.

The C_{pk} dart chart is a graph of standard deviation vs. average on which triangles are drawn to indicate specific C_{pk} ranges. This type of chart has been used in the past to compare and contrast different types of process capability indexes.[1] For continuous processes, monthly averages and standard deviations can be plotted on this chart. For parts industries, campaign averages and standard deviations can be plotted. Each plotted point on the chart represents a C_{pk} value. The triangles on the chart separate the C_{pk} values into categories from not-at-all capable to very capable. With continuous improvement, the plotted points will head in the direction of the inner triangle, where the largest values for the C_{pk} reside.

After several months or several campaigns worth of data have been collected on this chart, it can be given to customers to clearly summarize recent quality improvements. If the points plotted most recently fall in the smaller inner triangles, the customer will know you have improved process capability. The chart can also be used as an internal measure of continuous improvement. Managers and operations personnel can use it to search for trends indicating the magnitude and direction of change in the ability to meet customer specifications. Each plotted point on the chart must be based on a sufficiently large sample size to prevent a false conclusion that improvement has occurred. A good means for determining sufficient sample size is to consult a table for the lower confidence values of the C_{pk}.[2] One rule of thumb is that each point must be based on a sample size of 50 or more.

The C_{pk} dart chart has the added advantage of being a powerful learning tool. The ranges that the triangles outline bring home the true meaning of the C_{pk} statistic. To reach a certain C_{pk} value, the average must be close enough to target and the variability small enough so that the plotted point falls within the desired triangle.

Construction

A computer is not needed to make this simple chart. Just draw a vertical and horizontal axis on a piece of graph paper. Label the vertical axis "standard deviation" and label the horizontal axis "average." Put the lower specification limit (LSL) for your product measurement at one end of the horizontal axis and the upper specification limit (USL) at the other. You have already plotted the first two corners of one triangle. Now you must decide how many triangles you want to draw on the chart. No more than three triangles should be drawn to avoid cluttering the picture. Next, decide what C_{pk} values you want to lie within each triangle. Choose your most important C_{pk} goal for the inner triangle. For many companies, this goal is the standard 1.33 value that Ford uses as a minimum value to demonstrate a process is fully capable. For the outer triangle, choose a C_{pk} value that is close to where your process is currently operating. For the middle triangle, choose a C_{pk} value that is reasonably far along the path toward your most important C_{pk} goal. Once you have selected your C_{pk} values, use this formula to plot the apex of each triangle: $(USL + LSL)/2$ on the horizontal axis and $(USL - LSL)/6C_{pk}$ on the vertical axis. Once the corners and apex are plotted, draw in the triangles. The sides of the triangles represent combinations of the average and standard deviation where the C_{pk}s are exactly the values you have chosen. Any points that you plot within the triangles will have higher C_{pk}s than the values you have chosen.

Demonstration

Suppose your company, Widgets-Are-Us, makes widgets with a specified length of 20 feet to 40 feet. Your customer has requested that you implement a continuous improvement program with the primary goal of making your process fully capable within a year. Currently the process is not very close to being capable; the last C_{pk} you calculated was a miserable 0.4.

Your task is clear: reach a C_{pk} of 1.33 within a year. Thus, draw an inner triangle such that, when you plot points inside this triangle, the C_{pk} is 1.33 or greater. Currently your C_{pk} is a little below one-half, so draw the outer triangle such that, when you plot points within the triangle, the C_{pk} is 0.5 or greater. Just reaching the point where the 6-sigma limits meet the specification limits (C_{pk} of 1) would be a good improvement and is a reasonable goal. Therefore, draw the middle triangle such that, when you plot points within this triangle, your C_{pk} is 1 or greater. The inner triangle has its two corners at 20 and 40, and the apex is at $(40 + 20)/2 = 30$ and $(40 - 20)/(6 \times 1.33) = 2.5$. The middle triangle has the same corners, and the apex is at 30 and $(40 - 20)/(6 \times 1) = 3.33$. The outer triangle has the same corners, and the apex is at 30 and $(40 - 20)/6 \times 0.5 = 6.67$. Drawing in the lines to complete the triangles gives you the graph shown in Figure 9.16.

Once you have drawn the chart, you can collect the data on the widget process and plot the averages and standard deviations for the data. As Figure 9.16 shows, Widgets-Are-Us met the customer's requirement of becoming fully capable within a year. In fact, the process has improved so much that it is time to consider making a new chart with smaller triangles to track future improvement.

The C_{pk} dart chart is easy to draw and use. It effectively displays a company's improvements to customers, tracks improvements, and teaches the C_{pk} statistic.

References

1. Boyles, "The Taguchi Capability Index," pp. 17–26.
2. Chou, Owens, and Borrego, "Lower Confidence Limits on Process Capability Indices," pp. 223–29.

When this column was published in February 1993, John Buckfelder was the polypropylene quality coordinator at Solvay Polymers, Inc. in Houston, TX. Buckfelder received a doctorate in physical chemistry from Iowa State University in Ames. Jon Powell was the statistician at Solvay Polymers. He received a master's degree in statistics from Texas A&M University in College Station and a master's degree in business administration from the University of Houston in Texas. Powell was an American Society for Quality member and certified quality engineer.

Figure 9.16.

C_{pk} Dart Chart

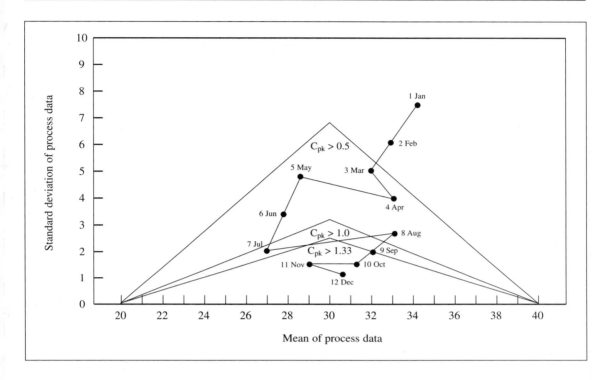

Pareto Analysis and Trend Charts: A Powerful Duo
by Roger E. Duffy

The Pareto principle states that a few causes (or, as J. M. Juran called them, the "vital few" causes) often account for most of an effect.[1] To find those vital few causes, data are usually collected and categorized by defect type or class, then the defect classes are ranked. Although this traditional Pareto analysis allows the most important defects to be addressed, it has several drawbacks:

- If there are small amounts of data, the Pareto diagram might not show much difference between the classes of defects.
- There might be variation over time in the occurrences of defects in a particular class. (For example, a serious problem last week might not be a problem this week, even if no action was taken to correct the problem.)
- If a Pareto diagram is used to present a ranking of defects over time, no information is available to assess the trend of individual defects or to assess their frequency of occurrence.

Figure 9.17.

Top 10 Final Inspection Rejects

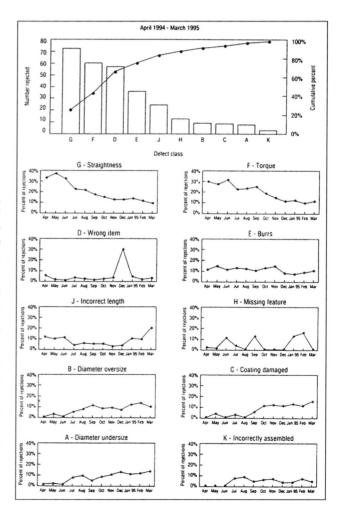

At Kerk Motion Products, I encountered these drawbacks when using Pareto diagrams to analyze defects in the processes used to manufacture motion control assemblies. Since it was difficult to determine the necessary corrective actions, I started preparing Pareto diagrams with trend charts using a 12-month, rolling data base. The data base is summarized monthly by defect class, and a Pareto diagram is produced. In addition, for each of the top 10 defect classes, a trend chart is created and placed below the Pareto diagram (see Figure 9.17).

With today's computers and software, maintaining a 12-month, rolling data base is easy and often can be automated. With this data base, Pareto diagrams and trend charts can be quickly produced for any specified period.

This combination of Pareto diagrams and trend charts has many benefits:

- The *real* vital few problems are identified. In Figure 9.17, defect class D would be considered a significant problem if the Pareto diagram were used alone. The trend chart, however, shows that the high rate of occurrence in December was a one-time event.
- How often defects occur is monitored. As Figure 9.17 shows, defects occur monthly in most of the classes, except for class H, where defects occur infrequently but at high levels.
- Potential problems can be acted on. Defect class C would not be considered one of the vital few using Pareto analysis, and typically no action would be taken. But the trend chart indicates that this defect's occurrence is increasing over time, thus allowing action to be taken before it becomes one of the vital few.
- Trend charts clearly show the effect of corrective actions. Although defect class G has caused the most rejections in the past 12 months, the trend chart shows that actions taken in May have substantially reduced the problem. In addition, the effectiveness of the corrective action initiated for defect class J levels off in December, indicating that the action might now be ineffective.
- Common classes of defects can more easily be compared. Defects relating to diameters (defect classes A and B) were low until June, when the trend of both started to increase.

Combining Pareto diagrams and trend charts provides a powerful analysis tool for quality professionals; more information is available than if they are used separately. This powerful duo enables quality professionals to quickly identify chronic problems and assess the long-term effectiveness of corrective actions.

Reference

1. Juran, *Juran's Quality Control Handbook*, pp. 22–19.

When this column was originally published in November 1995, Roger E. Duffy was the quality assurance manager at Kerk Motion Products, Inc. in Hollis, NH. He received an associate degree in quality assurance from the New Hampshire Technical College in Nashua. Duffy was an American Society for Quality senior member, certified quality engineer, and certified quality auditor.

Clearly Illustrate Multiple Measurables with the Web Chart

by Richard (Coach) M. Carangelo

One of the benefits of benchmarking is that you get to learn about new tools and techniques. During my travels in Europe, I visited a colleague in Belgium. In a discussion on measurables reporting, my colleague used a unique tool called the web chart. I like this chart so much that I've used it ever since and have introduced it to many managers, supervisors, and fellow quality practitioners.

The web chart clearly illustrates measurables at a glance. Since the center of the chart is the target for each measurable scale, it provides unambiguous data interpretations. If you need another measurable, you simply have to add a scale for it. Since the chart shows previous and current periods on the same chart, you can easily make comparisons between them. In addition, it can be used for any time period (e g., weekly, monthly, or yearly).

The web chart is easy to make:

1. Determine the number of measurables to be charted.
2. Group measurables by topics (such as customer satisfaction and continuous improvement).
3. Determine scales for each measurable.
4. Set the scales so that the targets are at the center of the chart. Depending on the accuracy required, decide whether you want to use tick marks or whether you simply want to write down the value next to the measurable's plotted point.
5. Set the angle between the scales so that they will be evenly spaced (for example: 7 scales = 360 degrees/8 spaces = 45 degrees).
6. If one or more scales are inverse (meaning that zero would be at the opposite end in comparison), divide the chart into two sections using a dotted line. Label one section "Center = 0" and the other "Center > 0." Place the scales in the appropriate sections.
7. Plot the data from the last period and connect them using a dotted line.
8. Plot the data from the current period and connect them using a solid line.
9. Label the chart accordingly.

Figure 9.18 contains an example of a web chart. This simplified example illustrates several measurables used by a management team to measure plant performance for that quarter. Any time period that suits a particular purpose can be used. For example, a weekly chart can be used by process owners on the production floor. Managers, on the other hand, might use an annual chart for strategy sessions.

The web chart is a simple, clear, and concise tool that illustrates multiple measurables and allows comparison between current and previous reporting periods. Once you try it, you'll always want your measurables to be caught in the web.

When this column was originally published in January 1995, Richard (Coach) M. Carangelo was the managing director of the International Quality Exchange in Easley, SC. Carangelo was an American Society for Quality member and certified quality engineer.

Figure 9.18.
The Web Chart

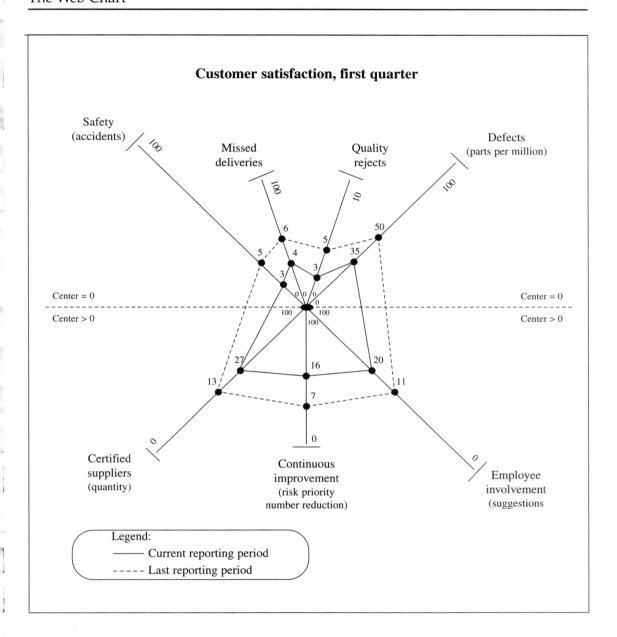

Customer satisfaction, first quarter

Safety
(accidents)
100

Missed
deliveries
100

Quality
rejects
10

Defects
(parts per million)
100

6
5
50
5
4
35
3
3

Center = 0
Center = 0

0 0 0
0
100 100
100

Center > 0
Center > 0

27
16
20
13
11
7

0

Certified
suppliers
(quantity)
0

Continuous
improvement
(risk priority
number reduction)

Employee
involvement
(suggestions
0

Legend:
——— Current reporting period
----- Last reporting period

Get Management's Attention by Focusing on Rejects

by Raymond Goldstein

What is the most effective way to present data for percent accepted to management? This question was tackled by me and the other members of my department. The answer became obvious after we gave the situation some thought. Clearly, very little needs to be done with products that have been accepted. Therefore, we decided to focus management's attention on the products that were being rejected.

The data shown in Figure 9.19 indicate a range of 90 percent to 98 percent for percent accepted. It focuses on what appears to be the good news. But the portion of the data requiring management attention is the difference between 90 percent and 100 percent: the percent rejected. So instead of using only 10 percent of the graph to plot the problem area, we decided to magnify the situation by a factor of 10 by plotting percent rejected instead of percent accepted. This provided a more discernible indication of the trends (Figure 9.20).

To further increase the usefulness of the chart, we added the unit cost of each rejection multiplied by the quantity of rejections. This provided an indication of the rejections' cost. A cumulative line further depicted the total rejection cost to enable a trade-off analysis of the cost of failures vs. the cost of corrective action. Thus, by focusing on

Figure 9.19.
Percent Accepted

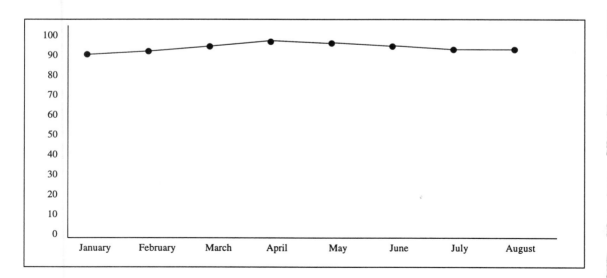

Figure 9.20.

Percent Rejected

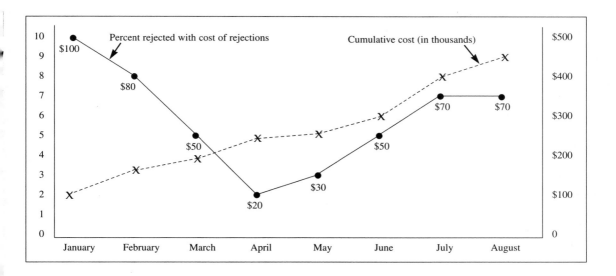

the problem area and its cost impact, the first step was taken toward reducing failure costs and improving manufacturing yields.

My experience indicates that this form of chart presentation better attracts management's attention and generates more responsive corrective action than a chart that merely presents good news in the form of high acceptance rates. The company from which I have retired has successfully applied this concept for more than five years.

When this column was originally published in January 1990, Raymond Goldstein was an American Society for Quality Fellow in Chatsworth, CA.

How to Document Quality

In the early 1990s, in my role as editor of *Quality Progress,* I (Brad Stratton) was walking the exhibit floor of the Quality Congress, the American Society for Quality's annual meeting. I struck up a conversation with a longtime exhibitor who did a fair amount of consulting and was well respected for his work. Among the topics we covered was the current rush for ISO 9000 registration.

I asked him how hot this trend was and what its longevity might be. He didn't answer the questions directly. Instead, he recited every hot trend from the quality field over the preceding 40 years. He concluded by saying that he expected ISO 9000 to have perhaps a few more years in the sun, then the masses would rush off to something else. But, he quickly added, he didn't want to be quoted on the subject because, of course, he was making a fair amount of money on standards-related consulting.

The prediction turned out to be incredibly inaccurate. As the 1990s close, ISO 9000 is still of great importance to thousands of organizations worldwide. It has become the de facto calling card for getting your foot in the door for international business. If you examine the advertising in the prominent quality-industry magazines, it will be clear that half (and sometimes more) of the advertising pertains to standards-related products or services. When I journeyed to Brazil in late 1997, people extensively talked about not only ISO 9000, but also the prospects of similar widespread acceptance for proposed industry-specific standards and ones relating to the environment and occupational safety.

With that in mind, we believe that the entries in this chapter have yet to age. Insights into how to approach documentation and how to avoid wasting time and effort in the process continue to be of value. The first two articles in this chapter provide such insight:

- If you're tired of explanations being described as some sort of pyramid, you're not alone. Christopher J. Cremer was when he wrote "The ISO 9000 Documentation Bike Ride." As the title suggests, an analogy goes a long way toward understanding.
- If you're repeatedly asked to provide the same company information, you can save time by creating a profile of your company. Richard W. Sherman tells how in "Company Profiles Provide Concise and Timely Information."

More information is often mistakenly perceived to mean better information. For example, on November 19, 1863, two major speakers delivered addresses at the dedication of the National Soldiers' Cemetery in Gettysburg, PA. One spoke for two hours, the other for three minutes. It is the latter address, spoken by Abraham Lincoln, that is among the most important speeches in U.S. history. Few people besides historians know who delivered the former (Edward Everett).[1]

This spirit of brevity runs through the next three entries in this chapter:

- "How to Avoid Creating the Dreaded 'Big Honkin' Binder" contains Richard Balano's insights into how not to create a document that is suitable for a punch line in a Dilbert cartoon.
- Akio Miura has audited quality systems at more than 50 companies, and he believes most procedure manuals are "too thick and complicated to be read by operating personnel." His article, "Don't Suffer Through Bad Manuals," offers seven suggestions for better documentation.
- Steven M. Lulis, in "Procedures: Prepare Them Right the First Time," endorses a spartan approach to procedure writing that he believes should reduce the number of procedures needing to be written by at least 20 percent.

Finally, Doug Riggins offers insights into "Meeting the Documentation Challenge in Small Businesses." Even without the luxury of having the full-time technical writers that many large companies have, small companies can still create the documents needed for registration.

Reference

1. Wills, *Lincoln at Gettyburg: The Words That Remade America,* p. 34.

The ISO 9000 Documentation Bike Ride

by Christopher J. Cremer

Companies beginning the journey toward ISO 9000 registration are often confused about the types of documentation to use and the level of detail that is needed for each type. A tool often used to explain ISO 9000 documentation is the documentation pyramid, which shows the quality policy at the peak of the pyramid, the quality system plan in the middle, and procedures and work instructions at the base. While this pyramid is accurate and easy to understand, it does not contain much information on the amount of detail best suited to each level. To help understand the level of detail needed, an analogy is helpful: think of ISO 9000 documentation as a bicycle ride to work.

The quality policy: the bike ride's goals

As just mentioned, the quality policy is at the top of the pyramid. But what amount of detail is needed at this level? To find out, let's apply the biking analogy to the quality policy. The policy would read, "I am committed to ride my bicycle to work and be on time every day." Just like an ISO 9000 quality policy, the biking quality policy is very general. It simply details:

- *The parties involved.* The policy indicates that you and your family (comparable to the organization seeking registration in an ISO 9000 quality policy) and your employer (comparable to the organization's customers) are involved.
- *Needs.* The policy reflects each party's needs. The "be on time every day" clause describes the employer's need for you to be to work on time. The "ride my bicycle to work" portion addresses you and your family's needs because it supports your goal to keep your job.
- *Commitment.* The policy indicates your commitment to riding your bike (comparable to an organization's commitment to quality).
- *Actions.* The policy describes what you are going to do (i.e., ride a bike) to meet the needs.
- *Goals.* The policy contains two objectives that are achievable and measurable: riding a bike to work every day and being on time every day. Goals are important because they will help determine whether the system is meeting both parties' needs.

One additional note about the biking quality policy is that you must tell your family members what you are planning to do so they understand and support your effort (or at least don't do anything to obstruct you, like accidentally damage your bike). In the same respect, ISO 9000 requires companies to ensure that the quality policy is understood and supported by all organizational levels.

The quality system plan: getting from here to there

The next level in the documentation pyramid is the quality system plan. The quality system plan is more detailed and focused than the quality policy. In essence, the quality system plan documents that the standard's requirements are being met. Each section in the standard should be represented by a section in the plan.

For example, ISO 9001 Subsection 4.3.2, Contract Review, requires that a company review contracts before acceptance to ensure that:[1]

- *The requirements are adequately defined.* In the bike analogy, this would mean defining what time is "on time" for being at work. In other words, the quality system plan would state that you are required to be at work by 7 A.M.
- *Any differences between the offer and contract are resolved.* Your quality system plan would document that there were no changes from the time you made a counter offer for the job and the time you accepted it.
- *The supplier has the capability to meet the requirements.* Your quality system plan would state that, before you decided to ride your bike to work, you made sure you could meet the requirement of being to work by 7 A.M.

If a section in a standard does not apply to an organization, you should state this and explain why. (For example, ISO 9001 Section 4.7, Control of Customer-Supplied Product, is not applicable in the biking analogy because the employer is not supplying the bike or any components.) If a section becomes applicable later, it should be added to the documentation, along with the appropriate procedures and work instructions.

Procedures and work instructions: where the rubber hits the road

Procedures and work instructions are at the base of the documentation pyramid. They describe how the requirements in the quality system plan are being met.

Each section in the quality system plan should have a procedure describing how its requirements will be met. For example, ISO 9001 Subsection 4.2.3, Quality Planning, indicates that suppliers should consider several activities in meeting product requirements, including:[2]

- *Preparation of quality plans.* In the bike analogy, the documentation for this point would discuss plans to ensure the quality of the product (i.e., the bike ride). The plans might include such specifics as what route will be taken to ensure the shortest trip or what time to wake up to get to work at 7 A.M.
- *Identification and acquisition of processes, equipment, skills, and such to achieve the required quality.* The documentation for this point would address any concerns that must be resolved before you start biking to work, such as whether you need to get a bike tune-up, some rain gear, or even a new bike. Resolution often requires research or testing.
- *Identification and preparation of quality records.* The documentation for this point would identify your timecard as the quality record because the quality of the bike ride is measured by you being to work by 7 A.M.

Work instructions contain the finest level of detail in quality system documentation. They give specific, step-by-step directions for completing tasks. They often include requirements for successful completion of the task and how that success is measured. For example, you might include a work instruction on how to shift gears on your bike. This work instruction, which supports the procedure on how to ride the bike, would describe how to shift, under what conditions gears should be changed, and how to tell if the bike is in the correct gear.

For simple operations, procedures and work instructions can be combined into one document. For instance, part of your safety check procedure might include verifying tire pressure. It would make sense to include the work instruction for adjusting tire pressure within this procedure. But for more detailed tasks, such as adjusting the brakes, the procedures and instructions should be separate. The procedure would indicate that you must check the brakes and then reference the work instruction. The work instruction would describe how to check the brakes, what tools to use, what replacement parts are needed, and so forth. It might also reference the owner's manual for specific tolerances.

Use an analogy

ISO 9000 documentation is often easier to understand if interpreted using a nontypical situation that removes you from the processes you work with every day. Riding your bike to work is one such analogy. It can help you explain the different levels of detail needed at each step in the documentation process.

References

1. *ANSI/ASQC Q9001-1994, Quality Systems—Model for Quality Assurance in Design, Development, Production, Installation, and Servicing.*
2. Ibid.

When this column was published in January 1997, Christopher J. Cremer was a corporate quality engineer at Modine Manufacturing Company in Racine, WI. He received a bachelor's degree in communication from Valparaiso University in Indiana. Cremer was an American Society for Quality member, certified quality engineer, and certified quality auditor.

Company Profiles Provide Concise and Timely Information
by Richard W. Sherman

Surveys and self-audits are commonly used to help assess suppliers' capabilities. While they can be beneficial in forging mutual understanding and trust, they can also be very time consuming and frustrating to complete.

Typically, these surveys and self-audits follow no standard format and can vary considerably in length and detail. In addition, they are not generally considered to be value-added activities. This is especially true when you consider the redundancy of the information requested.

Having completed more than 100 surveys and self-audits over the past few years, I have identified information commonly requested by them, such as my company's address, phone and fax numbers, key personnel, and types of facilities. Taking this information, I have developed a company profile (see Figure 10.1). As I complete a survey or self-audit, I reference the company profile whenever I come to a section asking for that information. A standard cover letter, which can quickly be customized to a specific customer, completes the process.

Figure 10.1.
The Company Profile

Company name:

Subsidiary of:

Acquired:

Headquarters address:

Phone:

Fax:

Total No. of U.S. employees:

Primary products:

Facilities

Type (e.g., headquarters, manufacturing)	Location	Square feet

Key Personnel

Name	Title	Reports to
	Vice president and general manager	
	Quality assurance manager	
	Research and development manager	
	Engineering manager	
	Manufacturing manager	
	Sales manager	
	Marketing manager	

Employees				Shifts	Union
Total	Production	Quality assurance	Quality control		

Quality systems approved: ISO 9001 (1994), MIL-I-45208A, MIL-STD-45662A, Ford Q1

The company profile also has other uses. It is a good vehicle to communicate general company information to customers, suppliers, and employees. The profile promotes a better understanding of the company's structure, thereby improving communication among all parties. Both customers and suppliers will know whom to contact directly in case of problems or inquiries. When a potential customer or supplier calls requesting information, employees will know who should receive the call, preventing the caller from being bounced around the organization in the attempt to reach the appropriate employee.

With today's word processing software, you can easily create and update a company profile that is professional looking and easy to read. The profile can be customized to fit a particular company's structure. You can add as much information as desired, but a good rule of thumb is to limit its length to one page. Several different profiles can even be created for different types of surveys. Some profiles might include such items as delivery terms or financial information.

Using the company profile, I have been able to cut survey completion time by more than 50 percent—and still provide accurate, concise, and up-to-date information. With a little training, this responsibility could even be delegated to another staff member.

When this column was published in March 1996, Richard W. Sherman was the quality assurance manager at Grace Specialty Polymers in Lexington, MA. He received a bachelor's degree in chemisty from Elmhurst College in Illinois. Sherman was an American Society for Quality senior member, certified quality manager, certified quality auditor, and certified quality engineer.

How to Avoid Creating the Dreaded "Big Honkin' Binder"

by Richard Balano

Every company that seeks ISO 9000 registration for its quality system is required to have a quality manual. Most quality manuals, however, are constructed quickly in preparation for an upcoming audit. This can result in confusing, nonvalue-added quality manuals that do not fulfill the spirit of ISO 9000.

In his cartoon strip "Dilbert," Scott Adams characterizes the compilation of a quality manual as the creation of a "big honkin' binder" of "insanely boring" departmental procedures to be routed to the first passerby, who will, in turn, treat it like a "dead raccoon." Although this characterization elicits chuckles, it has roots in reality. The quality manual need not be that way, however.

The rules

By following these nine rules, you can avoid creating a big honkin' binder:

1. *Plan the manual.* A comprehensive outline of what the manual will contain should be developed. (If you are having difficulties with this outline, read *ANSI/ISO/ASQC Q10013-1995, Guidelines for Quality Manuals.*[1] These guidelines contain excellent insight in how to develop a quality manual and show the level of detail needed.) All involved in the registration process should agree on the outline before any writing is done.

2. *Use cross-functional experts to write the manual.* Often the quality assurance department is left with the burden of writing the quality manual. It is unreasonable to assume one department has all of the knowledge needed. Thus, departments should write the sections that pertain to them. For example, the research and development department should write the section on design assurance practices (e.g., section 4.4 of ISO 9001), while purchasing should write the section on purchasing practices (e.g., section 4.5 of ISO 9001).

3. *Customize the manual to your business.* Most manual writers think they're finished once they have addressed all of the elements in the particular standard for which they are seeking registration. But every business has special activities or processes that employees should be aware of, and these special activities or processes should be included in the manual. In the medical device industry, for example, biocompatibility, sterilization, and regulatory affairs processes often exist in addition to normal business systems. Consequently, a medical device manufacturer should customize its quality manual with sections addressing these specific areas.

4. *Use the services of a technical writer.* Employees at all organizational levels should be able to understand the quality manual. Most manuals are not understandable, however, because they are written without regard to the users' needs. A useful strategy is to have a technical writer rewrite the final draft of the manual at a sixth-grade reading level. Using a technical writer is a wise investment because the resulting manual will be easy to understand and use.

5. *Have different types of employees review the manual.* After being written, most manuals are reviewed and approved by senior management. Although this is acceptable, a

more effective route is to also have different types of employees review the quality manual. Specifically, all interested parties (including quality assurance staff) should read the manual and provide input. In addition, a relatively new employee (or, at least, a human resources staff member) should review it, because if it doesn't make sense to a new employee, it is of no value.

6. *Give the manual to everyone.* Once the quality manual has been created, a decision regarding its distribution must be made. In some companies, only a handful of top-level executives are given a copy of the manual. This is a nice start, but these companies have not considered the employees on the manufacturing floor. Suppose that a shop-floor employee is interested in submitting a procedural change to improve his or her operation. Do you think this employee would visit a senior executive's office to review the quality manual first? It's not likely. More often, the employee would drop the matter entirely rather than disturb a senior executive. The distribution of the manual as well as basic instructions in its use must be widespread. Ideally, all employees should have the quality manual at their fingertips and be taught how to use it.

7. *Include quality manual training as part of new employee orientation.* Newly hired employees should be given a quality manual (or at least told where to find one). They should also be given basic instructions on what the manual contains and how to use it.

8. *Provide a system by which employees can suggest improvements to the manual.* Continuous improvement of the quality manual can be ensured by creating a simple suggestion form that employees can complete and submit to a quality systems management representative. If employees believe that their ideas are listened to and taken seriously, they will be quick to provide improvement feedback.

9. *Don't be secretive unless absolutely necessary.* Outside a company's walls, a quality manual need not be considered confidential since it usually does not provide much detail. Normally, it provides only references to documents that are detailed and possibly confidential. Instead, the quality manual should be viewed as a guide that customers and third-party auditing agencies can use to become familiar with the business. The company should be proud of the manual and encourage outsiders to read it.

An important document

A quality manual is a required element of a documented quality system and should be considered the flagship of your company's documents. It can help new employees quickly become effective at their jobs, ensure that all employees have the correct and latest information available, and impress customers and auditing agencies.

Reference

1. *ANSI/ISO/ASQC Q10013-1995, Guidelines for Quality Manuals.*

When this column was published in March 1997, Richard Balano was an auditor with the medical division of TÜV Rheinland of North America in Marlborough, MA. He received a bachelor's degree in technology from Purdue University in West Lafayette, IN. Balano was an American Society for Quality member and certified quality engineer.

Don't Suffer through Bad Manuals

by Akio Miura

A good manual is an indispensable handbook for both inexperienced and experienced employees. This goes for both procedural manuals for day-to-day tasks and instructional manuals that go with equipment.

The methods described within procedural manuals must let users work with speed and accuracy to save time, effort, materials, and utilities while simultaneously protecting them and the organization from every conceivable risk and danger. An instruction manual for a piece of equipment is no different. A well-written instruction manual does not force the reader to waste time trying to decipher cryptic directions nor force the reader to remember unnecessary details.

Unfortunately, there are many bad manuals. Despite their glossy covers, they are thick with unnecessary and confusing explanations. Often, if their directions were followed precisely, tasks would go unfinished and machines would simply not work. Such manuals have a much better use: kindling.

Most likely, these manuals turned out bad because either the people in charge of putting them together were unaware of the manuals' importance or the manuals were written by self-appointed writers who had little or no experience in the field. These writers might have been well-versed in writing other types of publications, but not manuals, where absolute precision and clarity are required.

In my career, I have audited the quality systems and quality manuals of more than 50 companies in Japan and the United Kingdom. At most companies, the manuals were too thick and complicated to be read. They were merely ornaments on bookshelves. I rewrote or corrected the procedural and equipment manuals for some of these companies.

As I have reworded these publications, so can others. Manuals should be written by responsible technical people who have a basic understanding of logic, technical writing, and editing. There is no substitute for writers having experience in the area that they will be addressing. Writers must also have complete knowledge of safety and all industry codes and standards. The most minor writing mistake could harm an employee or operation.

Seven suggestions for writing manuals

Once the proper people have been selected to prepare a manual, they should heed seven suggestions:

1. *Make the documentation clear, brief, plain, and specific.* This makes the manual easy to read and search. The manual must be complete so that all users will successfully achieve their objectives quickly and efficiently. Remember that each user has different level of experience and education.

2. *Make the manual concise.* There is one priority: The manual must be easy to carry.

3. *First write everything necessary.* This includes requirements for employees, material requirements, general cautions, and warnings. Then describe the flow of each

process, taking care to mention each step in the proper order. Use short, imperative sentences when possible.

Mark any indispensable procedures that must be remembered (such as the emergency stop for a piece of equipment) as such. Complicated procedures that are not urgent should be written in detailed, easy-to-follow steps. Users can refer to these steps at a later date as needed.

4. *Do not include anything unnecessary.* Remember that readers are eager to start and compete their work, so do not put them on hold with long introductions and explanations. Most employees are not being paid to study theories.

Similarly, in instructional manuals, do not include detailed explanations of the structure, principles, and mechanisms of equipment. Information that users do not have to remember is a nuisance. Including it in a manual can even be harmful. If a user stops reading a manual because it is cluttered with unnecessary information, the manual has defeated its purpose. Extraneous information can be included in a catalog or other publication that operators are not required to read.

5. *Include troubleshooting lists in the appropriate places.*

6. *Include sketches that show key points for operations.* However, avoid crowded illustrations and frivolous ornamentation.

7. *Use words and phrases that are understandable to all people.* Avoid technical jargon and expressions associated with new functions or technology. Jargon only confuses people—novices and experts alike.

An example of what a good manual can do

I was an executive director of a Japanese manufacturer for several years. The company's products were required to meet most major standards. During my tenure, I established a new quality assurance and production system to meet these standards. Along the way, I wrote or revised more than 200 manuals and in-house standards, simplifying and standardizing all operations.

After distributing the new manuals (which included revised standard procedures for specific jobs) most errors, reinvented wheels, and inadvertent duplication disappeared because complicated processes had been simplified at each step. In addition, customer complaints about nonconformances dropped to 1/40th of their previous total. Within three years, the company was approved by almost all major oil companies and large engineering firms in the United States and Europe.

Obviously, not all the success can be attributed to the revamped documents. But they do deserve a good share of the credit.

When this column was published in December 1989, Akio Miura was a quality assurance consultant in Tokyo. He received a bachelor's degree in mechanical engineering from Waseda University in Tokyo. Miura was a member of the American Society for Quality.

Procedures: Prepare Them Right the First Time
by Steven M. Lulis

Want to make your suppliers panic? Tell them you want to audit their systems. Prior to supplier audits, I've seen managers spend huge amounts of time preparing procedures, charts, and graphs to impress auditors and to explain how their businesses are run. When this ritual occurs before every audit, it signals that a supplier is not preparing its procedures right the first time.

Some suppliers have separate procedures for each customer, which produces volumes of paperwork. Other suppliers have procedures that conform to all of their customers' requirements but go overboard and produce volumes of just-in-case procedures—i.e., procedures that cover anything and everything in the plant, even when they are not needed.

Volumes of procedural paperwork aren't necessary. To increase the efficiency of your procedures—and thereby reduce paperwork and audit preparation time—follow these helpful tips:

- Use only the procedures that meet your most-stringent customer's needs. By doing so, your systems should satisfy all your customers and you won't have to keep changing the procedures to match whichever audit you happen to be involved in that week.
- Adopt a rule such as "Procedures will be written only when product and service quality are affected." All other materials can be used as instructional aids or supplements.
- Review current procedures and eliminate redundancy. Applications, functions, duties, and responsibilities can be combined if they are in the same area.
- Write procedures for the employees, not the customers. The procedures should explain, step by step, how tasks should be accomplished. When writing the procedures, use simple terms and keep them as short as possible. In other words, write to express, not impress.
- Further reduce the number of procedures by creating a main departmental procedure that generally explains your policies. All other materials can be listed as instructional aids or supplements.

Further efficiency

You can go a step further and enhance the efficiency of your procedural system using these ideas:

- Create a master procedure manual and master index containing all plant procedures.
- For each department, create a procedure manual and index that contains only those procedures that affect that specific department. A copy of each department's index should be kept in the master index.

- Create a simple sign-off form and place one behind each procedure in the department manuals. After employees read the procedure, have them sign and date the form. On the bottom of the form, leave a space in which employees can record any revisions they see necessary. In addition to getting employee feedback, this practice shows auditors that employees are involved in writing and revising procedures.
- Create another simple form for those in charge of reviewing the procedure manuals. After they have reviewed the department manuals for employee feedback, have them sign and date the form. Revisions to procedures have to be made only to the master procedure manual and index; photocopies can then be sent to the departments affected.

The results

These techniques can help reduce the number of procedures by at least 20 percent. My company has, for example, reduced the number of procedures by 23 percent and is continuing to review them for further reductions. The revised procedures have resulted in less material for the employees to read and understand, fewer subsequent procedure revisions, a reduction in the amount of audit preparation time, and less material that the auditors have to review. Most important, the company has realized these benefits without affecting its ability to meet customers' requirements.

When this column was published in March 1993, Steven M. Lulis was the assistant quality manager at Lakeport Plastics Inc., a division of the Huron Plastics Group, in Port Huron, MI. Lulis was an American Society for Quality member.

In ongoing continuous improvement efforts, change is the name of the game. Small companies that are responsive to their customers and the marketplace often have to change their process documentation. The challenge becomes even greater with ISO 9000 registration.

The burden of being small

Most small businesses, however, do not have full-time technical writers to convert process changes made during improvements into written procedures and to update or destroy old procedures. This duty generally defaults to process or quality engineers who are already hip deep in their daily operations.

H-R Industries has discovered a few actions that can help ease the documentation burden:

1. *Keep the quality manual as general as possible.* The manual should not contain procedures but rather policies that address different aspects of the quality program. For example, it could contain the organization's mission statement or a generic quality organizational chart with no names listed on it. Not including specific procedural items in the quality manual also saves the company money if it is registered to an ISO 9000 standard. The company will have more freedom to change and improve the manual without having to send its registrar a revised copy every month for review—reviews cost money.

2. *Write and maintain company procedures and the master list of company documents using a computer word processor.* It is much easier to revise a word processing file than to retype a document on a typewriter. It is advisable to use revision dates or numbers instead of letters, since a dynamic company can go through the alphabet quickly. It is also beneficial to use page numbers on all procedures in the event that, in an update, only one page needs to be revised. Finally, back up the files after every update.

3. *Include input from operators, production managers, and quality, maintenance, safety, and environment personnel when writing or updating procedures.* For a procedure to be effective, those who perform the procedure must help define it. The following requirements must also be met:

- The procedures must include what is expected of the operators in terms of quality characteristics, output, and records.
- The procedures must include a means for the operators to measure their performance against expectations.
- The procedures must include a means for the operators to act on any difference between performance and expectations.

4. *Use a computer to maintain other records, such as inspection and statistical process control data, corrective action requests, and customer complaints.* A data base or word processing file is an accepted form of record. A company must, however, include how to maintain and access those records in its procedures.

5. *Have master files for all procedures and records in a local area network, if possible.* This eliminates multiple copies of the same file having different revisions. The files should be protected with a password to prevent unauthorized changes.

The benefit of being small

Coordination and teamwork are essential to keeping up with the fast pace of documentation changes. Fortunately, this is much easier to do in a small company.

When this column was published in January 1994, Doug Riggins was the vice president of quality assurance at H-R Industries in Richardson, TX. He was an American Society for Quality senior member, certified quality engineer, and certified quality auditor.

How to Track and Improve Your Measurements

Finding the right tool to improve quality is often only one step of an improvement process. Overall success comes after using the right tool in tandem with the right approach, which might prove to be a difficult task.

The GM Truck and Bus Group Reliability Laboratories faced such a task. According to Bob Miles, a statistical method was needed to evaluate both the accuracy and machine error of coordinate measuring machines (CMMs). In "Evaluate CMMs Quickly and Automatically," he describes how a variable gage study and a machine checking gage did the job.

Any organization with hundreds of measuring instruments knows the challenge of keeping them properly adjusted to satisfy requirements in ISO 9001 and 9002. To satisfy the requirements without spending an inordinate amount of time on inspecting, measuring, and adjusting the instruments, Yves Van Nuland proposes "Maintaining Calibration Control with a Control Chart."

A similar problem that establishments could face is keeping track of hundreds of measurements. Rather than drowning in a sea of numbers, Teresa Dickinson suggests that you "Keep Track of Your Measures by Using a Measures Data Base." Not only can such a database organize operations, but it can also reduce redundancies and protect against key knowledge walking out the door when the person collecting the data retires or quits.

Evaluate CMMs Quickly and Automatically

by Bob Miles

The GM Truck and Bus Group Reliability Laboratories needed a statistical method that would quickly and automatically evaluate a coordinate measuring machine (CMM) in terms of the accuracy and the tolerance consumed by machine error. The accuracy of CMMs can be determined using various tools and by different methods. Lasers, step gages, and ball bars are commonly used for checking volumetric accuracy. There are also different methods for determining machine accuracy, such as the American Society of Mechanical Engineers' B89 Standards or the Coordinate Measuring Machine Manufacturers Association's specification. These tools and methods are suitable for annual calibrations but are not practical for quickly evaluating machine accuracy. Also, they do not relate accuracy to part tolerance. While people often speak in terms of machine accuracy, they should speak of machine error instead. With CMMs, the amount of machine error should determine what should or should not be inspected on a particular CMM.

Thus, it was decided to use a machine checking gage to measure machine error and a variability gage study for repeatability and reproducibility to determine accuracy. The machine checking gage is a device consisting of a counterbalanced rod that pivots on an upright column. The rod has a two-pronged fork on one end that rests on the CMM probe stylus ball. This allows the CMM to automatically rotate the rod 360° and measure it in various positions. The gage duplicates the function of a ball bar while adding flexibility of movement.

A CMM program was developed to measure the machine checking gage rod at three different elevations and eight different angles, repeated three times automatically under computer control. The gage was placed at three positions on the CMM to encompass an area large enough to represent a typical part. The CMM program was executed in each position.

The data were then entered into a computer spreadsheet set up to represent a modified gage repeatability and reproducibility data sheet (Figure 11.1). The Sample # column was used for different elevations and angles. Instead of three operators, the three positions for each measurement were used. Instead of three trials for each operator, those fields were changed to the measurements that were repeated three times at each position where the gage was placed on the CMM. The result was 90 measurements at 10 elevation-angle combinations that were compared at three different positions on the CMM and repeated three times.

Figure 11.1.
Gage Repeatability and Reproducibility Data Sheet (Long Method)

	1	2	3	4	5	6	7	8	9	10	11	12
Operator	A —				B —				C —			
Sample #	1st Trial	2nd Trial	3rd Trial	Range	1st Trial	2nd Trial	3rd Trial	Range	1st Trial	2nd Trial	3rd Trial	Range
1												
2												
3												
4												
5												
6												
7												
8												
9												
10												
Totals												

Sum $\overline{R}_A$ Sum $\overline{R}_B$ Sum $\overline{R}_C$

$\overline{X}_A$ $\overline{X}_B$ $\overline{X}_C$

$\overline{R}_A$	
$\overline{R}_B$	
$\overline{R}_C$	
Sum	
$\overline{R}$	

# Trials	D_4
2	3.27
3	2.58

$$(\overline{R}) \times (D_4) = UCL_R{}^*$$

$$(\underline{\quad}) \times (\underline{\quad}) = \underline{\quad}$$

Max. $\overline{X}$	
Min. $\overline{X}$	
X Diff.	

*Limit of individual R's. Circle those that are beyond this limit. Identify the cause and correct. Repeat these readings using the same appraiser and unit or discard values and reaverage and recompute R and the limiting value UCL_R from the remaining observations.

Notes: _____
_____

Once the data were entered into the spreadsheet, the part tolerance cell was changed to generate various percent gage repeatability and reproducibility values. Those values were graphed to show the amount of part tolerance consumed by the CMM at different tolerance levels (Figure 11.2). In the case of the *General Motors Statistical Process Control Manual,* gage repeatability and reproducibility values of 10 percent to 30 percent can be acceptable, depending on the factors involved, such as the importance of the application, gage cost, and cost of repair. Values of more than 30 percent are generally unacceptable and should be investigated to identify and correct the problem. Based on this criterion, a decision on what a particular CMM can inspect can be made intelligently.

Figure 11.2.
Repeatability and Reproducibility Study

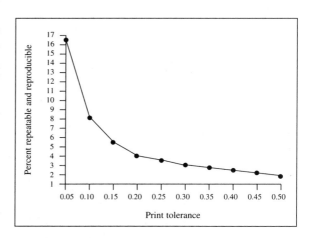

When this column was published in December 1988, Bob Miles was a supervisor for GM Truck and Bus Group, General Motors Corporation in Pontiac, MI. He received an associate's degree in liberal arts from Oakland Community College, Oakland County, MI. Miles was an American Society for Quality member and certified quality engineer.

Maintaining Calibration Control with a Control Chart

by Yves Van Nuland

"The supplier shall identify, calibrate, and adjust all inspection, measuring, and test equipment and devices that can affect product quality at prescribed intervals. . ."

—ISO 9001 requirement 4.11g and ISO 9002 requirement 4.10b

This basic requirement can lead to considerable practical problems in industries where hundreds of measuring instruments are used for process surveillance in a plant. Since disassembling the measuring instruments would be a major undertaking, usually few of them are calibrated.

Sometimes these instruments are installed in parallel, which is frequently the case for temperature indicators and pressure gauges. Typically one instrument is used for visual process indication, maintenance purposes, or safety reasons; the second instrument is connected to a process computer. In such cases, both instruments can be maintained under calibration control by means of a simple x-t chart or with a moving average chart.

The difference between the readings of each instrument's values (e.g., the temperature) represents a normal distribution. After about 30 readings, the mean value and the standard deviation can be calculated (see Figure 11.3). With this information, a follow-up chart can be established on which operators can plot the mean $\pm 3\sigma$.

The operators can then read the difference between both instruments and plot the data on a chart. As long as points fall within the 3σ lines, the instruments are okay. But as soon as one point falls beyond these control limits, one of the instruments is no longer under calibration control and requires corrective action (see Figure 11.4).

Following Al Jaehn's interpretation of a control chart, it is easy to identify, at an early stage, any smaller deviation (e.g., a slow increase of the measuring points as a function of time).[1] A moving average chart can also be used instead of an x-t chart, although the latter is recommended since it is easier for operators to use.

Figure 11.3.

The Values

Here are 35 readings for two temperature instruments: one is coupled to a process computer (T1) and the other is used for visual control (T2). The first 30 measurements are used to determine the mean value and the standard deviation. It should be noted that the second temperature instrument suddenly jumps 0.6°C starting on Day 31.

Unit: °C

Day	T1	T2	Difference
Day 1	84.3	84.6	0.3
Day 2	84.3	84.3	0.0
Day 3	84.5	84.6	0.1
Day 4	84.4	84.7	0.3
Day 5	84.3	84.6	0.3
Day 6	84.1	84.6	0.5
Day 7	84.7	84.9	0.2
Day 8	84.5	84.6	0.1
Day 9	84.2	84.5	0.3
Day 10	84.7	84.7	0.0
Day 11	84.5	84.4	−0.1
Day 12	84.2	84.7	0.5
Day 13	84.3	84.7	0.4
Day 14	84.3	84.4	0.1
Day 15	84.4	84.5	0.1
Day 16	84.8	84.7	−0.1
Day 17	84.0	84.4	0.4
Day 18	84.4	84.5	0.1
Day 19	84.3	84.5	0.2
Day 20	84.4	84.4	0.0
Day 21	84.4	84.5	0.1
Day 22	84.2	84.5	0.3
Day 23	84.4	84.6	0.2
Day 24	84.6	84.7	0.1
Day 25	84.1	84.5	0.4
Day 26	84.3	84.5	0.2
Day 27	84.4	84.8	0.4
Day 28	84.6	84.6	0.0
Day 29	84.4	84.6	0.2
Day 30	84.5	84.9	0.4
N = 30			
Average	84.38	84.58	0.2
Standard deviation	0.18	0.14	0.17
Day 31	84.6	85.2	0.6
Day 32	84.5	85.1	0.6
Day 33	84.4	84.9	0.5
Day 34	84.6	85.3	0.7
Day 35	84.3	85.0	0.7

Figure 11.4.

The Control Chart

The chart shows the difference (D) between two indicators as a function of time (days). The values with an "x" are abnormal points. Starting at measuring point 32, there is a deviation that indicates the instrument must be calibrated.

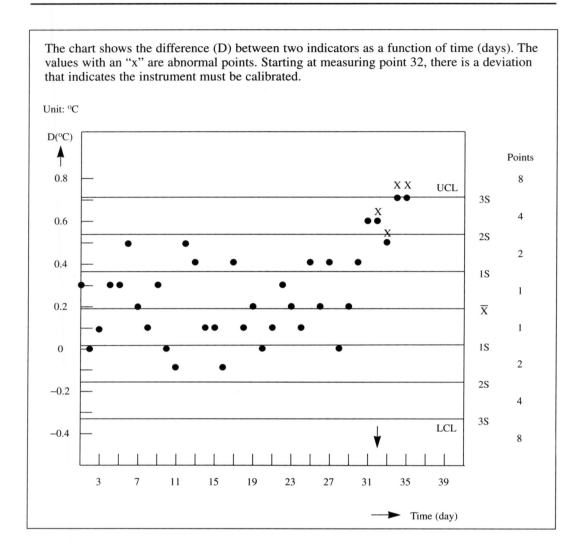

Unit: °C

Whenever there are many measuring instruments, it is obvious that many charts are also needed. Since the measurements are easily and quickly made, however, this need usually does not present any difficulties.

Although all the measurements do not have to be made under the same conditions (e.g., the same temperature of 85° C), it is essential that the calibration points fall within the working range of the process. They must fall within the measuring limits of the instruments and within the linear range.

Using a simple x-t chart or moving average chart to maintain calibration control provides important advantages since operators can dispose of reliable measuring data (because the x-t chart will indicate when the reading is no longer under control). It will help companies meet one requirement of ISO 9001 and 9002: having all their instruments under control.

Reference

1. Jaehn, "All-Purpose Chart Can Make SPC Easy."

When this column was published in March 1992, Yves Van Nuland was the quality manager at UCB Chemicals in Brussels, Belgium, and a professor at the University of Diepenbeek in Belgium. He was also the founder and chairman of Qualichem, the Belgian Center for Total Quality Management for the Chemical and Related Industries. Van Nuland received a doctorate in chemistry from the University of Leuven in Belgium. He was an American Society for Quality member.

Keep Track of Your Measures by Using a Measures Data Base

by Teresa Dickinson

Do you collect data to see how your processes are operating and to measure the results of your improvement initiatives? If so, statements of this type might be familiar to you:

- "We're collecting so much information, we just can't keep track of it all."
- "We put a lot of effort into getting this information and then found out that another group is collecting the same data."
- "When our manager left, we lost track of how she sourced the data for the monthly reports."

If this is the case, the solution might be to establish an electronic data base of measures.

The Commonwealth Scientific & Industrial Research Organization has jointly developed such a data base that is being successfully used by an Australian communications company. It contains the raw data for each measure and an appropriate graph. More important, for each measure, the data base also contains:

- A code name or number that uniquely identifies it
- Information about when the measure was first entered and most recently updated
- Its current status (e.g., being planned, operational, or lapsed)
- Details of which process improvement group or business unit owns the measure
- Information about who set it up and who is responsible for updating it. These fields contain people's names and phone numbers so they can be contacted directly.
- The measure's name and detailed operational definition, including subsequent inclusions and exclusions
- Details of how the data are collected for the measure. (For measures obtained from on-line computer systems, this includes the precise identifier of the report containing the data.)
- Information on how often the data are collected and reported and to whom this report is given

A company that wants to establish a measures data base has the option of having it custom written or purchasing a commercial data base program and then entering the information into it.

When a team wants to establish a new measure, it can search the data base using key words, dates, or other attributes to see whether a similar measure is already being used by another group in the organization. If a similar measure exists, the team could adopt or adapt that measure, or the team might want to contact the other group for more information. If no similar measure exists, the team can register its new one. This is done by completing an electronic registration form (see Figure 11.5). This form is then updated as necessary. When a measure becomes operational, the files containing the raw data and graphs are linked to the data base and can be accessed in conjunction with the registration information. The measures data base works equally well for high-level corporate measures (for example, customer satisfaction scores) and local measures (for example, a department's or team's effort to improve the time to process orders).

There are many benefits of using a measures data base. It increases communication between groups because each group knows the measures that other groups are using to monitor and improve performance. Another benefit is less duplicated effort, since it is often possible to use or adapt other groups' measures. The data base has also been found to reduce the effort required in choosing and establishing a measure because the registration form provides an effective check sheet of items to consider.

So, if keeping track of your measures is a hassle, establish an electronic measures data base.

When this column was published in September 1995, Teresa Dickinson was a statistician and quality consultant at the Division of Mathematics and Statistics of the Commonwealth Scientific and Industrial Research Organization in Clayton, Victoria, Australia. She received a master's degree in statistics from the University of Melbourne in Victoria, Australia. Dickinson was a member of the American Society for Quality.

Figure 11.5.

Example of a Completed Measures Registration Form

Part 1. Measure details	
Measure name:	Length of cut pipe from extrusion line 2
Date first entered:	10 October 1994
Last date amended:	17 October 1994
Status of measure:	Operational - data being collected now
Team setting up measure (team name or business unit and location):	QA department
Detailed measure definition:	Average and range of sample of cut pipe lengths, as per sampling plan described below

Part 2. Data collection details	
Method of data collection (system or manual):	Pipes to be removed as being stacked on pallets and measured manually using standard tape
Details of data source:	See sampling scheme
Person responsible for collecting data:	Line supervisor on duty (ext. 2231)
Sampling scheme (if used):	No pipes to be sampled from first 300 meters of cutting. Thereafter, 10 pipes are to be sampled per km of extrusion, one per 100m.
Location covered by the measure:	Extrusion line 2
Collection frequency:	10 per km of extruded pipe

Part 3. Reporting the data	
Person responsible for plotting data:	Line supervisor on duty (ext. 2231)
Person responsible for reporting data:	Line supervisor on duty
Reported to whom:	QA dept - Joe Smith
Plotting frequency:	One point per km of extrusion (i.e., per batch of 10 pipes)
Person responsible for reacting to data:	Special causes - line supervisor Assessment of level of variation - QA department
Actions to be taken:	Special causes - identify cause and rectify locally Most common actions are: - recalibrate cut length setting - replace broken cutting edge
Reporting frequency:	Once per shift
Method of display:	X bar, R chart

How to Measure Progress

Measuring activities is one challenge; measuring progress is quite another. Several years ago, I (Brad Stratton) traveled to an auto parts manufacturer. Each station in the assembly area had a metal rod on which one or two runs charts were hung. At determined intervals, the workers were tracking the performance of their stations. My hosts explained the purpose of the charts and showed how the data were being used to track and improve operations.

"But it's a good thing you didn't visit us last year," said one manager.

"Why is that?" I asked.

"See that wall over there?"

It was hard to miss the wall, so I nodded yes.

"It was covered with charts and graphs. We were tracking everything and learning nothing."

He went on to explain how they had gotten overzealous in their data collection. It took an experienced quality professional visiting from another office to analyze the situation and help guide the people so that they could turn data into information. This, in turn, allowed them to measure where they were improving.

The authors in this chapter are like the visiting quality professionals. They provide several examples of how to properly measure whether progress is being made.

For instance, Kris A. Rasmussen shows that flowcharts aren't just for process mapping anymore. He's found a new use for a familiar tool in "Flowcharts Can Show Process Improvements in Action."

Assessing strengths, weaknesses, and effectiveness are the ideas behind "Is Your SPC System Working Well?" Authors Raphael Costa and Marcello Eduardo Rodrigues describe a statistical process control system audit used at their refinery that looks at general system setup, operator procedures, foreman and supervisor procedures, and process engineer procedures.

Ronald Baltz and others at Henkel Corporation were intent on tracking the status of projects in "Measuring Progress in SPC Implementation." The grid they developed delivered what was originally expected—and more. They found their tool could show them problems that developed when shortcuts were taken during SPC implementation.

While few people will argue that tracking and measuring appropriate areas is useful, Dennis Grahn questions what should be done with "Our Magnificent Obsession with Measurement." His point? "We should understand the limitations that all mathematical analysis brings to any situation." His final suggestions for using good sense when attempting to measure progress are followed by a useful and diverse short bibliography.

Flowcharts Can Show Process Improvements in Action

by Kris A. Rasmussen

Using flowcharts to analyze work processes is gaining wide acceptance among quality practitioners. By modeling current work flows graphically, flowcharts can identify process improvement opportunities. But they can also be used for another purpose: to measure the effectiveness of process improvements as they occur. Try posting a large flowchart of a work process in a central location and using markers or magnets to track products as they move through the process.

Many products are delivered to my organization—the Data Network Systems Test group—for verification. The work process consists of three phases: test planning, test execution, and test reporting. A detailed flowchart of the work flows in each of these phases is posted close to the test engineers' work area (see Figure 12.1). A time log for each product is posted next to the flowchart. The responsible lead test engineer tracks each product scheduled for test through each step of the process by moving the product marker. The time each step takes is recorded in the log by the test engineer, along with relevant comments.

If process improvement opportunities or inaccuracies in the flowchart are identified by the test engineer, the appropriate section of the flowchart is modified using a red pencil. If the test team sees merit in the change, the flowchart is officially updated and redrawn, deploying the new process.

In addition to displaying the flowcharts and logs, appropriate measurements are posted. In the test systems area, for example, failure-find rates and test completion

Figure 12.1.

Flowchart to Analyze Work Process

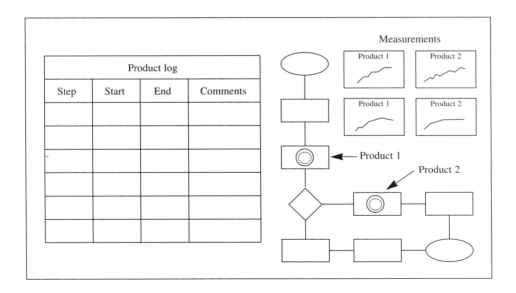

rates are posted alongside the project schedules. This helps keep the focus on process improvements without compromising the process output.

Using flowcharts to measure the effectiveness of process improvements has numerous advantages. The current status of all activities within the process can be seen at a glance. Knowing how long it takes to complete the process is useful for proposing process improvements and for making more accurate planning and scheduling estimates for future work. Training time for new employees is reduced because the graphical representation of the work process usually answers their question, "What's next?" Quality programs are no longer an extra activity but part of the group's daily work. Employee morale is also boosted because employees are empowered to recommend changes to their work processes.

As part of a total quality management program, this technique provides a clear picture of process improvements in action.

When this column was published in February 1992, Kris A. Rasmussen was the supervisor of the Data Networks Systems Test group of AT&T Paradyne in Middletown, NJ. He received a master's degree in computer engineering from the University of Lowell in Massachusetts.

How do you know whether your statistical process control (SPC) system is working effectively? How do you assess its strengths and weaknesses?

At the Alumar Alumina Refinery in Sao Luis, Maranhao, Brazil, where 1 million tons of alumina is produced each year, an in-house SPC system audit is used to provide quick and accurate answers to these questions.

Figure 12.2 shows the audit, which was designed and implemented by a team of area process engineers, area supervisors, and the plant statistical methods specialist. The questions are straightforward and are rated using the simple scoring system of Yes = 1 and No = 0. The final rating is achieved by adding the number of affirmative answers and dividing by the total number of applicable questions.

Figure 12.2.

SPC System Audit

Date: Sept. 29 Area: Power house Audit team: Marcello, Sergio, and Jose
Internal audit No.: 2

	Audit No. 1 2nd quarter		Audit No. 2 3rd quarter	
General setup				
Are all points correctly plotted and the calculations accurately done?	1		1	
Are the control and specification limits well determined and the numeric scale easy to read?	1	2	0	2
Is the log book filled out with all necessary information?	0		1	
Is the troubleshooting guide updated and easy to understand?	0		0	
Operator procedures				
Does the operator know what a control limit is?	1		1	
Does the operator know what a specification limit is?	1		1	
Does the operator know what a special cause is, how to identify it in the control chart, and how to deal with it?	1	4	1	5
Does the operator talk about SPC during shift changes and, when necessary, request the foreman's help?	0		1	
Is the operator acting on all out-of-control situations and reporting them in the log book?	0		0	
Are the charts being updated as soon as the information is available?	1		1	
Foreman and supervisor procedures				
Does the foreman check all parts during the shift?	0		1	
Does the foreman use the log book and stress the importance of updating it?	0		1	
Does the foreman know how to identify a special cause and lead operators to take action on it?	0	0	0	3
Does the foreman provide support and feedback to the operators based on the control charts?	0		0	
Does the foreman check the charts and log book daily?	0		1	
Process engineer procedures				
Are all variables tested against the normal distribution and are necessary adaptations taken?	0		1	
Is all information readily available, are the completed charts changed at the correct moment, and is the troubleshooting guide revised adequately?	1		1	
Is the process control situation evaluated, including test for randomness?	0		0	
Is the process capability evaluated correctly?	0	2	0	5
Are the control limits revised when necessary?	0		1	
Does the process engineer check the SPC variables' behavior daily?	1		1	
Are the operators' and foremen's technical doubts about SPC addressed and solved?	0		1	
Total positive	8		15	
Checked items	22		22	
Final rating	36%		68%	

The audit addresses four areas:

- The general setup of the SPC system
- The procedures that the operators follow
- The procedures that the foremen and supervisors follow
- The procedures that the process engineers follow

SPC system audits are performed quarterly and take about an hour to conduct. An assessment team—usually consisting of a representative from the area being assessed, a representative invited from another area, and the plant statistical methods specialist—conducts the audit by interviewing an operator, a shift foreman, the supervisor, and the area process engineer. The group interview is performed in front of the SPC bulletin board, which displays SPC control charts, in the area control room. All nonconforming situations that occurred are presented and discussed. The team also checks the control charts and log book and reviews SPC system procedures.

The team then prepares a one-page report that discusses nonconforming items, indicates the SPC system's strong points, and, when appropriate, suggests how to enhance the existing system. The opportunities for improvement are indicated by the negative answers. Since the audit is conducted quarterly, enough time is available to implement the suggested corrective actions. Their effectiveness is verified in the next audit.

The report might also discuss some audit items in more detail for clarification. For example, in Figure 12.2, the rating for the second question in the general setup section—Are the control and specification limits well determined and the numeric scale easy to read?—decreased in the third quarter. The report for this audit explained that the operator had forgotten to draw the lower control limit in the chart and that corrective action was immediate.

When completed, the audit report is given to the area superintendent, who is ultimately accountable for taking corrective actions and maintaining the SPC system's strong points. The report is also posted on the SPC bulletin board so that all shift operators and foremen can read it.

At the Alumar Alumina Refinery, the audit effectively tracks the SPC system's performance over time. By adapting it to your particular environment, it can also help you track your SPC system's performance.

When this column was published in December 1993, Raphael Costa was the technology and quality manager at Alumar Alumina Refinery in Sao Luis, Maranhao, Brazil. He received a bachelor's degree in chemical engineering from the State University of Campinas in Campinas, Sao Paulo, Brazil. Costa was a member of the American Society for Quality. Marcello Eduardo Rodrigues was a statistical methods/quality engineer at Alumar Alumina Refinery. He received a bachelor's degree in chemical engineering from Federal University of Rio de Janeiro in Brazil.

Measuring Progress in SPC Implementation
by Ronald Baltz

Measuring quality performance indicators is a key part of any company's total quality process. In addition to using traditional measurements such as percent of on-time deliveries, percent of in-spec production, and the number or type of customer complaints, Henkel Corporation has developed an objective way to track and communicate its progress in implementing statistical process control (SPC). The company uses a tool called the SPC status categories grid (Figure 12.3).

Employees from the Process Development Group and the Quality Assurance Department who had hands-on experience in SPC training and application worked together to

Figure 12.3.

The SPC Status Categories Grid

Phase 1	Phase 2	Phase 3	Phase 4
Project initiation	Understand process	SPC charting	Monitoring progress
Management planning and goal setting	Team flowcharting for process analysis	Control charting starting in work areas	Employee control of process
Department, business, and technical commitment	Cause-and-effect analysis	Special causes identified and removed	Reduced process time, errors, and adjustments
Quality team selected and active	Critical in-process parameters identified	Special causes identified and removed	Documented gains and improvement
Training in philosophy and tools of quality	Standard operating procedures review; equipment repair, preventive maintenance, and calibration	Control plans established	Reduced sampling and inspection
Process definition and selection	Process input and measurement evaluation	Process capability studies performed	Capability index greater than 1; process optimization
Critical characteristics identified	Static process data collection	Specification and process review	Planning for continuous improvement

All process improvements start in Phase 1, block 1. This system assumes that the activities in previous phases are active or completed. Phase 2, process understanding, is critical to success. The long-term goal is to reach Phase 4.

develop the grid. Initially, the group brainstormed the steps to take when establishing an SPC project and the desired results. The specific steps were then grouped into four phases:

- Phase 1: Project initiation
- Phase 2: Process understanding
- Phase 3: SPC charting
- Phase 4: Progress monitoring

In Phases 1 and 2, the internal customers and suppliers of the process being investigated participate in a quality improvement team with the operators. Their commitment is crucial; they must effectively apply quality tools to understand the process. Their ability to work as a team is also crucial; they must reach a consensus on the proper operating procedures and critical characteristics needed to control the process. The steps in these two phases are referred to as the project activities.

Once data collection has begun, the quality improvement team meets less frequently and the SPC implementation moves into what is called the process activities of Phases 3 and 4. In these phases, the operators establish control of the process. During specification and process review, they decide whether to continue monitoring the process or to reevaluate the procedures and control characteristics.

This system has given Henkel Corporation a uniform language with which to effectively communicate the status of the process improvement efforts at several locations. It has proven to be an excellent training tool for manufacturing and administrative personnel. The modular approach allows the company to look at SPC overall as well as to elaborate on specific blocks in the grid. Each block can be expanded into a flowchart of responsibilities and activities that take place therein.

When the company evaluated existing SPC activities against the new grid, it discovered an unexpected benefit: the areas omitted or needing more attention were quickly identified, clearly revealing the pitfalls that can result from taking shortcuts during SPC implementation. For this reason, there are no time limits given for moving from phase to phase in the grid.

The SPC status categories grid provides standardized terminology for SPC, a training tool, a guide for measuring progress, and a checklist for troubleshooting implementation problems. As employees gain more experience in using the grid to implement SPC, it will be modified and improved.

When this column was published in May 1992, Ronald Baltz was the quality control manager for Henkel Corporation's Organic Products Group in Mauldin, SC. He received a master's degree in analytical chemistry from Villanova University in Villanova, PA. Baltz was an American Society for Quality member and certified quality engineer.

The Magnificent Obsession with Measurement

by Dennis Grahn

The adage "In God we trust—all others bring numerical data" seems to be the rallying cry for companies. Companies spend great amounts of time and effort trying to numerically quantify and measure everything they can so they can run their businesses by the numbers.

Clearly, it is important to try to quantify, measure, and focus on improving certain key business measures, such as financial performance, levels of service and delivery, and conformance to product specifications. The value of a good set of reliable metrics in some of these areas is extremely high in most businesses. But can companies carry this obsession with numerical quantification and measurement too far?

I believe so. In running an organization strictly by the numbers, it is possible to ignore aspects that are difficult or even impractical to measure quantitatively. In focusing too much on measured performance areas, companies might neglect other areas of greater importance as they relate to business success and long-term survival.

I don't want to diminish the value of numerical measurements when they are appropriate. Rather, I want to point out that some of the most critical issues in any business can be assessed with only information that is difficult to measure quantitatively. Moreover, there are issues that can only be assessed qualitatively, yet also might be critically important.

Perhaps it would be easier to clarify this point using some specific examples, given here in three categories:

Category 1

Category 1 issues are fairly easy to quantify and accurately measure. Such issues include number of customers gained and lost, number of customer complaints and reasons for complaints, number of on-time deliveries, incidents of shipping damage, product dimensions, training events (number of classes, seminars, or college courses attended), number of employee involvement teams (or self-managing work teams), employee turnover, financial performance, and operational efficiency.

Category 2

Category 2 issues are more difficult to quantify and accurately measure. Examples of Category 2 issues include customer satisfaction, real causes of customer complaints (and effectiveness of solutions), product visual quality (aesthetics), product reliability and safety, adequacy of product packaging, employee assessment of training value, effectiveness of employee involvement teams, clarity of organizational purpose, real reasons for employee turnover, clarity of communication, and overall operational effectiveness.

Category 3

It is very difficult, if not impossible, to quantify and measure Category 3 issues in meaningful ways. Using numbers to codify levels of these issues is still a subjective assessment, not an objective measurement. Category 3 issues include customer delight and loyalty; customer perceived value (of products and services); product fitness for use; prevention of customer dissatisfaction; trust and mutual respect (extending to customers as well as employees); employee morale and sense of teamwork; effectiveness of communication; effect, relevance, and real value of training events; personal growth and development of stakeholders; effectiveness of leadership development; strategic business effectiveness; and meaningfulness of purpose.

These are just a few examples that apply to almost all businesses. Most leading-edge, causal issues (i.e., issues that cause performance rather than measure after-the-fact results) are in Categories 2 and 3. Perhaps the only way to truly judge progress in these areas is through objective assessments (i.e., assessments based on established facts and alignment with principles) and subjective assessments (i.e., assessments based on values, beliefs, and alignment with purpose). Trying to measure them numerically could be a waste of time and, worse, might misrepresent what is really happening.

Some people might see these differences as merely semantics. Others might believe that if something cannot be quantified and measured, real, tangible progress cannot be achieved. But before drawing a conclusion, you want to examine some different viewpoints on the limitations of objective measurements.[1]

It can be argued, for instance, that each time you attempt to represent something by using and manipulating numbers, you actually leave behind more information than you gain. For example, suppose I were to describe a bottle of Samuel Adams stout numerically. I could say that it is 7 inches long, 2 inches in diameter, 16 fluid ounces, and 40° F. I could go further by giving a numerical description for the viscosity, alkalinity, and opacity of the contents. I could even be qualitative by rating its taste and smell on a scale of 1 to 10. But what tells you more, all of these numbers or the simple statement "a bottle of Samuel Adams stout"?

The same is true with any product or service. Trying to describe anything strictly by the numbers leaves behind far more information than is gained. This does not mean you shouldn't attempt to quantify and measure products or service. Rather, you should understand the limitations that all mathematical analyses bring to any situation. Then you can use this method of analysis as an aid to good judgment instead of as a tool with which to be obsessed.

Here are a few final suggestions:

- Don't allow an obsession with numbers and measurement to blind you to critical subjective issues.
- Be aware that people typically present data that support their own subjective positions. Often they are oblivious to conflicting data.
- If the issue is extremely important, have a number of people with diverse viewpoints present their conflicting data. Then practice Stephen Covey's habit No. 4 ("Think win/win"), No. 5 ("Seek first to understand, and then to be understood"), and No. 6 ("Synergize") as a group.[2]

- Use caution when attempting numerical measurements on issues that fall under Category 2 and, particularly, Category 3. As Jarrett Rosenbert writes, it is easy to become "seduced by the numbers and assume that they represent an objective reality in the same way that production numbers or stock prices do."[3]
- Good judgment and intuition are among the most valuable human capabilities. Don't discredit or undervalue them. Data and information should be used to enhance, not supersede, them.

References

1. For different viewpoints on the limitations of objective measurements, read Kuhn, *The Structure of Scientific Revolutions*; Nietzsche, *The Will to Power: An Attempted Transvaluation of All Values*; Rorty, *Philosophy and the Mirror of Nature*; and Wheatley, *Leadership and the New Science: Learning About Organization from an Orderly Universe*.
2. Covey, *The 7 Habits of Highly Effective People.*
3. Rosenbert, "Five Myths About Customer Satisfaction."

When this column was published in November 1997, Dennis Grahn was the director of corporate quality management at Menasha Corporation in Neenah, WI. He received a master's degree in business administration from Lake Forest College in Illinois. Grahn was a member of the American Society for Quality.

How to Sample

Sampling is not exactly the topic you'd expect to find in national news, but it was there in early 1998 when the director of the U.S. Census Bureau, Martha Farnsworth Riche, resigned. According to a report in the *Washington Post,* Riche resigned in part because she was frustrated with the continuing political skirmish over how to conduct the 2000 census.[1] The bureau plans to collect a questionnaire from every U.S. household. As with any survey, some people won't respond. In those cases, the bureau plans to contact a statistically representative sample of people. A total population figure would be arrived at by combining respondent and nonrespondent information.

Democrats are said to favor such an arrangement because it better counts people in urban areas, whom Democrats typically represent. Republicans, according to the *Washington Post,* say that such a process is subject to manipulation, less accurate than a traditional head count, and unconstitutional.

It's too bad that W. Edwards Deming isn't around to enjoy this story. The revered quality and statistical expert, who died in 1993 at the age of 93, did a tour of duty at the U.S. Census Bureau and was credited with developing what might have been the first application of statistical quality control procedures to a nonmanufacturing problem: the 1940 U.S. census.[2] His short recollection of his Census Bureau experiences in his book *Out of the Crisis* explains how people need a better understanding of census-taking methods before they criticize them.[3]

It is doubtful that the authors in this chapter will be at the center of any controversy with their approaches to sampling, probably because their managers have an appreciation of what sampling can do for them.

Lyle Dockendorf, in "Choosing Appropriate Sample Subgroup Sizes for Control Charts," shares what has been learned by the Statistical Competency Center at IBM-Rochester in Minnesota.

In "Matrix Can Help Improve Audit Sampling," Milton J. Kowalewski explains how a completed matrix can provide indicators of unacceptable end product or process root causes.

One problem related to statistical sampling, according to D.B.N. Murthy, is that shop-floor personnel might consider it too complex, so they discard statistical sampling and use less precise methods, such as recollections of past experiences. To guard against this, he created a simplified approach to sampling, which he explains in "A Statistical Recipe for Success."

References

1. Vobejda, "Embattled Census Director Quits: Riche Leaves in Midst of Sampling Dispute, Preparations for 2000 Count."
2. Stratton, "Gone but Never Forgotten."
3. Deming, *Out of the Crisis*, pp. 281–85.

Choosing Appropriate Sample Subgroup Sizes for Control Charts
by Lyle Dockendorf

Most texts on statistical process control don't address how to choose an appropriate subgroup sample size for control charts. As a result, a default value of four or five is usually chosen. Although this approach might be adequate when first evaluating a process, it ignores the effects on quality when used continuously.

The Statistical Competency Center at IBM-Rochester in Minnesota has simplified the task of choosing a correct sample size by developing charts that clearly show the relationship between process shifts and the sensitivity of control charts to detect them using different subgroup sample sizes. The chart in Figure 13.1 illustrates the probability of seeing the next plotted point outside the 3-sigma control limits (a point out of control) when the process has shifted some number of process standard deviations.

To effectively use these charts, you need to relate the capability of the process to the quality requirements. For example, suppose you have a process with a $C_{pk} = 1.5$ (indicating there are 4.5 standard deviations between the mean and one of the specification limits) that is producing at a defect level of 3.4 parts per million (ppm). The quality requirement is that a sustained operation at 1,350 ppm is unacceptable. This corresponds to a $C_{pk} = 1$ (the mean is 3 standard deviations away from one of the specification limits). Thus, a sustained shift in the mean of 4.5 – 3 = 1.5 standard deviation units is deemed unacceptable and needs to be protected against.

Figure 13.1.

Probability of Detecting a Shift in Mean in the Next Subgroup for Various Control Chart Subgroups of Size n

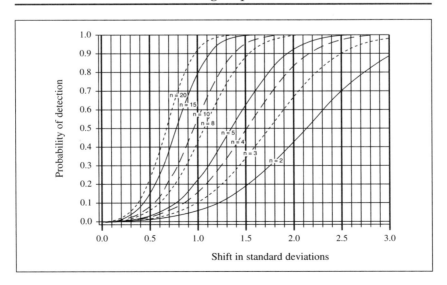

You can apply this knowledge using Figure 13.1. If the control chart being used has a sample size of five and the process has shifted 1.5 standard deviations (to an unacceptable quality level), there is only a 64 percent chance of seeing the next plotted point outside the control limits. If you want close to a 90 percent chance of detecting such a shift in the next subgroup, you must use a sample size of at least eight. As you can see from the chart, a sample size of five has a 90 percent chance of detecting a shift only if it is at least 1.9 standard deviations.

To detect smaller shifts in the mean requires an ever-increasing sample size. For example, to detect shifts of 1 standard deviation requires sample sizes approaching 20. From a cost basis, this might be unacceptable. Practically, it might be sufficient to ensure that mean shifts are detected in a predetermined amount of time. You then might be able to use additional control chart criteria based on patterns of several successive points.

The chart in Figure 13.2 quantifies the sensitivity of different subgroup sizes in detecting shifts in means in the next three samples. It is based on applying the criterion of either having two out of three points beyond the 2-sigma warning limits or having a single point outside the 3-sigma limits. As the chart shows, if you can tolerate a shift in mean of 1.5 standard deviations for a short time, a subgroup size of three might be appropriate, because there is a 90 percent probability of detecting that shift in the next three subgroups.

Figure 13.2.

Probability of Detecting a Shift in Mean in the Next Three Subgroups Using the "Two Points out of Three in the Warning Zone" Rule for Various Control Chart Subgroups of Size n

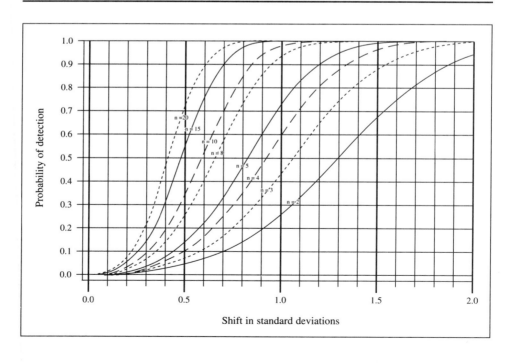

When these probability charts are used to set up control charts, it is important to consider both the control chart's sensitivity and the frequency with which the subgroups are taken. Knowing the probability of detecting important mean shifts greatly simplifies this procedure.

When this column was published in October 1992, Lyle Dockendorf was a staff statistician at the Statistical Competency Center, IBM-Rochester, MN. He received a master's degree in physics from the University of Minnesota at Minneapolis. Dockendorf was a member of the American Society for Quality.

Matrix Can Help Improve Audit Sampling
by Milton J. Kowalewski

I use Nicholas L. Squeglia's sampling plans for audits.[1] His plans provide tables and figures necessary to select sample sizes designed to result in equal or greater consumer protection with less inspection than MIL-STD-105-D plans. After I select sample sizes, I use random number generation to determine which items to review. To adequately review the files or samples selected, I divide the procedures used into parts. Each part is assigned a significant (S) or minor (M) weighting (Figure 13.3). Once I complete the classification, I evaluate each product against each part of the procedure used to develop the

Figure 13.3.
Audit Sampling Matrix

		Item: Test procedures									
Effect on	File No.	7	12	19	36	51	54	57	60	74	Total checklist unsatisfactory results
Task	Question No.										
S	8.2.1 1	A	N/A	N/A	U	A	A	N/A	A	A	1/6
S	8.2.2 2	A	N/A	N/A	A	A	A	N/A	A	A	0/6
S	8.2.3 3	U	N/A	N/A	U	A	A	N/A	A	A	2/6
S	8.2.4 4	A	N/A	A	U	A	A	N/A	A	A	1/7
M	8.2.5 5	N/A	N/A	N/A	A	U	A	N/A	A	N/A	1/4
S	8.2.6 6	U	N/A	N/A	U	A	N/A	N/A	A	A	2/5
S	8.3 7	N/A	A	N/A	N/A	N/A	N/A	A	N/A	N/A	0/2
S	8.3.1 8	N/A	A	N/A	N/A	N/A	N/A	A	N/A	N/A	0/2
M	8.3.2 9	N/A	U	N/A	N/A	N/A	N/A	N/A	N/A	N/A	1/1
S	8.4.1 10	N/A	N/A	N/A	N/A	N/A	N/A	N/A	N/A	N/A	0/0
S	8.5.1 11	N/A	N/A	N/A	N/A	N/A	N/A	N/A	N/A	N/A	0/0
Totals	Per file	2/5	1/3	0/1	4/6	1/6	0/5	0/2	0/6	0/5	8/39

A = Acceptable
U = Unacceptable
S = Significant
M = Minor
N/A = Not applicable to sample

Audit No. 87-002-E
Date 2/18

product. I either accept (A) the product of each part of the procedure or identify each part as unacceptable (U) or nonapplicable (N/A) to that part of the procedure.

Each time I decide to accept (A), reject (U), or identify as N/A, I enter the appropriate letters on the audit sampling matrix. Entries from left to right represent the performance of each part of the procedure and, from top to bottom, the suitability of each item.

I then accumulate the columns and rows to derive a fraction represented by the number of unacceptable (U) entries in the numerator over the total number of entries representing the acceptable (A) and rejected (U) entries in the denominator.

A review of the completed audit sampling matrixes for each evaluated item provides indicators of unacceptable end product or process root causes. These causes are represented by fractions with numerators greater than zero in either the part row or item column. In addition, the significance is determined by individual weighting of the significant vs. minor impact elements.

Tasks resulting in columns and rows with zero in the numerator represent acceptable end products.

The example audit sampling matrix (Figure 13.3) identifies eight unacceptable steps of the 39 reviewed. Of these eight, six are for the following significant steps of the audited test procedure: 8.2.1, 8.2.3, 8.2.4, and 8.2.6. Four of these six significant U's are in one file: No. 36. Information revealed from completion of the audit sampling matrix is very useful to the auditor when preparing the audit report.

Reference

1. Squeglia, *Zero Acceptance Number (C=O) Acceptance Plans.*

When this column was published in September 1990, Milton J. Kowalewski was a principal quality assurance consultant for UNC Geotech in Grand Junction, CO. Kowalewski was an American Society for Quality member and certified quality engineer.

A Statistical Recipe for Success

by D. B. N. Murthy

Many organizational decisions are made ad hoc or made based on past practices. People are averse to using data not tried out in actual practice. That is why many prominent statistical tables are gathering dust: They are feared as too complex. At the same time, valuable resources are squandered because trial-and-error methods are used during tests.

This was the situation at one of my past jobs. There was an urgent need to instill a sense of scientific experimentation. But it could not be too complicated for use by the shop-floor personnel and others not well versed in statistical methodology.

After some consultation, it was decided to put a great deal of information in a small amount of space. Using both sides of a 6-inch-by-9-inch sheet of heavy paper, a quality cookbook with a single recipe was created. Like all recipes, there were ingredients and the method to combine those ingredients.

The front side had the ingredients: a simple table (Figure 13.4). A certain amount of flexibility was built into the table to avoid complaints of insufficient samples. On the back side was the recipe method: explanations and examples of actual use (Figure 13.5). To stress the importance of key terms (such as reliability and confidence level), definitions were included. Moreover, the fact that large sample sizes were needed for special purposes only was highlighted.

The table was accepted by many people because it was so simple to understand and easy to operate. As workers gained more confidence, the use of the table became universal.

Figure 13.4.

The Ingredients

Sample sizes for test/trial for making decisions				
Reliability required for test/trial	Maximum % defective expected/ permitted	Confidence level (%) required for test/trial		
		80%	90%	95%
		Number of tests/trials		
For special purposes only				
0.995	0.5	320	460	600
0.994	0.6	270	380	500
0.993	0.7	230	330	430
0.992	0.8	200	290	370
0.991	0.9	180	260	330
For normal use				
0.99	1.0	160	230	300
0.98	2.0	80	115	150
0.97	3.0	50	80	100
0.96	4.0	40	60	75
0.95	5.0	30	45	60
0.94	6.0	25	40	50
0.93	7.0	22	30	40
0.92	8.0	20	28	35
0.91	9.0	18	25	32
0.90	10.0	15	22	30
0.89	11.0	14	20	26
0.88	12.0	13	18	24
0.87	13.0	12	17	22
0.86	14.0	11	16	20
0.85	15.0	10	15	19
0.80	20.0	7	11	14
0.75	25.0	6	8	11
0.70	30.0	5	7	9
0.65	35.0	4	6	7
0.60	40.0	4	5	6
0.50	50.0	3	4	5

In fact, any introduction of a change in raw material, process, or machines could be done only after sufficient trials were conducted using the table.

The table was printed and distributed to all supervisors and managers. A circular was issued urging everyone to adopt the table because of its advantages. These advantages included reducing costs and improving the reliability of the final product. Use of the table eventually became the norm for determining the sample size before making a final decision.

When this column was published in June 1989, D. B. N. Murthy was a quality consultant based in Pune, India. Murthy was an American Society for Quality senior member and certified quality engineer.

Figure 13.5.

The Method

Scope and use of the table

1. Sample sizes should be determined prior to conducting a test/trial to decide suitability of a particular tool, raw material, component, piece part, assembly, or process. This is essential in view of cost, time, and risk involved.
2. Choice of sample size depends on confidence and reliability required.
3. Confidence level of 80 percent is considered fair, 90 percent is good, and 95 percent is very good. Normally, use the 90 percent confidence level.
4. No failures are permitted in the number of tests/trials. If failures occur, the expected reliability is lower.
5. If sufficient samples as per the table are not available, it is permissible to start with a smaller sample size and then accumulate test data progressively depending on availability of samples.
6. The table is based on a binomial sampling plan.
7. *Reliability:* The probability of performance without failures under stated conditions for stated time.
   Confidence level: Certainty (confidence) with which test/trial results can be interpreted.

How to Audit

Quality auditing became popular in the 1990s, thanks to the rush to ISO 9000 registration. Its usefulness, of course, has enjoyed a longer life. Classic texts released prior to the 1990s, such as *Total Quality Control* and *Juran's Quality Control Handbook,* both devote sections to the topic.[1,2]

No matter when auditing procedures were instituted, certain challenges existed. Mike Micklewright discusses the most basic one in "Make 'em Laugh, Make 'em Laugh, Make 'em Laugh." People need to be prepared for an audit and what to expect. Micklewright believes that a little humor will help these processes along.

Edmund S. Fine has preparation in mind, too, in "Zen and the Art of Quality Auditing." To determine whether systems being audited are complete, he recommends that auditors be prepared, inquisitive, and resourceful.

Weighing in one more time on being properly prepared is Robert W. Brown. His article, "How to Develop a More Effective Checklist," covers not only what an auditing checklist should look like, but also how the questions should be worded. He advises staying away from questions that can be answered with a yes or no.

The Zenith Pumps Division of Parker Hannifin Corporation takes a democratic approach to auditing. As can be gleaned from the title, "The More, the Merrier—and the More Effective," this company believes broad involvement is important to an audit. Thomas J. Warling explains how the task is handled en masse.

What happens if one's group is audited and the results are less than what had been hoped? "Death and the Quality Audit," Fine's second One Good Idea in this chapter, suggests dealing with the results as one might deal with impending death. The article isn't as morbid as this might sound because the process Fine suggests puts one back on the path toward continuous improvement.

References

1. Feigenbaum, *Total Quality Control,* pp. 290–97.
2. Frank M. Gryna, "Quality Assurance," in J. M. Juran, *Juran's Quality Control Handbook,* section 9.

Make 'em Laugh, Make 'em Laugh, Make 'em Laugh

by Mike Micklewright

To determine whether a company's quality system conforms to the appropriate criteria, third-party auditors primarily collect evidence from two sources: documents and discussions with employees. It is ironic that most companies spend hundreds of hours preparing documentation but virtually no time preparing employees.

This lack of preparation causes employees to become stressed, which is manifested in many ways, from losing sleep the night before to not being able to hold down breakfast the day of the audit. Some employees even take vacation during the scheduled audit to avoid the stress.

For the employees' well-being (and for the audit's success), companies must prepare their employees—the auditees—for the audit. They are entitled to know what to expect.

Time to move on

A company preparing for an audit will, at some point, hit the point of diminishing returns, especially from the standpoint of documentation. If the quality system is not in place and if there is a major nonconformance one week prior to the audit, it is likely too late to make any acceptable last-minute changes. At this point, companies must relax their documentation efforts and instead conduct a training session that will prepare employees for the audit.

The training session should begin with a pep talk. Management should let employees know that the company wins or loses together—that the outcome is not any one individual's doing. One wrong comment, one uncontrolled document, one unanswered question, or one procedure not followed correctly is not going to cause a company to fail an audit. It is the accumulation of negative evidence or the lack of a complete system that will result in failing the audit.

Next, employees should be given information that will help them feel at ease when being audited. This part of the training can be uninspiring and boring—but it doesn't have to be. To excite employees and prepare them for the audit, companies should involve them in the training, make the training humorous, and when possible, use real audit situations and examples from internal audits. The key is to use techniques that will help employees remember important points. One such method is the Goofus and Gallant technique.

Goofus and Gallant

Do you recall waiting in the dentist's office, flipping through *Highlights* magazine? One magazine feature is the Goofus and Gallant cartoon. In this cartoon, Goofus reacts to everyday situations in the wrong manner, while Gallant reacts to the same situations in the appropriate way. For example, given the situation that asparagus is served at dinner, Goofus throws his asparagus on the floor for Fido to eat and tells his mom that dinner was very good, while Gallant eats all of his asparagus (even though he doesn't like it) because he knows it's important to eat a healthy meal and he wants to make his mom feel good.

Training exercises based on the characters of Goofus and Gallant can be videotaped. Following a prepared script (but allowing for some ad-libbing), the performers can act out Goofus and Gallant auditing scenes. (The scenes can also be performed live at the training session, with volunteers from the audience reading the prepared scripts.) Goofus and Gallant can be used to:

- Reenact experiences observed during internal audits so that employees can relate to real-life situations
- Review typical auditor questions and proper auditee answers
- Review a company's quality manual, policies, procedures, work instructions, and records so that employees know their whereabouts and understand their meaning
- Review training procedures and records to make sure that employees are following the correct procedures (such as never using uncalibrated gages)
- Show employees how to look for uncontrolled documents
- Make sure procedures are correct and records are being kept

Normally, 10 to 15 topics will prepare employees for the upcoming audit.

This videotape becomes a key tool in the training session. First, the Goofus scene—which will have an inappropriate response—should be presented, followed by a discussion. Auditees should be asked: "What was wrong with this response?" and "What would be a more appropriate response?" Then, the Gallant scene—the more appropriate response—should be shown. After this scene, what was learned should be summarized to reinforce the points. This summary should be brief, containing no more than four points.

A Goofus and Gallant training session is very productive because:

- Many important points will be remembered.
- It covers wrong or typical answers vs. more appropriate answers.
- It lets auditees know what they might encounter.
- It offers entertainment and a moment of relaxation while emphasizing that no one person will be the cause if the company fails the audit.

Other humorous techniques

The Goofus and Gallant technique is successful because it incorporates humor. There is no better way to get people to listen to and remember a presentation than through the use of humor. Other humorous devices that can be used separately or incorporated into the Goofus and Gallant technique include:

- *Exaggeration.* Making a big deal out of the wrong responses can be humorous. For example, exaggeration can be used with the Goofus and Gallant technique to coach employees on how much information they should provide to auditors. In the Goofus scene, an auditor asks a supervisor (i.e., Goofus) a simple question on an internal audit that was conducted. The supervisor proceeds to ramble on about what a pain the internal auditors were and how audit recommendations were sometimes not followed. Through exaggeration, the point that employees should only answer the question and say no more is successfully demonstrated.

- *Role playing.* To get points across, employees can role play. For example, they can become an auditor and share their perspectives on audits or they can become an uncalibrated gage or an uncontrolled document that is used by some and ignored by others.
- *Association.* Relating two actions or objects that normally have nothing to do with each other can make learning fun. For example, the consequences of using an uncalibrated gage to measure products can be related to getting pulled over by the police for speeding (even though you weren't) because the cop was using an uncalibrated radar gun.

How dry it is—not

Although the auditing process is a powerful tool, it is normally a dry subject. But it doesn't have to be if people use their imagination. With humor, management can make every employee understand the value of auditing a company's quality system and realize that conformance to a standard is not just a paperwork exercise.

For the employees' welfare, management must prepare them for the impending audit to diminish the fear of the unknown and to create an understanding of the goodness of the process. Employees need to understand that they are not being audited, but rather the system is being audited. Humor and the use of interactive training will accomplish these goals.

When this column was published in August 1996, Mike Micklewright was president of QualityQuest in Arlington Heights, IL. He received a bachelor's degree in engineering from the University of Illinois in Urbana. Micklewright was an American Society for Quality member, certified quality engineer, and certified quality auditor.

Zen and the Art of Quality Auditing

by Edmund S. Fine

In my student days, my compatriots dabbled in oriental philosophies. One tenet that made a lasting impression was the answer to a Zen riddle: What is the sound of one hand clapping? The sound of one hand clapping was explained to me as the absence of an expected behavior. Keeping this principle in mind has been an immense aid in determining the goodness of quality systems. In other words, when auditing a quality system, auditors need to look for the absence of expected system elements.

It is relatively easy to determine whether a hardware manufacturer has a major element missing from its quality system, For example, failing to segregate suspected defective material from known good material is a discrepancy that will alert even the most inexperienced auditor that something is amiss. It is also fairly easy to spot weaknesses such as a supplier rating system that does not account for problems detected after a part has been accepted. It is much more difficult, however, to spot an omission of an infrequently used element (such as the lack of a person trained in design and analysis of experiments or improper test tiers) unless you are lucky enough to be there on the right day.

Auditors usually have time constraints and must make judgments rapidly. Thus, they are faced with a dilemma: how to evaluate a quality system without the luxury of spending an extended period of time examining it. To solve this dilemma, auditors must be both prepared and inquisitive.

Be prepared

An important auditing tool is a checklist (against a standard such as ISO 9002 or MIL-Q-9858A), which can be used to ensure that all major elements are covered. If there is no appropriate standard, use the closest applicable one as a guideline to create a checklist.

Auditors can precoordinate a checklist with the company being audited; often this results in self-directed improvements being made before the audit. But auditors need to be careful. Companies might have a superb set of standards for one product and none for any others. Since it is human nature (and common sense) for auditees to show their best examples, they will present only the good ones. In such cases, auditors should praise the good examples but probe and ask for additional ones.

Be inquisitive

An effective investigating technique is to ask questions that cannot be answered with a yes or a no. Words like "describe," "demonstrate," and "show" can help uncover the depth and breadth of subsystems. Rarely will a quality engineer answer "no" to the question, "Do you have a calibration system?" But by rephrasing the question as "Describe your calibration system," missing pieces might be revealed.

System implementation deficiencies can be discovered by comparing manuals, presentations, or procedures with actual practices. Recently, I sat through an impressive half-hour presentation on Company X's new computerized statistical process control (SPC) system. Unfortunately, an informal walk through the shop later that day showed no trace of even the manual operator-recorded histogram charts cited as Company X's starting point. The computerized SPC computation system, which had allegedly superseded the manual system, was also nowhere to be found. Healthy skepticism is the proper attitude. When in doubt, check it out!

Be resourceful

After an auditor has found out what is not there, the results must be presented to someone who can effect changes. The report, written or oral, must specifically document what is missing, why it is needed, and where it fits into the current system. If possible, quotes from the governing standard, including paragraph numbers, should be used to strengthen the report.

Getting deficiencies corrected usually goes against common sense: In general, the more glaring a problem, the easier it is to get it corrected. Large, costly discrepancies are usually seized by management—often corrections are begun before the audit is complete. Minor or subtle problems, however, are more difficult to get corrected. In such cases, the best course is to plant a hint and let the auditee think that the corrective action is his or her own idea.

Remembering the riddle of one hand clapping is a healthy auditing mind-set. It will help increase the efficiency and effectiveness of quality audits. Ignoring this Zen concept might cause an auditor to miss subtle but important deficiencies in a quality system. Therefore, it is wise to listen for the sound of one hand clapping when auditing a quality system.

When this column was published in August 1994, Edmund S. Fine was a senior product assurance engineer at Sverdrup Corporation at Eglin Air Force Base, FL. He received a master's degree in industrial engineering from New York University in New York City. Fine was a senior member of the American Society for Quality.

<table>
<tr><td>Idea
86</td><td><h1>How to Develop a More Effective Audit Checklist</h1> by Robert W. Brown </td></tr>
</table>

Idea 86	# How to Develop a More Effective Audit Checklist *by Robert W. Brown*

An essential part of planning and preparing for any type of audit involves developing an appropriate checklist. An effective, easy-to-use checklist will include evaluation criteria, questions to be answered, information to be verified, reference sources for requirements or audit points, and space for recording objective evidence.

Over the years, a common failure of most audit checklists has been the style of the question being asked. Typically, the majority of questions can be answered with a simple yes or no. Such answers can be gained from sitting in someone's office without getting out on the shop floor, where the action and objective evidence are found.

A more effective style, particularly for inexperienced auditors, is to phrase the question or audit point so that a narrative response is required. By using words and phrases—such as "describe," "what," "how," "who," "where," "when," "review and verify," "assure that," "identify," and "show the evidence"—much more definitive information can be obtained than by asking yes-no questions. Such phrases as "review and verify" actually give direction to the auditor to review objective evidence and verify that the requirements are being met.

Here are several examples of how to change traditional yes-no questions into the narrative style. These examples are based on ANSI/ASQC Q9001 requirements:

1. *Traditional:* Are the quality policy and supporting procedures known and understood by staff at all levels?

Narrative: Interview personnel at all levels and determine whether the quality policy is known and understood.

2. *Traditional:* Does the quality manual outline the structure of quality system documentation?

Narrative: How is the quality system documentation structure outlined in the quality manual?

3. *Traditional:* Are formal design reviews conducted?

Narrative: What evidence shows that formal documented design reviews are planned and conducted?

4. *Traditional:* Is verification at the subcontractor's premises specified in purchasing documents?

Narrative: What contractual provision is there for the supplier to verify purchased products at the subcontractor's facility?

5. *Traditional:* Are records maintained for qualified processes, equipment, and personnel?

Narrative: What evidence shows that records for qualified processes, equipment, and personnel are on file?

6. *Traditional:* Are there safeguards to prevent unauthorized changes or adjustments to inspection, measuring, and test equipment?

Narrative: What method is used to ensure that adjustments to inspection, measuring, and test equipment cannot be made?

7. *Traditional:* Are there adequate procedures to prevent the unintended use or installation of nonconforming products?

Narrative: Describe the controls that prevent nonconforming products from unintended use or installation.

If it is necessary to ask a yes-no question, the auditor should expand on it. Take, for example, the question: "Have the responsibility and authority of all personnel whose actions affect quality been defined and documented?" Assuming the answer is yes, two follow-up questions should be asked: "Where are those responsibilities and authority documented?" and "May I see that document?"

Lockheed Martin Space Information Systems has used the narrative approach in preparing its checklist that covers the ANSI/ASQC Q9000 requirements. The checklist is used to perform both internal and external audits. Figure 14.1 shows a portion of that checklist. Because of the narrative responses required, this checklist provides credible evidence that the investigation has been thorough.

When this column was published in February 1997, Robert W. Brown was a quality engineer at Lockheed Martin Space Information Systems in Houston, TX. He received a bachelor's degree in aerospace technology from Kent State University in Ohio. Brown was a member of the American Society for Quality.

Figure 14.1.
An Effective Audit Checklist

Reference document ANSI/ASQC Q9001	Requirement	Contact	Objective evidence	Compliance S	D	NA	NC No.
4.2 Quality system 4.2.1 General	A. Verify that a quality manual exists and record the title, document number, and issue date.						
	B. Verify that the manual includes or makes reference to the quality system procedures.						
	C. How is the quality system documentation structure outlined in the manual?						
	D. Where are documented quality system procedures maintained to ensure that products conform to specified requirements?						
4.2.2 Quality system procedures	A. Who is responsible for verifying that the quality system procedures are consistent with the requirements of the ANSI/ASQC Q9000 or ISO 9000 series standard?						
	B. How does the organization determine that the quality system and procedures are effectively implemented?						
4.2.3 Quality planning	A. Where has the organization defined and documented how requirements for quality will be met?						

Organization audited: _____ Auditor: _____ Element audited: _____ Audit date: _____

Key: S = Satisfactory   D = Deficient   NA = Not applicable   NC No. = Nonconformance number

The More, the Merrier—and the More Effective

by Thomas J. Warling

In most organizations, the responsibility for conducting internal quality audits lies entirely with the quality assurance (QA) function and its staff of trained auditors. The effectiveness and efficiency of audits, however, can be greatly enhanced by having a large number of employees participating to some degree in the internal auditing process.

The Zenith Pumps Division of Parker Hannifin Corporation found this out first-hand. While preparing its quality system for compliance to ISO 9001, it decided to design the internal audit function so that employees from every sector of the business would be trained to conduct different components of the quality system audits, with assistance from the QA function.

To properly implement an internal auditing system of this magnitude, the division had to establish and coordinate several components, such as audit checklists, auditor training, audit schedules, reporting format, and results follow-up. These components had to be agreed to by all involved and needed to be integrated effectively. In addition, the entire system had to be documented.

To begin, the division created an audit checklist for each process. These checklists are concisely written guidelines that outline the processes' procedures and related work instructions. They help auditors determine the important items to review (but the auditors are not limited to those items). The checklists are permanently attached to procedure documentation to ensure their continued compatibility with future procedural revisions.

After the checklists were created, the division focused on selecting and training internal auditors. All department managers were asked to select conscientious employees who were willing to be part of the initial training class. These employees had no previous audit experience and, except in their areas of responsibility, had limited exposure to the quality system and ISO 9001. Each employee was given training in:

- The purpose of QA, ISO 9000, and the internal audit process
- The audit process, including audit preparation, performance, conduct, reporting, follow-up, and closure
- The definitions of audit terms
- The ISO 9001 and ISO 10011 standards
- Audit checklists and their use
- How the initial audits would be performed
- Areas of special concern

The initial audits conducted by these newly trained auditors were carefully reviewed by the trainers to ensure the quality of the audit in terms of its scope, sampling size, objective evidence presented, reporting format, and findings. Overall auditor performance was also noted. Where deemed necessary, additional training was given. As skills were demonstrated, the trainers recommended individuals for inclusion on a qualified auditors list. In other words, these auditors achieved internal auditor certification.

Currently, about half of the division's hourly and salaried employees have been certified as internal quality auditors. Having this many auditors available means that most conduct two to four audits annually. This usually does not overtax the individuals or affect their normal job functions. When audits are particularly involved or require considerable expertise, QA staff members either help the internal quality auditors conduct the audit or conduct the audits themselves.

Next, the QA function developed a master audit schedule. This computer-generated schedule outlines the frequency with which audits are given for the various areas, the processes to be audited next, the dates of those audits, and the assigned auditors. It also notifies those who will be involved in upcoming audits, including the auditors, their direct supervisors, and the leaders of those departments affected. The notifications are printed and distributed weekly and are usually given at least four weeks in advance to allow everyone sufficient time for planning.

As the audits are completed, the reports are forwarded to the QA function for review. QA staff members then update the master audit schedule, noting whether a particular process passed the audit, requires follow-up, or needs to have another audit scheduled.

Audit reports are also reviewed by the department manager responsible for the process being audited. In the event of a dispute between the auditor and auditee over the audit results, effectiveness of practices, need for corrective action, or another issue, the QA function helps resolve the dispute, if needed. This is important since department managers must include internal quality audit results in biannual reports that summarize their quality-system management practices and performance. These reports are reviewed by the division's general manager.

Zenith Pumps Division's internal auditing system has been in place at its Sanford, NC, and Monterrey, Mexico, facilities for more than four years, during which it has been continually fine-tuned. In addition to helping the division become registered to ISO 9001, the internal auditing system has produced many benefits, including:

- Since more employees are directly involved in the internal auditing system, they better understand ISO 9001's requirements and benefits, which, in turn, generates support for ISO 9001 throughout all organizational levels.
- Having employees from different functions performing audits in areas independent of their duties has given them new insight into the organization as a whole. As they share this new understanding with others, interdepartmental communication and cooperation are enhanced.
- Many good suggestions and improvement ideas have been generated. Having an individual look into unfamiliar processes and procedures with an unbiased, independent view can sometimes be helpful in obtaining fresh ideas.
- Employees are more adept at and less fearful of third-party audits. Since they know how to conduct audits, they know what to expect when they are being audited.
- A comprehensive audit system has been implemented without an increase in staff.

The success of the division's internal auditing system has not only been recognized internally but also externally. Auditors from third-party certification organizations have noted the system's effectiveness while conducting ISO 9001 reassessments at both the Sanford and Monterrey facilities.

When this column was published in August 1997, Thomas J. Warling was the manufacturing manager of the Zenith Pumps Division of Parker Hannifin Corporation in Sanford, NC. He received a bachelor's degree in management from Ohio University in Athens. Warling was an American Society for Quality senior member, certified quality auditor, certified quality engineer, and certified quality manager.

Death and the Quality Audit

by Edmund S. Fine

In her classic book *On Death and Dying,* Elisabeth Kubler-Ross describes five emotions that people experience serially when faced with their impending death.[1] These emotions—denial, anger, bargaining, depression, and acceptance—are quite similar to those that a supplier faces when presented with results from a customer's audit indicating a subpar quality system. Learning to expect these emotions and learning how to cope with them can help both the auditor and auditee ease the pain of transition from an inadequate or obsolete quality system to an acceptable system, much as an understanding of Kubler-Ross' work can ease the agony of dying.

Denial

The first stage of the process is for the supplier to deny that a problem exists at all. "Our quality system simply can't be as bad as the auditor has rated it! The XYZ Corp. thinks our products are the greatest—we even received their quality award." This sort of thinking is common, and usually a certification or quality award that was given out several years ago (and not followed up since) is presented to justify the position. The denial usually extends to the top of the corporate ladder; no one wants to believe that his or her company's quality system is substandard.

Experience has shown that one way to get the supplier past this stage is to suggest that its own quality assurance (QA) staff perform an audit as if it were examining a potential supplier. If the audit is done to the same standard, the results will be quite similar to those found by the auditor. This internal verification is often necessary to motivate the supplier to progress to the next phase.

Anger

After the supplier has realized that the auditor has indeed found genuine system deficiencies, the usual reaction is for the president to want to fire the entire QA group and replace it with competent staff or to fire the internal auditor who has verified the problems found in the original audit. The reaction might also take the form of a heated discussion between the president and the supervisor of the external auditor. This anger, like the denial phase, is genuine and should not be dismissed lightly.

This stage is more difficult to deal with than denial, since anger is a more active emotion. If misdirected, it can cause permanent and irreparable damage to a company's internal structure by causing the termination or demotion of good employees. Anger can, however, be used constructively if it can be focused on the systemic problems found by the audit rather than on the people who might prove to be innocent victims of a poor system. If employees are indeed the problem, anger might compel management to make some long-overdue personnel changes. The best way to deal with this stage is to try to focus the anger where it will make a positive contribution to improving the deficient quality system.

Bargaining

Once the anger has died down, management will try to make a deal with the auditor, such as, "Can't we have just a few more months so that we can finish this order? We'll fix the system then." Of course, when the few months are up, another similar request will be made. This stalling is a last attempt to avoid real change.

The auditor has to be firm but reasonable when coping with this stage. He or she cannot be totally inflexible. The auditor's company needs the supplier's parts to continue production, but it cannot accept bad products or perpetuate an unacceptable quality system in which marginal products are fed into production. A cautious approach incorporating a tight, classic receiving inspection is recommended to keep the production line running. Meanwhile, the company must continue to insist that the supplier institute the changes necessary to improve the deficient quality system. Patience and persistence will eventually overcome procrastination, and the supplier will start to repair its quality system.

Depression

A few months into a "get well" program, management will despair over correcting the deficiencies. Minor glitches appear to be large stumbling blocks. The QA staff and upper management both outwardly exhibit signs of stress, snapping at anyone who dares to cross them. Daily QA activities become a burden. Both internal and external quality indexes might take nosedives. Not only is there no progress in improving the current system, but the system appears to be devolving to an even poorer state than was found by the audit.

At this stage, the auditor has to become a cheerleader and facilitator. Rather than continuing to emphasize the need for global improvement, the auditor must focus on what has already been done and is currently being done to improve the quality system.

Within the supplier's facility, the QA staff must highlight little gains. Even small reductions in customer complaints or improvements in internal quality indexes can serve as evidence that the improvement efforts are beginning to work. This is the time to institute (if it's not already in place) a reward-and-recognition system to make some of the gains tangible and help carry the organization through this difficult stage.

Acceptance

One day, the supplier wakes up and realizes that the phone has not started ringing at 7:30 A.M. with customer complaints; the cost of poor quality has decreased substantially; and the sales force is not continually calling to expedite late orders. The improved efficiency and quality levels indicate that the changes required to satisfy the audit have been made. The supplier has now reached the stage at which the improvements required to satisfy the audit have positively changed the way it does business. Since the manufacturing system consistently delivers acceptable products in a timely fashion, the auditor is now thought of favorably as a catalyst rather than perceived as the enemy. It is up to management and the QA staff to see that these changes are institutionalized so that the production system does not revert to old ways.

An ongoing process

It is best to think of the five-step acceptance process as an iterative one because quality systems that are currently state of the art might become obsolete in a few years. For example, major aerospace companies that have based their quality systems on military standards (such as MIL-Q-9858A) are now rapidly switching to the ISO 9000 series standards. Some day that, too, will be superseded by a newer standard, as manufacturing concepts grow and change. This will necessitate yet another wholesale evolution in the way in which companies do business, and another excursion through this five-phase acceptance process.

Reference

1. Kubler-Ross, *On Death and Dying.*

When this column was published in January 1996, Edmund S. Fine was a senior product assurance engineer at Sverdrup Corporation at Eglin Air Force Base, FL. He received a master's degree in industrial engineering from New York University in New York City. Fine was a senior member of the American Society for Quality.

How to Turn Problems into Opportunities

Turning a problem into something positive is difficult because people are, for lack of a better word, people. Who likes to be told they've made a mistake? Worse yet, who willingly takes responsibility for a mistake?

But to be honest, how often is one person really responsible for making a mistake? In our experiences, it was often a system that prevented a person from being successful. Our favorite example is a situation we both lived through. In the early 1990s, *Quality Progress* had a monstrous problem: It couldn't review manuscripts submitted by external authors in a reasonable period of time. It was taking an average of more than 450 days to undertake an initial review of an article.

Fortunately, no one jumped forward to blame others. A team of four people, two from the magazine's staff (Debbie Magerowski and Brad Stratton) and two American Society for Quality members (Jill Phelps Kern and Christine Robinson), sat down one day to assess the situation. What resulted from the discussion on that day and in days to follow was a new system designed to deal with the current monthly volume of manuscripts (about 30) rather than the volume for which the old system was designed (fewer than 10 a month).

Within a few months, the initial review time was slashed to 100 days. The system was continually refined in the following years, and by mid-1997, the work was routinely being done in less than 50 days.

At no time was fault assessed. All we did was work toward creating a new system based on what we had learned from the old one. In retrospect, it is fortunate that neither the headquarters nor volunteer leadership of ASQ lost patience with us or looked for a responsible party to blame. Everyone was willing to wait and turn a problem into an opportunity.

The authors in this chapter have similar attitudes. Edmund S. Fine, who has two articles in this group, has a lot to say about the proper attitude for turning problems into opportunities. "There's Gold in Them Thar Failures!" calls for people to pay careful attention to what might appear to be random events. By paying attention and analyzing information received, a company might make major discoveries—and savings.

By taking "A Common Sense Approach to Corrective Action Systems," Mark R. Miller writes that his company was able to create a simple corrective action report form that eventually helped it identify and solve persistent problems. Among these difficulties were recurring engineering and manufacturing errors, internal-handling and plant-layout deficiencies, and ineffective accounting procedures.

Customers can be the best source of information about product problems—if an organization has its ears open. Fine's "Are You Listening to Your Customers?" proposes a four-step checklist to use when responding to what others are saying.

Ken Paxton closes the chapter with a nice slap of reality. "Corrective Action in the Real World" provides a step-by-step plan that isn't like most checklists you might have encountered. You'll realize that this isn't a typical fill-in-the-blank form by reviewing his four suggested steps:

- Stay calm!
- Ask "Why?" when a cause is discovered.
- Be specific.
- What's the point?

<table>
<tr><td>

Idea
89

</td><td>

There's Gold in Them Thar Failures!
by Edmund S. Fine

</td></tr>
</table>

An explicit task of the quality assurance (QA) function is to prevent defective products. Tools commonly used to achieve this goal include design reviews, process capability analyses for key product characteristics, failure mode effects analyses, and 6-sigma and zero-defects programs. Despite the best efforts of the QA, design, and manufacturing functions, however, defective products, or failures, do happen.

It is obvious that expensive or frequently recurring failures must be analyzed so that root causes can be identified and corrective actions can be taken. What is not so obvious is the benefit of analyzing apparent random failures that occur during early product testing and infrequent failures (particularly in inexpensive products) that occur while the product is in the customers' hands. The usual reaction has been to ignore early design failures and infrequent field failures since they do not seem to affect production or profits. This reaction is short-sighted. By ignoring these problems, companies are discarding "gold"—that is, they are discarding valuable data that can be used to continuously improve products.

Discovering the gold

Engineers who are pushing hard to qualify a design sometimes try to minimize the effects of a malfunction by calling it a "random event." They wait for a second occurrence before deciding that a problem is genuine. But, since early testing is often conducted on a very small number of units, this can be a costly practice. For example, if one out of 10 testing units has experienced a "random event," there could potentially be "random events" in 10% of the products. Thus, if an early design failure is ignored, defective products might be produced and shipped. Fixing defective products in the field is costly to both the bottom line and customer satisfaction.

Quality personnel must let design engineers know that encountering early design failures is like discovering gold. Early failures can guide design engineers toward a more robust product with minimal investment.

Gold can also be discovered in infrequent field failures. An analysis of such failures might reveal that a customer is using the product in an unforeseen manner. For example, one company with a progressive test program found that a customer was experiencing machine wear-out far faster than had been predicted by internal tests. Although the marketing department had indicated that the normal use would be about 40 hours per week, a field engineer discovered that this customer was using the product during all three shifts, seven days a week—in other words, 168 hours per week. As a result, the customer, not the internal test program, had the "high time" units. The customer needed replacement parts much earlier and more frequently than had been predicted by the test program.

This customer's failures were worth their weight in gold because they obviated the need for continuing the internal testing. They enabled the company to make the product's design more robust based on actual operating data.

There is also gold to be found in the return of inexpensive products. For example, the usual reaction of customers who buy a defective ballpoint pen is to discard it and replace it with one from another manufacturer. Occasionally, customers get angry enough to send back the defective product. These few returns must be regarded as tip-of-the-iceberg events. They must be analyzed to determine the root cause so that corrective action can be taken.

In enlightened companies, line employees (i.e., those involved in the process being investigated) analyze and correct problems. Not only is this a more effective and efficient way to solve problems, it also has the additional benefit of being a motivational process. For example, some factories have line employees compose response letters to the offended customers. In these letters, the employees explain what had gone wrong and how they will prevent the problem's recurrence. Even in a traditional environment in which the QA department is held accountable, this gold must not be discarded.

Mining the gold

Realizing that there is gold in early design and infrequent field failures is only the first step in its retrieval. To refine the ore and get to the gold, a company must use an orderly, defined process to extract the root causes of problems. The QA function is the logical group to lead the failure investigation process team because, by its very nature, it is impartial—there is no inherent bias to arbitrarily assign a failure's root cause to the design or manufacturing function. QA personnel are also the most familiar with the tools needed to effectively isolate a problem's root cause. In addition, once the root cause is determined, they often have the technical and interpersonal skills needed to effect prompt and permanent remediation.

To take advantage of available gold, QA personnel must convince the design and production functions to treat early design and infrequent field failures as valuable tools rather than disruptive annoyances. If unexpected gold in the form of failures appears, companies must try to mine it and use it wisely.

When this column was published in April 1996, Edmund S. Fine was a senior engineer at Sverdrup Corporation in Huntsville, AL. He received a master's degree in industrial engineering from New York University in New York City. Fine was a senior member of the American Society for Quality.

A Common Sense Approach to Corrective Action Systems

by Mark R. Miller

A necessary element in quality assurance (QA) processes is a well-defined, effective corrective action system. The corrective action system must drive case-by-case problem solving, broad-based preventive action, and long-term continuous improvement.

Clearing/Niagara, located in Buffalo, NY, has developed a corporatewide system to correct errors and improve operations. The company designs and manufactures machine tools and associated equipment for the metal-forming industry. Many of its products are custom-engineered metal-forming presses that are built to customer specifications.

Clearing/Niagara's corrective action feedback system begins with an originator— anyone within the organization who discovers a nonconformance in a design or manufacturing process. The originator completes a corrective action report (CAR) packet (see Figure 15.1). These multiple-copy packets are numbered to allow all nonconformances to be tracked, eliminating the possibility of forgotten or ignored reports. The completed CAR includes all pertinent data associated with the nonconformance. The CAR's major advantage is that all nonconformance situations—such as rework, scrap, rejects of outside purchases, and change requests—can be handled by one all-purpose problem-solving procedure.

The originator passes the completed packet to the QA department, where the numbered form is logged in as received in a spreadsheet. The QA department ensures that the report is complete and provides any necessary supporting documentation before distributing the packet to the department responsible for the nonconformance. This procedure is ideal since the responsibility for correction lies directly with the department creating the nonconformance.

The responsible department then investigates the situation and implements corrective or preventive action. Information regarding the action taken is recorded at the bottom of the report. The feedback copy is returned to the QA department signaling that the matter has been resolved.

The QA department determines whether the action is sufficient. If it is, the feedback copy is logged in as received and distributed to the originator, who gains the satisfaction that action has been taken to address the nonconformance. At this point, the feedback loop is closed. Periodic audits of closed reports are conducted to determine whether the action was suitable and long lasting.

The CAR log kept by the QA department is the key to the system. Traceability and repeat situations are monitored by manipulating data in the spreadsheet. The policy at Clearing/Niagara is that all CARs must be responded to within 30 calendar days of receipt, unless urgency dictates otherwise. Since CAR packets are numbered, the QA department is able to detect those reports that have not been acted on. Most important, the QA department is able to distinguish nonconformance trends with respect to part numbers, suppliers, or factory order numbers by sorting data within the CAR log using the spreadsheet commands. Data arranged by the spreadsheet commands clearly focus on areas that should be targeted for attention.

Figure 15.1.
The CAR Packet

Corrective Action Report				2133
❏ Rework	❏ Reject	❏ Scrap	❏ Change request	❏ Other _____

To	Quantity ordered	Quantity received	Quantity rejected
Part name	Part No.	Assembly order No.	Shop order No.

Description of discrepant characteristic

	Move to department

Disposition
- ❏ Returned to you for rework   ❏ Reworked at your expense   ❏ Other _____
- ❏ Returned to you for evaluation   ❏ Used as is

Vendor name	Purchase order No.	Item No.

Originated by _____ Date _____ Return parts to _____

Reason for problem	Clock No. _____ Machine No. _____
❏ Operator ❏ Lost ❏ Setup ❏ Routing	Responsible individual's signature
❏ Machine ❏ Drawing ❏ Tooling ❏ Other	_____
❏ Handling ❏ Vendor ❏ Material _____	Charge

Instructions to correct	FOR OFFICE USE ONLY ON SCRAP
	Replace on shop order No. _____
	Posted to stock record _____ by
	_____

Dispositioned by _____ Date _____

Steps taken to prevent recurrence

Reponsible department_____ Date _____

Copy distribution	FOR OFFICE USE ONLY ON REWORK
White Work copy/production control	
Green Responsible individual	Made on shop order No. _____ Operator_____
Yellow Responsible department file	Operator No. _____ Date performed _____
Pink Feedback copy	
Goldenrod Originator copy	Superintendent's signature _____

Identifying trends is particularly useful for organizations dealing with applications in which it is difficult to use statistical techniques, such as low-volume production, custom-engineered products, and many different components in a product. Clearing/Niagara has identified and solved many persistent problems that were previously difficult to quantify, such as recurring engineering and manufacturing errors, internal-handling and plant-layout deficiencies, and ineffective accounting procedures. A system fostering small, incremental improvements has evolved.

Over a nine-month period, 803 reports have been logged in at Clearing/Niagara, which translates to about four reports per day. Eighty percent of the logged reports have initiated successful implementation of corrective action and closure of the feedback loop. All outstanding reports are continuously tracked to ensure the loop is closed.

A comprehensive history of nonconformances is updated daily. This library of nonconformances, coupled with cost-of-quality data, has yielded extremely useful, detailed summary reports. These case-specific summaries are used as a management tool in directing well-informed, precise product and system improvements.

Finally, an environment of increased communication and quality awareness has developed due to the CAR system. Departments and individuals have become sensitive to the concerns of other areas within the organization as well as to the concerns of the most important individual: the customer.

When this column was published in February 1995, Mark R. Miller was the quality assurance engineer at Clearing/Niagara in Buffalo, NY. He received a bachelor's degree in mechanical engineering from the State University of New York in Buffalo. Miller was a member of the American Society for Quality.

<table>
<tr><td>Idea
91</td><td><h1>Are You Listening to Your Customers?</h1> by Edmund S. Fine </td></tr>
</table>

It is an unfortunate fact that problems will occur during the operation of any manufacturing or service system, regardless of product or industry. The true measure of the goodness of a system is how well it copes with reported anomalies. The following steps can be used as a checklist to assess your system.

1. Acknowledge

Let your customer know promptly that you received his or her complaint, it is being investigated, and how long the investigation should take. If a complaint does not contain sufficient information, the acknowledgment letter should request additional information. Remember that your customers might have no idea what those funny numbers and letters on the container mean (your lot or date codes), but they are important to you for problem isolation and resolution.

2. Investigate

Not all complaints are valid. There are dishonest people, people whose expectations are unreasonable, and people who do not obey cautions and warnings. For example, if an ink marker is labeled "permanent" and a complaint is received from a consumer who used the marker and cannot remove the ink from a surface, the complaint probably should be rejected.

3. Communicate

If you have decided that a complaint is invalid or unsubstantiated, tell your customer why you have come to that decision. Don't use platitudes or insult the customer's intelligence. Above all, don't take a belligerent or condescending tone; to do so only invites the customer to take his business elsewhere, to call his lawyer, or both. Address the problem directly and explain in detail why you are rejecting the complaint.

If you have decided that a complaint is valid, tell your customer what went wrong with the system to allow the delivery of defective goods or services, apologize for the problem, and explain what is being done to preclude future occurrences of the problem. Often, this validation of a complaint and the generation of a positive corrective action will do more to retain a customer than anything else your company can do. A customer who has purchased an underfilled container of your product, for example, will probably be glad to know that you have installed automatic scales in the production line that ejects bottles that fall outside the weight limits. This will help ensure that the customer will never encounter that problem again.

4. Compensate

Try to make your customer view the problem and its resolution as a positive, or at least neutral, experience. You have already gotten negative points because your system has slipped. You can, however, regain some of the points by telling your customer how grateful you are to him or her for having uncovered a gap in your system. You can gain more points by promptly replacing the defective product or refunding the customer's money, and even more by compensating your customer for additional expenses that he or she incurred. Above all, you will win points by describing your systemic changes that make it very unlikely that the problem will ever be seen again, by the customer or anyone else. If you are lucky, you might gain a really loyal customer as a result of effectively correcting a systemic error.

Above all, don't delegate the task of coping with customer complaints to a low-level clerk without a review by a qualified supervisor. Moreover, be sure that your decisions on complaint validity are correct. Unless you are a monopoly, your customers do have a choice of whom to procure future services or products from. Carefully listening to your wronged customers will give you a chance of retaining their future business. If a company loses too many customers through shoddy products or services, it won't survive. Offended customers can hold grudges for a long time and spread the news of the offense to business associates, friends, and relatives. Make sure that your system measures up, and help your organization retain its customer base in spite of adversity.

Problems happen. How you deal with them will determine the future of your business.

When this column was published in January 1998, Edmund S. Fine was associate principal engineer at Sverdrup Technology in Huntsville, AL. He received a master's degree in industrial engineering from New York University in New York City. Fine was a senior member of the American Society for Quality.

<table>
<tr><td>

**Idea
92**

</td><td>

Corrective Action in the Real World

by Ken Paxton

</td></tr>
</table>

When I have been the recipient of customers' corrective action requests (CARs), I have completed them on time. More than once, customers have responded with surprised delight when they realized that someone was actually complying with their stated requests. Their surprise is indicative of a gap that frequently exists between the customer's desire and the supplier's intent regarding corrective actions. Such gaps might exist because of:

- *Status.* In the real world, it can sometimes be difficult to get a supplier's cooperation when a CAR is issued by a relatively minor customer. For example, I once followed up on a CAR sent to a supplier only to find out that the recipient, a vice president who was responsible for the department involved, did not take any action by the requested due date. When asked why, he replied, "I never take those things seriously. They are after the fact and don't really accomplish anything." Although I quickly performed some on-the-spot corrective action training, the message did not get across until the CAR was passed up to the company's president. It is doubtful this would have been necessary if my company were one of the supplier's largest customers.
- *Misunderstandings.* In the real world, misunderstandings about the customer-supplier relationship sometimes exist on both sides. Some customers might expect a supplier to invest the time needed to solve problems without their assistance because they believe that they don't have the expertise to help. (Theoretically, a customer might offer to act as a facilitator, but, in practice, this would likely be construed as meddling.) On the other hand, suppliers might not be willing to invest the time needed to solve what they believe is a customer's problem.

So how can the gap between the supplier and customer be minimized? One approach is to hold training sessions on the corrective action process. But, in the real world, not every customer is able to provide this training, despite how beneficial it could prove to be.

Another approach is to use the corrective action guidelines in Figure 15.2. These guidelines, which can be used for both external and internal suppliers, are attached to the CAR. The guidelines quickly clear the air regarding what objectives to pursue and what pitfalls to avoid. They stimulate asking the right questions and begin the process of sorting through existing information, acquiring knowledge, and plotting a course of corrective action.

The corrective action guidelines are not meant to replace training and education programs designed to increase the effectiveness of corrective action systems. Rather, the guidelines provide a tool for the CAR initiator who has limited resources. They also increase the chance of success for both parties.

Figure 15.2.
Corrective Action Guidelines

Congratulations! You have been selected as our next corrective action owner. The following suggestions can help you generate the most successful solutions possible.

1. Stay calm!
As the owner, you are not expected to be a lone ranger, doing all of the investigation and solving all of the problems unaided. Instead, your objective is to gather together those who are most likely to offer the best contributions toward:
- Fixing what is defective
- Discovering what has gone wrong
- Developing procedures to prevent it from happening again

Important: Guard against the first reaction to a corrective action request, which is to fire the operator. The operator might very well be the individual who can contribute the most to solving the real problem. Throwing blame around is a good way to get people to hate you, not help you.

Important: Operators do make mistakes, just like the rest of us. The point is to discover what can be done to eliminate the causes of those mistakes (other than random human error).

2. Ask "Why?" when a cause is discovered.
Often something went wrong, which caused something else to go wrong, which finally messed up some parts. You want to discover all of the bad parts or processes; be aware that some might try to hide out.

Example: Cause = worn vise jaws

This failure is going to be fixed by repairing the vise jaws, but if you don't ask "Why?" the failure can and will happen again. You should ask such questions as, "Why didn't we find out about the worn vise jaws before defective parts were made? Did the jaws wear out due to natural causes, or were they used improperly?

Important: Corrective action is intended to produce permanent solutions.

3. Be specific.
Avoid listing an ambiguous cause, such as "bad tool," because it could refer to a variety of actual causes. To be specific, you might ask:
- Was the tool calibrated? If not, why? (Maybe calibration doesn't exist for the tool.)
- Did the operators use the tool they were given? If not, why? (Maybe they knew better, but fear kept them from speaking out.)
- Was the tool used properly? If not, why? (Maybe the leader was too busy to train the operators.)
- Was the tool maintained? If not, why? (Maybe it was considered too expensive to have it serviced.)

(Note: All of these responses imply the need for management change. This is very common.)

4. What's the point?
- The goal is to solve all of the causes so the problems cannot happen again.
- Once a cause is discovered, you can ask: Does this cause affect anything else? When the answer is yes, you might be able to fix a problem before bad parts are made.

If you have any questions about this CAR or these guidelines please call right away.

When this column was published in May 1996, Ken Paxton was the fly height control manager at Read-Rite Corporation in Milpitas, CA. Formerly, he was the quality assurance manager at Autocam California in Hayward, CA. Paxton was an American Society for Quality senior member, certified quality engineer, and certified quality auditor.

How to Build Lasting Customer-Supplier Relationships

People intent on getting their bosses to pay attention to quality improvement efforts had best learn to speak the language of management: money. Phil Crosby first made that point in 1979, but it was no less important when he presented it in a different way in 1992.[1,2] It could be argued that the idea is just as important today.

It is doubtful that improving customer-supplier relationships is often thought of as a way to make a sizable improvement in the bottom line. But what if an organization closely involved suppliers in all phases of operations? Could large savings be achieved, say $3.7 billion over eight years? If you asked that question of the Chrysler Corporation in mid-1997, the answer would have been a resounding "yes."

On June 5, 1997, Chrysler announced that its SCORE (Supplier Cost Reduction Effort) campaign had reached its 1997 target of $1.2 billion in cost savings 60 days ahead of schedule.[3] The program, established in 1989, challenges Chrysler suppliers to continuously seek out and identify opportunities to lower costs in the vehicle manufacturing process. With the success of the Chrysler program in mind, it is worth examining what the authors in this chapter have to offer about building lasting customer-supplier relationships.

Compaq Computer Corporation was looking to forge deeper relationships in "Agree to Tackle the Quality Challenge as Partners." Joel A. Skellie describes the basic language behind the partnership agreement that Compaq signed with key suppliers of critical components.

Using an idea advocated by its namesake, Philip Crosby Associates Inc. hosted an annual supplier day. Patrick Fiorentino explains in "Supplier Day Helps Forge Customer-Supplier Partnerships" the five steps his company used to improve relationships in an interesting, informative, and entertaining way.

Getting what is needed on schedule is a challenge nearly every organization faces. Winston D. Greer writes that this can be done by "Qualifying Suppliers' Delivery Performance." A seven-step approach allows his company to work with suppliers to identify improvement opportunities that will benefit all parties.

Inspection is rarely a progressive form of quality improvement. Skellie and coauthor Phung Ngo developed an alternative. They describe this alternative in "Use Statistical Process Monitoring Instead of Inspection."

It is often tempting to fire a supplier and seek a new one. But what if there are no other domestic suppliers and selecting an international alternative would be too slow? Faced with this situation, A. K. Chakraborty developed "Four Steps to Improve Your Supplier."

"Customers and Suppliers Must Focus on Each Other" is E. Muesch's recollection of how Johnson & Johnson Baby Products Company changed its approach to suppliers. It developed a technique called a focused quality improvement that allowed it to create joint partnerships and resolve problems in a manageable way: one at a time.

References

1. Crosby, *Quality Is Free.*
2. Stratton, "What Does the Boss Read?"
3. "Suppliers Team with Chrysler for $1.2 Billion in Cost Savings," *Quality Progress.*

Idea 93

Agree to Tackle the Quality Challenge as Partners

by Joel A. Skellie

Today's emphasis in procurement quality is the partnership between a customer and its key suppliers. Compaq Computer Corporation has chosen to document this relationship in a partnership agreement containing a balance of corrective action and prevention procedures.

Some of the company's commodity teams have negotiated partnership agreements with a number of key suppliers of critical components, specifically memory and ASIC, with plans to expand to other commodities. The results have been extraordinary: an 80 percent reduction in lot reject rate in memory and an increase in coplanarity C_{pk} from 0.8 to 1.33. These results have translated into reduced costs by minimizing shortages, raw material rework, board rework, delayed or lost sales, and delays in new product announcements.

This agreement is routinely referenced by both parties and serves as a working document to be modified and renegotiated each year. As shown in the partnership agreement boilerplate (Figure 16.1), there are seven sections to the agreement. The three fundamental sections are goals, continuous improvement process, and communication.

Goals

Based on corporate goals, quantifiable goal levels are stated in the areas of quality reliability, delivery, and service. These goals are stated by year for a two- to four-year period. In addition, the means by which performance will be measured against these goals is outlined. In one agreement, for example, Compaq requested that the lot reject rate go from 7.5 percent in 1989 to 3.5 percent in 1990 to 1 percent in 1991 to 0.5 percent in 1992.

The purpose of this section is to prevent misunderstood requirements through the communication of expectations and performance measurement methods. Although the current year's goals are inflexible, goals for future years are negotiated with the suppliers.

Continuous improvement process

This section is divided in two subsections. The first benchmarks the supplier's performance in the areas described in the goals section. For those areas where performance is not meeting the goal levels, a quality improvement growth curve (on semilog graph paper) is developed. In the previously cited example for lot reject rate (which Compaq considers the most important index), the desired improvements are plotted quarterly. Methods used to achieve this improvement rate are outlined. This subsection is negotiated with the supplier.

The second subsection indicates milestones that a supplier must meet to achieve preferred supplier status. Preferred suppliers are targeted for a larger percentage of

Figure 16.1.

Partnership Agreement Boilerplate

Sign-off sheets
- Compaq Quality Policy and approval signatures
- Supplier Operating Policy and approval signatures

Purpose and scope
- State the primary objective (continuous improvement)
- Define "partnership" and its mutually beneficial attributes
- Define "agreement" (gentleman's, not legal)
- Define the applicable commodities

Abbreviations, definitions, and references
- Spell out acronyms used in the document
- Define terms used at Compaq
- Note sources for referenced documents (e.g., specifications)

Goals
- State time period (e.g., rolling four or five years)
- State goals (by years) for quality, reliability, delivery, and service

Continuous improvement process
- State benefits to Compaq and the supplier at completion of each phase:
  —Phase I: Reach current year's goals by improving lot acceptance rate (LAR) and on-time delivery
  —Phase II: Reach qualified status on approved vendor list (AVL)
  —Phase III: Reach certified status on AVL

Communication
- Identify key contacts for Compaq and the supplier
- Identify information exchange process
- Define periodic reports requested from the supplier
- Define periodic reports to be published by Compaq

Appendixes
- LAR improvement growth curve
- On-time delivery improvement growth curve
- Back-up data to LAR and delivery performance
- Definition of qualified AVL status
- Definition of certified AVL status
- Supplier's process flow diagram (including administrative)

---

order placements and a lower percentage of order cuts. In addition, preferred suppliers are usually on a skip-lot or dock-to-stock inspection mode.

The purpose of the continuous improvement process section is to identify specific corrective actions needed to align supplier performance with stated goals. It also emphasizes the mutually beneficial aspect of the partnership agreement.

Communication

Two-way communication and openness have always been stressed in Compaq's relationships with suppliers. In this section, the communication process is analyzed and specifically defined for a particular supplier commodity. The key contacts are listed for both the customer and supplier, and alternate methods of communication are identified. Desired meeting and report content and frequency are negotiated and documented in this section.

The purpose of this section is to stress the importance of communication in both preventive and corrective action activities. It also affixes accountability for the communication process within each party and documents needed data for each to operate efficiently.

The target

In a corporate culture that empowers the working level by giving it total commodity responsibility and authority, the partnership agreement serves to document the business plan for the customer and the supplier. The negotiation of these three areas is a fundamental step in managing risk and eventually reaching dock-to-stock inspection status.

When this column was published in February 1990, Joel A. Skellie was staff quality engineer in the Supplier Quality Engineering Department for Compaq Computer Corporation in Houston, TX. He received a bachelor's degree from Texas A&M University. Skellie was a member of the American Society for Quality.

Supplier Day Helps Forge Customer-Supplier Partnerships
by Patrick Fiorentino

Many companies realize that the integrity of customer-supplier partnerships significantly affects product quality and, ultimately, company profitability. Delivering defect-free products and services on time does not happen by accident or coincidence but through deliberate cultivation of long-term customer-supplier relationships. Such relationships must be built on mutual trust, respect, and benefit. Having a supplier day is a useful way for purchasing and materials management professionals to help forge this partnership.

What exactly is a supplier day? Simply put, it is an education process in which the customer conveys information to the supplier, with the ultimate goal of improving the relationship. It is an event that should be interesting, informative, and a little entertaining.

At the quality management consulting firm of Philip Crosby Associates (PCA), Inc., supplier day is an annual event that began in the early 1980s. Considerable resources have been put into planning and executing supplier day activities. The process has five steps.

Step 1

The first step is establishing specific objectives for the day. Improving the customer-supplier relationship is a time-intensive process. Setting and accomplishing intermediate objectives can be viewed as steps along the way. Although the objectives need not be complex, they should be as detailed and measurable as possible.

For example, when PCA was having problems with deliveries, a portion of the day was devoted to a demonstration of the effect that late deliveries had on PCA's customer commitments. A measurement of past-due orders was taken before and after the supplier day to gauge the demonstration's effectiveness.

Step 2

Planning the agenda is the second step. The most significant part of planning the agenda is speaker selection. Start by deciding what topics best address the objectives for the day. Then choose speakers based on those topics.

Although the objectives and topics vary from year to year at PCA, there are three agenda items that remain constant:

- The keynote speaker is always a company chairman or president. This shows that commitment to improving the customer-supplier relationship starts at the highest level.
- A workshop is always held to generate feedback from suppliers. This workshop usually results in a written list of comments, concerns, or complaints about PCA from each supplier. These lists are categorized and converted into specific action assignments for PCA personnel to address.

- A PCA senior executive makes a presentation on the business outlook for the next year, including new products being developed. Virtually all suppliers have a vested interest in their customers' future business activities. This information not only allows suppliers to plan for the effective use of their own resources, but it also makes them feel they are part of the customers' strategic processes.

Step 3

The third step is selecting a theme for the event. Supplier day generally features several speakers. A common theme provides focus and keeps the presentations from appearing fragmented. It is important that all speakers incorporate the theme's message into their addresses. Printing the theme in all materials adds continuity to the day.

Step 4

Planning the meeting mechanics is the fourth step. There are dozens of details that must be addressed to ensure smooth execution of supplier day. Some of the more notable details are the location, invitations, agenda, seating, audio-visual needs, menu, awareness gifts, handouts, and media coverage.

Step 5

The last step is completing post-event activities. When the supplier day is over, hold a meeting as soon as possible to discuss what was liked and disliked. Document any changes that should be incorporated into next year's supplier day. In addition, complete any remaining administrative action tasks, such as sending thank you letters to guest speakers and assigning corrective action for workshop comments.

Building a long-term, mutually beneficial partnership is the ultimate goal of all customer-supplier relationships. Supplier days can play an important role in this journey. Proper planning and execution will help ensure a successful event.

When this column was published in May 1991, Patrick Fiorentino was the materials manager for Philip Crosby Associates, Inc. in Winter Park, FL. He received a bachelor's degree in business administration from the University of Connecticut in Storrs.

Qualifying Suppliers' Delivery Performance

by Winston D. Greer

Material requirements planning (MRP) and just-in-time (JIT) manufacturing help minimize work-in-progress and final inventories. This, in turn, reduces the cost of doing business. When MRP and JIT are applied to the purchased materials and services facets of a business, quantifying suppliers' delivery performance in terms of days early or days late presents no difficulty. But qualifying MRP and JIT performance assessment data so that they can be combined with other performance indicators can be problematic.

Wright Medical Technology, an orthopedic implant manufacturer, has developed an integrated approach to qualifying data. With this approach, the company establishes an acceptable delivery interval from the negotiated delivery data (essentially a "tolerance band" for deliveries), measures suppliers' variance from the nominal delivery, and assesses delivery performance.

How it's calculated

A seven-step approach is used to qualify suppliers' delivery performance:

Step 1. Define the measurement criteria in terms of business days. Exclude nonwork days, such as holidays and weekends.

Step 2. Establish an acceptable delivery interval for scheduled deliveries. For example, an acceptable delivery performance could be a lot received within the interval of (3, 1)—in other words, three days early to one day late, including the scheduled day of delivery. This results in an acceptable delivery interval of five "lot" days.

Step 3. Calculate the number of penalty lot days. When a lot delivery is within the delivery interval, no penalty lot days are given. When a lot delivery is outside the acceptable delivery interval, the following formulas are used to calculate the penalty:

- If the delivery is too early: number of days early – number of allowable days early = penalty lot days.
- If the delivery is too late: number of days late – number of allowable days late = penalty lot days.
- The maximum number of penalty lot days for a single lot is restricted to the number of lot days in the interval.

For instance, suppose Supplier X, which has an acceptable delivery interval of (3, 1), delivers five lots. Here are its penalty lot days:

- Lot 1: three days early (within interval) = 0 penalty lot days
- Lot 2: one day late (within interval) = 0 penalty lot days
- Lot 3: four days early = 4 – 3 = 1 penalty lot day
- Lot 4: two days late = 2 – 1 = 1 penalty lot day
- Lot 5: 18 days early = 18 – 3 = 5 penalty lot days (the rule for maximum number of penalty lot days for a single lot goes into effect)

Step 4. Add up the penalty lot days for the total number of lots received. For example, Supplier X has a total of seven penalty lot days $(0 + 0 + 1 + 1 + 5)$ for five lots.

Step 5. Multiply the total number of lots received by the number of days in the acceptable delivery interval to get the total acceptable lot days. For example, Supplier X has a total of 25 total acceptable lot days (5 lots × 5 days).

Step 6. Divide the number of penalty lot days by the total acceptable lot days to obtain a penalty percentage rating. For example, Supplier X has a percentage rating of 28 percent (7 penalty lot days/25 lot days).

Step 7. Subtract the penalty percentage rating from 100 percent (which represents the situation in which all lots are received within the interval) to obtain the delivery performance rating for the period. For example, Supplier X has a 72 percent delivery performance (100 percent − 28 percent).

If the maximum number of penalty lot days is not limited to the number of days in the interval, step 7 could result in a negative percentage rating. This restriction effectively weights the delivery performance between individual lots for a given supplier as well as the delivery ratings between suppliers within a supplier base (when computing a delivery rating for the entire base).

The reporting of delivery performance ratings should follow the same reporting schedules used for other performance indicators. That way, the delivery rating can be weighted and summed with other performance indicators so that individual and combined supplier overall performance ratings can be obtained. For example, suppose that Supplier X's delivery performance rating is 72 percent and its quality performance rating is 100 percent, and they were weighted 35 percent and 65 percent, respectively. Supplier X would have an overall rating of 90.2 percent [(72 percent × 35 percent) + (100 percent × 65 percent)].

How it's used

Once you use this seven-step approach to quantify suppliers' delivery performance, you can use this information to achieve continuous improvement. Specifically, you can use the information to:

- Identify and eliminate assignable causes that prevent on-time deliveries
- Use Pareto analysis to identify suppliers with the largest improvement opportunities
- Compare overall ratings to reduce supplier-base redundancies
- Determine which existing, otherwise comparable, suppliers to use for new products
- Reduce the interval tolerance band to reflect increased accuracy as improvements are implemented

When this column was published in February 1994, Winston D. Greer was the quality assurance manager of the Medical Specialties Division of Smith & Nephew Richards in Bartlett, TN. He received a bachelor's degree in quality assurance from the University of South Alabama in Mobile. Greer was an American Society for Quality senior member, certified quality engineer, and certified reliability engineer.

Use Statistical Process Monitoring Instead of Inspection

by Joel A. Skellie and Phung Ngo

Dock-to-stock, sometimes called ship-to-stock, is the process by which incoming products can bypass inspection because the quality of the supplier's products has been ensured. To achieve dock-to-stock, the customer must have confidence in its supplier's quality management systems and process controls. At Compaq Computer Corporation, this means confidence in the supplier's system and controls for both mechanical dimensions and electrical parameters. We have helped develop a practical, objective way to determine whether the stability and capability of processes producing electrical characteristics are sufficient to eliminate electrical testing of incoming lots.

SPM vs. SPC

Statistical process monitoring (SPM) is the use of statistics to evaluate a supplier's process at the customer's facility. The purpose of this variables data analysis is monitoring, not controlling, as it is in SPC. SPM is both a preventive tool (based on X-bar and S chart trends with subsequent feedback to supplier) and a tool to determine the extent of testing required for future lots (based on stability and capability).

Electrical vs. mechanical analysis

SPM criteria for critical electrical parameters differ greatly from the criteria used for critical mechanical parameters because the specification limits for electrical parameters are typically much wider than those for mechanical parameters. In the analysis of mechanical variables data, in which form and fit are the sole concern, tolerances are extremely tight (compared to a process spread of ±3 sigma) and acceptable performance depends on process stability (statistical control) and process capability. Typical requirements might be a stable process and a C_{pk} greater than or equal to 1.33.

But, for electrical variables data analysis in which function is the sole concern, tolerances are relatively loose; many parameters have only an upper or lower spec limit (as in most timing parameters of memory devices). These circumstances lend themselves to a special case for electrical parameters in which the process is capable but not stable. To illustrate this point, Figure 16.2 shows X-bar and S charts for a particular electrical parameter that is fully capable (CPU > 2.0) but not stable. Although the fact that the process is not stable indicates that the behavior of future lots will be unpredictable, the performance range is so far from the spec limit that requiring stability is impractical in this particular case.

It is important to note a departure from traditional SPC approaches in this SPM model for electrical evaluation. Although traditional SPC techniques dictate that process stability be established prior to calculating process capability indexes, this model uses a quick-and-dirty CPU calculation used as a snapshot capability index.

Figure 16.2.
Statistical Process Monitor (SPM) Chart

SPM chart

Supplier: ABC
Part number: 987654

Parameter: TDW Vcc max
Specification: 20 ns max

Lot number	1	2	3	4	5	6	7	8	9	10	11	12	13	14	15	16	17	18	19	20
Date	4/12	4/29	5/9	5/19	6/9	6/18	7/1	7/9	7/27	8/7	8/19	9/2	9/12	9/24	10/3	10/15	10/21	10/31	11/7	11/15
Average	14.1	14.4	12.7	14.0	13.7	14.2	14.4	14.1	13.7	14.0	13.9	13.8	14.1	14.0	13.7	14.0	14.3	13.8	14.1	13.5
Standard deviation	0.81	0.71	0.98	0.56	0.47	0.53	0.58	0.71	0.62	0.82	0.59	0.63	0.76	0.60	0.79	0.66	0.54	0.65	0.80	0.71
CPU	2.4	2.6	2.5	3.6	4.5	3.6	3.2	2.8	3.4	2.4	3.4	3.3	2.6	3.3	2.7	3.0	3.5	3.2	2.5	3.1

Average chart using S

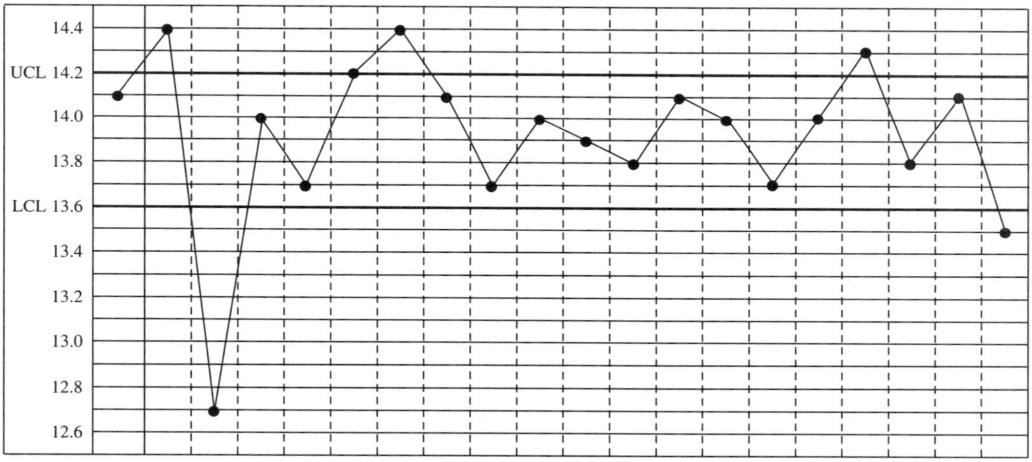

Standard deviation chart

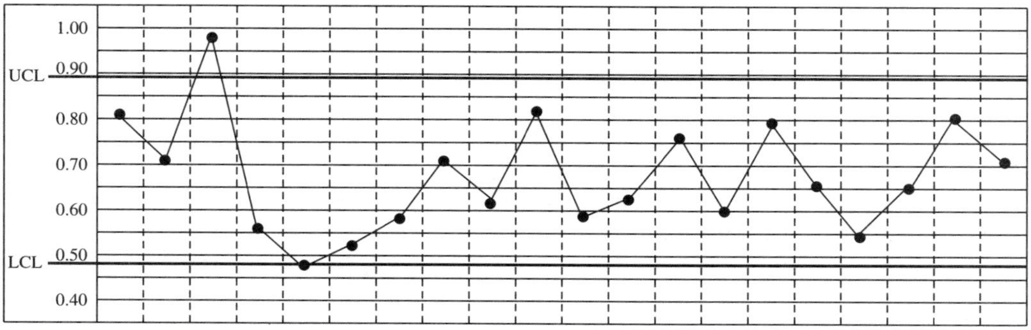

A look at the decision table

Figure 16.3 contains a decision table that can be used to determine what actions are needed depending on the capability and stability results for electrical parameters. The boxes that contain the phrase "dock-to-stock" indicate that the process is deemed adequate to provide products that consistently conform to specifications without the need for incoming electrical testing.

The three levels of corrective action are a means to prioritize responses based on risk. Level 1 is the highest risk. Any process that does not allow the customer to eliminate incoming inspection is defined as needing corrective action of both containment (screening) and permanent corrective action (elimination of root cause). The exact corrective action taken is left to the discretion of the supplier quality engineer.

Figure 16.3.

SPM Decision Table

Process stability	Snapshot process capability, C_{pk}*		
	< 1.4	1.4 - 1.8	> 1.8
Stable	Corrective action level 2	Dock to stock	Dock to stock
Not stable	Corrective action level 1	Corrective action level 3	Dock to stock
* CPU or CPL in the case of one-sided spec limits			

For example, corrective action level 1 occurs when a process is found to be unstable and incapable (C_{pk} < 1.4). Under these process conditions, an unacceptable level of nonconforming parts per million is a given. This would be the worst condition; thus, developing a corrective action for it receives highest priority.

The C_{pk} values of 1.4 and 1.8 were chosen as decision points based on several factors:

- Theoretical calculations translate these C_{pk} values to nonconforming parts per million of 17 and 0.06, respectively. These levels of nonconforming parts per million are so low that generally they're acceptable for manufacturing use.
- A process that is not stable requires a higher C_{pk} to compensate for the lack of stability.
- Although process capability indexes, such as C_{pk}, are only approximate measures of quality levels, our experience shows these theoretical approximations correlate well with actual manufacturing quality levels.

As an example, for a process that is stable with a C_{pk} of 1.4, incoming inspection can be confidently eliminated based on the acceptability of 17 nonconforming parts per million and on the low probability that a stable, statistically monitored process would result in a higher number of nonconforming parts per million because the process is centered 4.2 sigma from the limits.

To determine whether electrical testing can be eliminated, variables data are accumulated on 50 devices per lot for at least 20 lots. Once 20 consecutive lots meet the dock-to-stock criteria of Figure 16.3, electrical testing is eliminated.

The method gets results

Using this SPM model, we have been able to deviate from the traditional and archaic sampling by attributes. The old sampling technique forced us to remove parts to be tested from their package. Once this was done, the parts could not be repackaged; they were unusable. Therefore, SPM has produced major cost savings because scrap is eliminated. Other cost savings have resulted from reduced manufacturing overhead costs—including indirect labor (test operators) and indirect materials (fewer tester repairs)—and reduced inspection cycle time. All told, the power of statistical analysis of variables data saves us tens of thousands of dollars each month.

When this column was published in June 1990, Joel A. Skellie was staff quality engineer in the Supplier Quality Engineering Department for Compaq Computer Corporation in Houston, TX. He holds a bachelor's degree from Texas A&M University. Skellie was a member of the American Society for Quality. Phung Ngo was sustaining reliability engineer in the Component Reliability Engineering Department for Compaq. He earned a bachelor's degree from the University of Cincinnati. Ngo was an American Society for Quality member and certified quality engineer.

Four Steps to Improve Your Supplier

by A. K. Chakraborty

A company was having serious nonconformance problems with a component that it purchased from a supplier, so it sent one of its quality assurance engineers to the supplier's headquarters for an on-the-spot inspection. The engineer came back empty-handed. He had rejected the whole lot that was about to be dispatched. This created a crisis, since there was no other domestic supplier for that component.

The only solution that company's senior officials proposed was to begin importing the component, which meant a long lead time and a possible halt in production. However, as a faculty member of the Statistical Quality Control and Organizational Research Division of the Indian Statistical Institute, I suggested a different approach for this client: a four-step process to develop the current supplier.

Agreeing to try my approach, the senior officials discussed the plan with the supplier. It agreed to take these necessary steps for improvement. After following them, the supplier gradually went from having an entire lot being rejected to 100 percent acceptance. Here's how the supplier accomplished this vast improvement.

Step 1: Know the present status

A format was developed to determine the present status. Dimensions were measured and recorded. The supplier discovered that the component's diameter and length varied greatly.

Step 2: Search for a solution

Logical thinking told the supplier that the high variability was likely produced in an early step in the process. The process flowchart showed that the manufacturing process included an induction hardening stage for a part in that component. Experience has shown that induction hardening creates a good amount of variation. The supplier decided to grind that component after it hardened to reduce the variation. A few pieces were tested with this modified process. Although variation was reduced, there was still a number of components out of specification. The process capability for the modified procedure was 0.077mm, but the specified tolerance was 0.051mm.

Step 3: Go for a breakthrough

The problem was reviewed again from various angles. Grinding after hardening should have evened out any differences that might have existed. But the fact that a lot of variation still existed suggested that there must be a problem with the grinding machine itself. A thorough check took place. This investigation revealed that the grinding and feeder wheels along with their accessories had to be changed. Once done, measurements were taken on new components that went through the manufacturing process. Process capability took a nose-dive to 0.008mm.

Step 4: Sustain the achievement

The main responsibility at this point was to properly maintain this process capability. A precontrol chart was developed. Employees were given instructions on how to draw the chart and how it could help maintain the achieved process capability. They were asked to maintain the process themselves. To make their jobs simpler, suitable go/no-go gages were developed. Within six months, the supplier could guarantee that any component checked would satisfy the specification.

A happy ending

Both the supplier and the customer were happy. The customer was able to stay on schedule using a 100 percent fault-free component, while the supplier was able to keep the customer's business. In addition, solving the variation problem saved the customer from importing the item. Patience and hard work allowed both organizations to succeed.

When this column was published in April 1989, A. K. Chakraborty was on the faculty of the Statistical Quality Control (SQC) and Organizational Research (OR) Division of the Indian Statistical Institute in Madras, India. He received a master's degree in statistics and a post master's degree diploma in SQC and OR from the Indian Statistical Institute in Calcutta.

Customers and Suppliers Must Focus on Each Other
by E. Muesch

Companies must go beyond making futile demands of their suppliers. Traditionally, suppliers want to please their customers and will appear to meet buyers' expectations for the short term. But if agreed-on improvements don't survive the test of time, customers experience disillusionment and frustration. Without a game plan, both suppliers and customers are dead in the water.

This situation is a candidate for focused quality improvement (FQI). FQI is the ability to work with a supplier in a joint partnership to resolve one problem at a time. The term FQI was coined by Santosh Jiwrajka, director of quality services at Johnson & Johnson Baby Products Company, Royston, GA, while he was working with a supplier that had so many problems that the situation seemed unresolvable. Jiwrajka's approach of resolving one issue at a time made the situation manageable. Asking someone to move a building all at once is much different than requesting it be moved one brick at a time. If you make any job manageable, it will be managed.

From intimidation to cooperation

Prior to the new concepts of world-class manufacturing, a supplier could easily be intimidated with the mention of another supplier. The partnership between customer and supplier is a new concept to many companies, including Johnson & Johnson Baby Products Company. Today, many companies have learned that consolidating their businesses with fewer suppliers lowers prices and eliminates redundant systems. However, the demands on this relationship are greater than ever. This has led to an understanding that a long-term partnership between supplier and customer is mutually beneficial. It has created a new working relationship that encourages both parties to share information and technology. The supplier can no longer be thought of as just another raw material; instead, it must be considered as an organizational extension of the customer. Relationships must now be nurtured, problems identified, resources shared, and resolutions planned.

Openness between the supplier and the customer is the foundation on which FQI is built. Both must agree on the area to be improved, milestones for this improvement, and a schedule. A contact person within each group will route important information between the organizations. The customer must recognize the importance of a long-term commitment to doing business with a developed (over time) high-quality supplier. All customers and suppliers have organizational and procedural weaknesses. Following a mutual recognition that both can benefit from their new relationship, they can share resources to make improvements and reduce problems.

When results don't match intentions

During a recent visit of a supplier that was chosen for FQI, a team recognized the supplier had made significant gains in the areas of documenting correct procedures for good manufacturing practices, components listings, and other general quality assurance checks and procedures. However, during a floor tour of the supplier's facility, two major problems occurred: incorrectly notched sleeves and a label mix-up at the inspection station.

During the final review, the audit team shared its observation that the supplier made the intellectual inquiry and commitment but failed at practical implementation of its procedures and therefore was unable to accomplish its purpose. The supplier was noticeably disappointed, but wanted to know what went wrong after so much effort and what needed to be done next.

Policies require vision, but implementation requires old-fashioned hard work. Johnson & Johnson invited the supplier to the facility where its products were used to provide a model process for the supplier to imitate. The reason for this invitation was simple: Johnson & Johnson was asking a company to change its culture. The invitation to come to a Johnson & Johnson facility would allow the supplier to see the benefits of that culture firsthand. Top, middle, and lower management were invited, as were line personnel.

Johnson & Johnson's strategy was simple:

- Have each level of operation at the supplier meet and interact with its counterpart at Johnson & Johnson.
- Keep the atmosphere friendly and light. Johnson & Johnson didn't want to make the supplier feel liable for past problems. When the mood is upbeat, suppliers are more receptive to what they see.
- Hold the in-house training program over two days. During the first day, emphasize theory; during the second day, demonstrate practical implementation.
- Agree on a new supplier audit date.

When the supplier's personnel arrived on the first day, they were given a tour of the facility. General introductions followed in a conference room. After this, there was a review of past, present, and future Johnson & Johnson quality services. This review emphasized the Johnson & Johnson quality philosophies and their implementation, both in that facility and the corporation. The rest of the day was spent discussing Johnson & Johnson departments and the tools they used.

The second day stressed the practical application of label mix-up prevention and the general control of material flow. The supplier heard presentations by each department manager, giving the supplier the added opportunity to see firsthand what was previously hard to explain at a conference table. The Johnson & Johnson managers had prepared for several days so that they could focus on what they believed the supplier needed to know most.

The managers also told the supplier that it wasn't so long ago that Johnson & Johnson had experienced similar internal problems. This openness helped create a bond between customer and supplier—a crucial element for success. An example of this honesty was when a veteran Johnson & Johnson manager openly discussed how he resisted many changes and was often the last to support now-popular company culture and management practices. The supplier identified with this manager and realized that if he could adapt, its managers could also. This manager was a source of strength to the supplier's senior management for making changes within its own middle and lower management ranks.

At the end of the second day, all those involved in the training seminar reassembled with the supplier in the conference room to wrap up the session. This final gathering was another chance to raise questions and get answers. Before the meeting ended, the supplier agreed to implement the needed improvements by a proposed date and Johnson & Johnson agreed to send another audit team to the supplier's facility.

The supplier's visit ended as it started—with friendly handshakes. While it is too early to claim complete success, the previous problems have been eliminated and no new major problems have occurred. Johnson & Johnson plans to audit this supplier again.

FQI guidelines

The first requirement in FQI is not to select the perfect supplier, but to select the supplier you want to do business with for the long term. Another requirement is to use your internal resources to help the supplier overcome its problems, one at a time. At first, a costly problem that is deemed manageable for focused improvement should be selected. When the supplier recognizes the customer's desire for a long-term commitment, cooperation is likely to improve. The greatest contribution that you can make to changing a supplier's practices is first to change your attitude. Until you think of suppliers as extensions of your company—in whom you must be prepared to invest time and resources—you will have only limited success.

FQI has three specific requirements: open communication, clear goals, and clear measurement. These three major requirements are the building blocks of FQI. The ultimate criterion of FQI's success is not whether problems are eliminated, but rather whether the supplier becomes a conduit of future innovation for both the customer and supplier.

When this column was published in October 1989, E. Muesch was the manager of technical services for Johnson & Johnson Baby Products in Royston, GA.

How to Break into New Frontiers

J. M. Juran often wrote about making breakthroughs, but no place was he more succinct about the subject than in the famous *Juran's Quality Control Handbook*. He writes that when setting objectives, people must decide whether to maintain status quo or go for a breakthrough.[1] Both alternatives can serve worthwhile purposes, but his books on breakthroughs make it evident that he prefers seeking breakthroughs.[2,3]

While not following Juran's lead in the purest form, the authors in this chapter have the same thinking in mind. The status quo is not good enough, and a breakthrough is needed. In their cases, they are taking traditional quality ideas and recasting them to create an entirely new tool for their own purpose.

"A New Use for an Old Tool" by Sharon Johnson and Michael Reagan describes how a state-operated hospital transformed the familiar flowchart into a process tracking device. The idea has taken a bureaucratic process and made it manageable.

Deborah Donndelinger and Barbara Van Dine have found a human resources application for the cause-and-effect diagram, which is traditionally used to structure brainstorming sessions or sort ideas into useful categories.[4] In "Use the Cause-and-Effect Diagram to Manage Conflict," they describe how to use the diagram to objectively and systematically deal with emotionally charged issues.

It is fitting that this chapter closes where it began, with the ideas of J. M. Juran. "A Trilogy for Personal Effectiveness" by Thomas Johnson starts with Juran's trilogy, moves on to Stephen R. Covey's seven habits, and borrows from Harry V. Roberts's personal checklist. From these ideas, Johnson arrives at a personal planning calendar that works best for him.

References

1. Juran, *Juran's Quality Control Handbook*, pp. 5.20–5.21.
2. Juran, *Managerial Breakthrough: A New Concept of the Manager's Job*.
3. Juran, *Managerial Breakthrough: The Classic Book on Improving Management Performance*.
4. Tague, *The Quality Toolbox*, p. 132.

A New Use for an Old Tool

by Sharon Johnson and Michael Reagan

Quality practitioners often employ a variety of tools in their work. One of the most popular is the flowchart. Over the years, quality professionals have found many uses for flowcharts. The Brainerd Regional Human Services Center (BRHSC), a state-operated mental hospital in central Minnesota, has discovered yet another.

Although flowcharts appear in many variations, each chart performs one of two basic functions:

1. It describes work as observers perceive it to occur in reality. This function allows people to use flowcharts for such purposes as identifying opportunities for process improvement, analyzing root causes of problems, structuring discussions during problem solving, and communicating processes to others.

2. It describes a process as it is intended to work. This function allows people to use flowcharts for such purposes as communicating expectations to workers, planning work flow and resources, and designing new processes. It is under this function that BRHSC has found another use of the flowchart: as a tracking device.

Like any other hospital, BRHSC receives income from third-party payers, such as insurance companies, health plans, and government programs. Occasionally, these payers might deny a claim for payment. This sometimes occurs when an insurance carrier reviews the patient's record and decides that the care was not medically necessary. Such decisions are usually judgment calls involving an interpretation of the facts. For this reason, hospitals have the opportunity to appeal the decision and argue for paying the claim.

The appeals process involves several people and several documents. At any one moment, several cases can be in various stages of completion, thus making it difficult to remember the current status of any particular case. Previously, an update on a case necessitated a time-consuming review of the patient's insurance file. Now, flowcharts are used, eliminating the need for this lengthy review.

Here is how the flowchart process works: BRHSC routes letters of denial to the secretary in the utilization review department. She sets up a case file consisting of a manila folder into which she places all of the documents relating to the case. She keeps a supply of flowcharts of the appeals process at her desk and staples a copy to the outside of each folder as she sets up the file. As each step in the flow is completed, the secretary uses a highlighting marker to color in the corresponding shape on the flowchart. Anyone can then see at a glance, without wading through all of the paperwork, which steps are completed and which remain to be done. The secretary also notes the completion date for each step or any deadlines on the flowchart next to the shape.

Figure 17.1 contains a sample flowchart for a file. It indicates that the secretary has established the file. It also shows that the medical records department has provided the record and that the physician has reviewed the case, dictated an appeal letter, and sent

Figure 17.1.

Flowchart of the Third-Party Denial Process

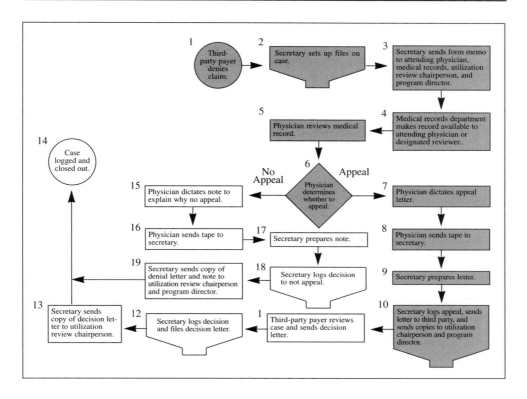

the dictation tape to the secretary. The secretary, in turn, has typed and sent the letter as well as updated the log. Overall, BRHSC has completed the first 10 steps and is now waiting for the third-party payer to review the appeal.

The decision to appeal and the composition of the appeal letter is the responsibility of the attending physician. The secretary uses a brief form letter to inform the doctor of the denial. She sends the form letter, a copy of the insurance company's letter of denial, and a copy of the flowchart to the appropriate physician. The secretary also highlights the first four steps to show their completion. This helps the physician remember what he or she is expected to do. It also tactfully communicates that the ball is in his or her court.

Using a flowchart as a tracking tool has saved time and made the appeals process run much smoother for BRHSC's utilization review department. It has also provided an easy way to communicate how far a process has progressed. It is one more handy use for a wonderful multipurpose tool.

When this column was published in November 1996, Sharon Johnson was a senior clerk stenographer in the utilization review department of the Brainerd Regional Human Services Center in Brainerd, MN. Michael Reagan was the director of quality improvement at the Brainerd Regional Human Services Center. He received a master's degree in special education at St. Cloud State University in Minnesota. Reagan was an American Society for Quality member and certified quality auditor.

Use the Cause-and-Effect Diagram to Manage Conflict

by Deborah Donndelinger and Barbara Van Dine

As organizations implement quality management initiatives, much training is devoted to the basic tools of quality and process improvement. Teams are taught how to use these tools to improve their work processes but often are not taught how to apply them to other nontraditional work situations, such as human interactions. Specifically, one tool—the cause-and-effect diagram—can be used to address conflict issues between individuals and departments at all levels of the organization. As team consultants and facilitators, we have used the cause-and-effect diagram in a variety of conflict situations, involving such parties as managers, team members, supervisors, and staff.

The cause-and-effect diagram, also known as the fishbone or Ishikawa diagram, is designed to examine the causes of a particular issue, problem, or process. In the case of a conflict between individuals or departments, this tool provides a more objective method for identifying and resolving the causes of conflict. The steps for using this technique will be outlined using a fictitious team situation involving two individuals, Bob and Doug, who work in different departments and are having trouble getting along on a team:

Step 1. Identify the stakeholders in the conflict situation. The stakeholders are those who are involved in the conflict or those who are being affected by it. In the example here, the stakeholders are Bob, Doug, and the team leader to start, although the conflict affects the entire team.

Step 2. Hold a meeting of the stakeholders to identify the causes of the conflict and construct the cause-and-effect diagram. This meeting is most successful if all individuals meet together, although it can initially be done in separate sessions if the emotional level is too high. It is also important to have this session facilitated by a third party to ensure equal participation opportunities for all involved and to maintain a focus on the topic. Sometimes one side is not aware of the conflict. In this case, the people aware of the conflict can create the cause-and-effect diagram and then use the diagram as a basis for discussion with the other parties.

To construct the cause-and-effect diagram, the stakeholders should start with a diagram showing only the major bones and then brainstorm possible causes, adding them to the diagram as smaller bones. Traditionally, the major bones are labeled as man (or people), machines, materials, and methods; however, these might vary depending on the situation. For example, "technology" might be a more appropriate heading than "machines" and "work environment" might be more appropriate than "materials." A fifth bone can even be added for the culture. In the case of Bob and Doug, the entire team met and developed the cause-and-effect diagram in Figure 17.2.

Step 3. Prioritize the top causes. Once the causes have been identified, it is important for the group to prioritize the top causes. Multivoting works best. There are many variations of multivoting. The simplest one is where each person is allocated a set number of points, typically 10. Each person votes by distributing the points among the causes. Ten points can be assigned to one cause, one point can be assigned to 10 causes, or any

Figure 17.2.

The Cause-and-Effect Diagram for Bob and Doug

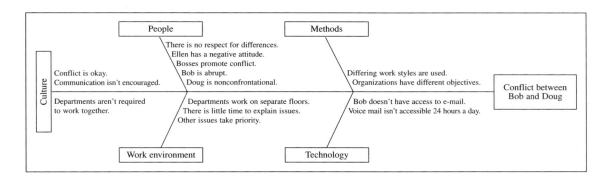

other combination as long as the person only uses 10 points. After every person votes, the results are tallied. Depending on the number of causes, three to five items on which to begin working should be chosen. In Bob and Doug's case, the top causes are "Communication isn't encouraged," "Bob doesn't have access to e-mail," and "Voice mail isn't accessible 24 hours a day."

Step 4. Develop an action plan. An action plan should be developed to break down barriers. This plan must be agreed to by all involved. For example, since not having access to e-mail is a root cause of problems between Bob and Doug, an action to connect all parties by e-mail or to find an alternate communication method could be developed.

The real benefit of using the cause-and-effect diagram to address conflicts is its objective and systematic approach for dealing with often emotionally charged issues. Identifying causes helps eliminate finger pointing and helps identify processes that might be contributing to the conflict. The resulting action plan produces concrete steps to resolve the conflict.

In addition, in our use of the cause-and-effect diagram, we have found that many conflict situations are the result of misunderstandings or poor communication. In such cases, there might not be a need to develop a detailed action plan; simply having the discussion might resolve the issue.

When this column was published in June 1996, Deborah Donndelinger was the manager of quality education at the University of Maryland Medical System in Baltimore. She received a master's degree in industrial engineering and operations research from Virginia Tech in Blacksburg. Donndelinger was a member of the American Society for Quality. Barbara Van Dine was president of Tri-Source Training Resources in Westminster, CA. She received a master's degree in educational psychology from California State University in Dominguez Hills.

A Trilogy for Personal Effectiveness

by Thomas Johnson

A person's life is a system of interconnected processes that serve a variety of customers. As with any system, the quality or effectiveness of your life depends on proper attention to the trilogy espoused by J. M. Juran:[1]

- *Planning.* You must plan your efforts and allocate your time to meet well-understood objectives.
- *Control.* You must perform and control your actions to fulfill your plans consistently.
- *Improvement.* You must continually progress to achieve your potential.

Just as systems thinking is a key element for improving quality and gaining knowledge, systems thinking is needed for managing personal time.[2] Thus, I have been searching for a tool to bring the trilogy of planning, performance, and progress (i.e., planning, control, and improvement) to better manage my time.

In his book *The 7 Habits of Highly Effective People*, Stephen Covey includes elements of the trilogy but emphasizes planning by weekly scheduling of your priorities after examining your core values.[3] In Covey's system, personal core values are expressed in a few defining roles, such as spouse, parent, professional leader, or community server. The effective person has explicit goals associated with each role for each time period. Other time management systems, such as the Franklin system, emphasize daily performance by prioritizing your schedule, again after examining your core values.[4]

More recently, Harry Roberts introduced the personal checklist as a tool for personal improvement.[5] The personal checklist—an adaptation of the well-known quality tool, the check sheet—helps people monitor their performance against personal priorities. Roberts implies that people should consider their values but does not integrate the check sheet into a complete system parallel to Juran's trilogy.

For years, I used a generic weekly planner with the entire week's calendar in view on my desk. As projects and schedules became more complex, however, the details became too much to maintain in constant view, so I began using a generic daily planner. The daily planner worked well for keeping the moment's activities on track, but since it did not have a conveniently located weekly planning sheet, I often became frustrated. The daily view is superior for maintaining performance, while the weekly view is superior for planning priorities.

To achieve a weekly overview based on scheduling priorities while keeping the daily schedule, I devised a form to supplement my 5.5-in.-by-8.5-in. daily planner. As Figure 17.3 shows, the form includes a weekly overview and a planning sheet. When inserted into the daily planner, the weekly overview stays in view; the planning sheet is covered by the pages of the daily planner, but it is easy to turn back to the planning sheet for review. This supplement worked well for planning and performance, but a tool for monitoring progress was missing and I certainly did not want another notebook on my desk.

Figure 17.3.
Planning Form for Personal Trilogy

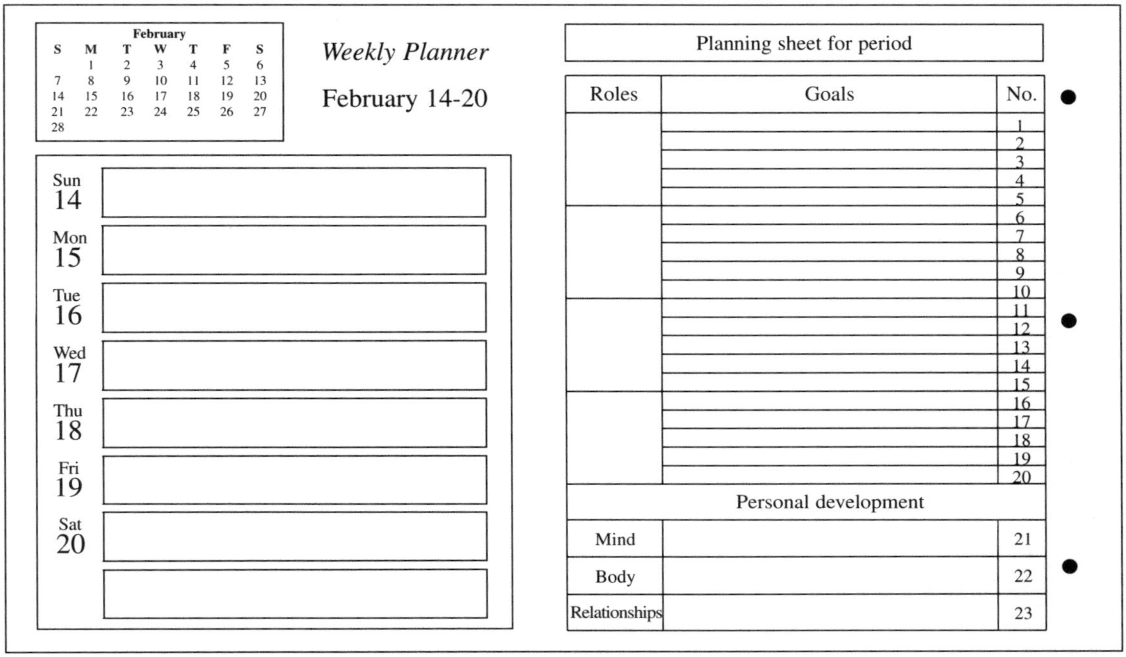

The back of the supplemental form proved to be a handy place for a personal improvement check sheet. I slightly modified Roberts's checklist since I prefer to speak in terms of opportunities rather than problems (see Figure 17.4). Thus, I used the heading "Opportunity for Improvement (OFI)," a term adopted from Milliken & Co. An OFI can be positive (such as "Check e-mail twice a day") or negative (such as "Failed to answer phone before third ring"). As in Roberts's system, I enter a mark for each occurrence of an OFI, producing a total count to track my improvement over time.

By turning to the back of the weekly calendar, I have ready access to the check sheet. When in use, the check sheet lies on a smooth surface for easy writing. When not in use, the check sheet is not visible to others.

The forms in Figures 17.3 and 17.4 can be produced easily with a standard word processing program. (I use Wordperfect.) A good, inexpensive program for producing the calendar is called Calendar Creator Plus.

If the weekly calendar is to be to the left of the daily planner (as I use it), it is important that the elements (the calendar, planning sheet, OFI definitions, check sheet, and holes for the binder rings) be arranged as shown in Figures 17.3 and 17.4. If the weekly calendar is to be to the right of the daily planner, the elements should be placed in the mirror image of those in Figures 17.3 and 17.4.

With this double-sided supplement added each week, my daily planner is now a complete tool to implement the trilogy of planning, performance, and progress for my personal time management system.

Figure 17.4.

Progress Form for Personal Trilogy

	Definitions of Opportunity for Improvement (OFI) categories
●	
●	
●	

Personal progress check sheet   Week of _____

OFI category	Sun	Mon	Tue	Wed	Thu	Fri	Sat	Total
Total								

References

1. Juran, *Juran on Planning for Quality*, pp. 11–13.
2. Senge, *The Fifth Discipline: The Art and Practice of the Learning Organization*, and Deming, *Out of the Crisis.*
3. Covey, *The 7 Habits of Highly Effective People.*
4. Winwood, *Time Management: An Introduction to the Franklin System.*
5. Roberts, "Using Personal Checklists to Facilitate TQM."

When this column was published in May 1994, Thomas Johnson was a professor of agricultural and resource economics, statistics, and biomathematics at North Carolina State University in Raleigh. He received a doctorate in economics and statistics from North Carolina State University in Raleigh. Johnson was a member of the American Society for Quality.

Epilogue

There is no shortage of good ideas. If this book got you thinking about a special improvement that you have undertaken, we hope you'll share it with *Quality Progress* magazine. It continues to accept submissions for the One Good Idea column, and in 1998, broadened the scope to consider bad ideas (as in "I can't believe we did this!").

Good or bad ideas can be sent to:
One Good Idea
ASQ/*Quality Progress*
P.O. Box 3005
Milwaukee, WI 53201-3005

If you want to check out the latest author guidelines for submitting articles to *Quality Progress*, request them by calling 800-248-1946 or (414) 272-8575. The guidelines can also be found on the World Wide Web at qualityprogress.asq.org.

Bibliography

Akao, Y., editor. (1990) *Quality Function Deployment*. Productivity Press, Cambridge, MA.

Alsup, Fred, and Ricky M. Watso. (1993) *Practical Statistical Process Control: A Tool for Quality Manufacturing and Services*. Van Nostrand-Rinehold, New York.

ANSI/ASQC Q9001-1994, Quality Systems—Model for Quality Assurance in Design, Development, Production, Installation, and Servicing. American Society for Quality, Milwaukee.

ANSI/ISO/ASQC Q10013-1995, Guidelines for Quality Manuals. American Society for Quality, Milwaukee.

AT&T Statistical Quality Control Handbook. (1956) Delmar Printing Company, Charlotte.

Beauregard, M.R., R.J. Mikulak, and B.A. Olson. (1992) *A Practical Guide to Statistical Quality Improvement*. Van Nostrand Reinhold, New York.

Box, George E.P., and Norman R. Draper. (1969) *Evolutionary Operation*. John Wiley & Sons, New York.

Boyles, Russell A. "The Taguchi Capability Index." *Journal of Quality Technology*, January 1991.

Campanella, Jack, editor, *Principles of Quality Costs*, second edition. ASQ Quality Press, Milwaukee.

Cartin, Thomas J. (1993) *Principles & Practices of TQM*. ASQ Quality Press, Milwaukee.

Chou, Youn-Min, D.B. Owens, and Salvador A. Borrego. "Lower Confidence Limits on Process Capability Indices." *Journal of Quality Technology*, July 1990.

Covey, Stephen R. (1989) *The 7 Habits of Highly Effective People*. Simon and Schuster, New York.

Crosby, Philip B. (1979) *Quality Is Free*. McGraw-Hill, New York.

Deming, W. Edwards. (1993) *The New Economics for Industry, Government, Education*. Massachusetts Institute of Technology's Center for Advanced Engineering Study, Cambridge, MA.

Deming, W. Edwards. (1986) *Out of the Crisis*. Massachusetts Institute of Technology's Center for Advanced Engineering Study, Cambridge, MA.

Duncan, Acheson J. (1986) *Quality Control and Industrial Statistics*, fifth edition. Richard D. Irwin, Homewood, IL.

Feigenbaum, Armand V. (1983) *Total Quality Control*, third edition. McGraw-Hill Book Co., New York.

Fiero, Janet. "The Crawford Slip Method." *Quality Progress*, May 1992.

Gabor, Andrea. (1990) *The Man Who Discovered Quality*. Times Books, New York.

Galloway, Dianne. (1994) *Mapping Work Processes*. ASQ Quality Press, Milwaukee.

Grant, Eugene L., and Richard S. Leavenworth. (1988) *Statistical Quality Control*, sixth edition. McGraw-Hill Book Co., New York.

Gunter, Berton H. "The Use and Abuse of C_{pk}." *Quality Progress*, January, March, May, and July 1989.

Harry, Mikel J. (1987) *The Nature of Six Sigma Quality*. Motorola booklet available from Motorola Communications Sector, 1301 E. Algonquin Rd., Schaumburg, IL 60196.

Ishikawa, Kaoru. (1990) *Introduction to Quality Control*. Chapman and Hall, London, UK.

Ishikawa, Kaoru. (1985) *What Is Total Quality Control? The Japanese Way*. Prentice Hall Inc., Englewood Cliffs, NJ.

Jaehn, Al. "All-Purpose Chart Can Make SPC Easy." *Quality Progress*, February 1989.

Janecke, K.M. (1995) "Upside Down VE, Study Analysis Sessions." Society of American Value Engineers Proceedings.

Joiner, Brian L. (1994) *Fourth Generation Management*. McGraw-Hill Inc., New York.

Juran, J.M. (1995) *Managerial Breakthrough: The Classic Book on Improving Management Performance*, second edition. McGraw-Hill, New York.

Juran, J.M. (1964) *Managerial Breakthrough: A New Concept of the Manager's Job*. McGraw-Hill, New York.

Juran, J.M. (1988) *Juran on Planning for Quality*. The Free Press, New York.

Juran, J.M., editor in chief, and Frank M. Gryna, associate editor. (1988) *Juran's Quality Control Handbook*, fourth edition. McGraw-Hill Book Co., New York.

Kübler-Ross, Elisabeth. (1969) *On Death and Dying*. Macmillan, New York.

Kuhn, Thomas. (1970) *The Structure of Scientific Revolutions*, second edition. University of Chicago Press, Chicago.

Mackowiak, Philip A., Steven S. Wasserman, and Myron M. Levin. "A Critical Appraisal of 98.6° F, the Upper Limit of the Normal Body Temperature, and Other Legacies of Carl Reinhold August Wunderlich." *Journal of the American Medical Association*. Vol. 268, No. 12, Sept. 23–30, 1992.

Mizuno, Shigeru. (1988) *Management for Quality Improvement—The Seven New QC Tools*. Productivity Press, Cambridge, MA.

Moran, J., R. Talbot, and R. Benson. (1990) *A Guide to Graphical Problem-Solving Processes*. ASQ Quality Press, Milwaukee.

Nathanson, Craig. "Are You a Total Quality Person?" *Quality Progress*, September 1993.

Nietzsche, Friedrich Wilhelm (Wille Zur Macht). (1913) *The Will to Power: An Attempted Transvaluation of All Values*. Translated by Anthony M. Ludovici. T.N. Foulis, London.

Parker, G.E. (1989) "Applying Understanding of Individual Behavior and Team Dynamics Within the Value Engineering Process." Society of American Value Engineers Proceedings.

Phillips, Gary. (1990) *SPC for Low Volume Manufacturing*. GPS Technologies, Troy, MI.

Pitt, Hy. (1994) *SPC for the Rest of Us*. Addison-Wesley Publishing Co., Reading, MA.

Pyzdek, Thomas. "Process Control for Short and Small Runs." *Quality Progress*, April 1993.

Raoff, J. "Body Temperature: Don't Look for 98.6°F." *Science News*, Sept. 26, 1992.

Roberts, Harry V. "Using Personal Checklists to Facilitate TQM." *Quality Progress*, June 1993.

Rorty, Richard. (1979) *Philosophy and the Mirror of Nature*. Princeton University Press, Princeton, NJ.

Rosenbert, Jarrett. "Five Myths About Customer Satisfaction." *Quality Progress*, December 1996.

Ryan, John. "A Job with Many Vacancies." *Quality Progress*, October 1990.

Senge, Peter M. (1990) *The Fifth Discipline: The Art and Practice of the Learning Organization*. Doubleday/Currency, New York.

Siegel, Robert. Interview of Robert Kallstrom on "All Things Considered," National Public Radio, Dec. 11, 1997.

Shewhart, Walter A. (1980) *Economic Control of Quality of Manufactured Product*, 50th anniversary commemorative reissue. ASQ Quality Press, Milwaukee.

Shewhart, Walter A. (1939) *Statistical Method from the Viewpoint of Quality Control*. Graduate School, Department of Agriculture, Washington, DC. (Reprinted by Dover in 1986.)

Squeglia, Nicholas L. *Zero Acceptance Number (C=O) Acceptance Plans*, third edition. ASQ Quality Press, Milwaukee.

Stratton, Brad. "Gone but Never Forgotten." *Quality Progress*, March 1994.

Stratton, Brad. "What Does the Boss Read?" *Quality Progress*, June 1992.

"Suppliers Team with Chrysler for $1.2 Billion in Cost Savings." *Quality Progress*, September 1997.

Tague, Nancy R. (1995) *The Quality Toolbox*. ASQ Quality Press, Milwaukee.

Triggers—Skill-Building Exercises for Teams. (1987) Rieker Management Systems, Los Gatos, CA.

Tufte, Edward R. (1997) *Visual Explanations: Images and Quantities, Evidence and Narrative*. Graphics Press, Cheshire, CT.

Tufte, Edward R. (1992) *The Visual Display of Quantitative Information*. Graphics Press, Chesire, CT.

Tufte, Edward R. (1990) *Envisioning Information*. Graphics Press, Chesire, CT.

Vobejda, Barbara. "Embattled Census Director Quits: Riche Leaves in Midst of Sampling Dispute, Preparations for 2000 Count." *Washington Post*, Jan. 13, 1998.

Walton, Mary. (1986) *The Deming Management Method*. The Putman Publishing Group, New York.

Wheatley, Margaret J. (1992) *Leadership and the New Science: Learning About Organization from an Orderly Universe*. Berrett-Koehler, San Francisco.

Wheeler, Donald J., and David S. Chambers. (1985) *Understanding Statistical Process Control*. SPC Press, Knoxville, TN.

Wills, Garry. (1992) *Lincoln at Gettysburg: The Words That Remade America*. Touchstone Books, New York.

Winwood, Richard I. (1990) *Time Management: An Introduction to the Franklin System*. Franklin International Institute, Salt Lake City.

Index

A

acceptance sampling, 68–69
act phase, 5
active listening, 95
agenda, 96–97
alliterative approach, promotion of quality and, 107
analysis tools, 120
annunciator report, 137–139
attribute charts, 163–164
audit sampling, improving, 218–219
auditing, 223–236
    checklist, development, 229–230
    critical audit, dealing with, 234–236
    employee involvement, 231–233
    employee preparation, 224–226
    tips for, 227–228
awards, promotion of quality and, 112–113

B

bead box exercise, 57
body temperature exercise, 55–56
brainstorming, 102–103
breakthroughs, achieving, 267–274
    cause-and-effect diagram, 270–271
    conflict management, 270–271
    personal effectiveness, 272–274
    tools, redesign, 268–269
Buchanan Scale, 27–28

C

calibration control, maintaining, 195–197
catchball exercise, 86–87
cause-and-effect diagram, 270–271
charts
    attribute charts, 163–164
    control chart, calibration control and, 195–197
    C_{pk} dart charts, 165–167
    data, charting, 143–173
    dot method C-chart, 158–162
    EMWA control chart, 156–157
    flowcharts, control charts and, 145–146
    flowcharting path, 7

    measuring progress, flowcharts and, 203–204
    Pareto analysis, trend charts and, 168–169
    short-run average charts, tips for, 153–155
    training for quality, flowcharts and, 63–65
    web chart, 170–171
    zone control chart, 147–149
check phase, 5
checklist, development, 229–230
cheese exercise, 51–52
communicate-listen-act system, 29–30
communication, quality and, 17–30
    Buchanan Scale, 27–28
    communicate-listen-act system, 29–30
customer-supplier relationships and, 252–253
    Menasha Excellence Process, 27
    poor quality, 23–24
    six principles, 21–22
    Socratic method, 25–26
company profiles, 180–181
conflict management, 270–271
contingency force analysis, 128–130
continuous improvement process, 251–252
control chart, calibration control and, 195–197
co-op programs, 38–39
    human growth, 38
    professional development, 39
coordinate measuring machine (CMM), evaluation of, 192–194
COPIS, 13–17
    implementation suggestions, 14
    steps, 13–14
corrective action
    reality and, 246–247
    systems, 241–243
C_{pk} dart charts, 165–167
critical audit, dealing with, 234–236
customer
    customer-supplier relationships, 249–266
    feedback, obtaining, 81–82
    listening to, 244–245